Gene and Georgia 1
great friends !
with warmest ~~ "

CKWebb

1-707-537-1623

ANDRÉE
and the EDUCATION
of a UNIVERSITY PRESIDENT

ANDRÉE
and the EDUCATION
of a UNIVERSITY PRESIDENT

C.R. WEBB

Personal History
PRODUCTIONS LLC

Other Books by C. R. Webb

Western Civilization, vol. 1 (with Paul B. Schaeffer) 1949,1958, D. Van
    Nostrand Company.
Western Civilization, vol. 2 (with Franklin C. Palm), 1949, 1958, D.
    Van Nostrand Company.
A Workbook in Western Civilization (2 vols.), 1949, Wm. C. Brown Co.
The Past As Prologue (with Everett U. Crosby), 1973, Appleton-
    Century-Crofts.

ISBN 978-0-9965590-3-4

Produced by Personal History Productions LLC
www.personalhistoryproductions.com
707.539.5559

*To our son, Richard, renowned artist, great
friend, my best and most discerning critic*

"It's better to know some of the questions than all of the answers."

    ♦ James Thurber

CONTENTS

Part Two

ACKNOWLEDGMENTS

$\mathcal{W}$ords of appreciation being due, I'd like to salute and to thank those who contributed in so many ways to the conception, writing, and production of this book.

Luther A. Nichols, Jr., West Coast editor, emeritus, of Doubleday & Company, for prodding me and constantly checking my progress; Debra Riker, for carefully reproducing the original typescript in triplicate and insisting I finish the book; Dr. William Hanchett, professor of History, San Diego State University, for his oft-repeated demand, "write that damn book!" and for his decades of moral support; Jack Bonno, for launching this tome in honor of his sister; Dr. Kathleen McGrory, erstwhile academic vice president at Eastern Connecticut State University and former president of Hartford College for Women, for steady support and encouragement along with a generous supply of writing and publishing tips; Dr. James Lacey, professor emeritus, Eastern Connecticut State University, for inspiring me with a series of beautifully written mystery novels; my son, Richard, for reading the entire manuscript and offering valuable critical advice and guidance on its contents; finally, my publisher, Personal History Productions LLC, for consistently capable service, and particularly—for an outstanding job patiently discharged with sensitivity, thoroughness, and great skill—my editor, Andi Reese Brady.

PROLOGUE

Her name was Andrée: *Ohn-thray* as her mother always intoned it, a short burst rising sharply, but ending in the faintest diminuendo. Though hearing this lilting call from early childhood, Andrée would soon be content to adopt a simple, even-syllabled *On Dray*.

Most of her friends easily mastered this more or less standard *American* pronunciation. Some of them, however, were slow to adjust to foreign touches such as accent marks and the double-*e*.

None of their tongue-twisting ills afflicted a certain linguistically talented neighbor on Garber Street, near the Claremont Hotel in Berkeley. There, Andrée lived with her family and frolicked on the grounds of Emerson School, close by.

Ohn-thray! Ohn-thray! Vienne ici, the obstreperous neighbor would shrill, perfectly accented, the second syllable stressed a bit more than the first. When Andrée often returned unexpectedly from play, her perplexed mother insisted she had not called her. Animated and prolonged discussion inevitably followed, daughter suspecting parental amnesia, mother convinced of childish hallucinations. The two endured awkward moments daily until, at last, they caught the teasing tormenter in the act.

Together in the kitchen one morning, they heard the familiar summons, *Ohn-thray! Ohn-thray! Vienne ici*: the articulate command of an overachieving parrot.

INTRODUCTION

The persnickety parrot, and the street on which he vocalized, have a bearing on the words that follow. My lifelong friend, Luther A. Nichols, well-known local author and publisher, lived most of his childhood on Garber Street. He and I and J Ward, who enters this narrative later, spent many hours on the nearby playground of Emerson Elementary School; assuredly, that same playground where a little French girl cavorted and a mischievous parrot connived.

Andrée and her mother, moreover, would soon be rid of the silver-tongued warbler, since they moved frequently. Gabriel D. Bonno, father and husband, respectively, of the two, was a professor, and chairman of the French Department at the University of California. Official duties in that capacity, scholarly research, and long-standing commitments to the French government took him abroad often.

Trips to France usually involved a search for new rental quarters upon the return to California. In fact, Andrée was past her 20th birthday before the family owned a home. Thus she lived in two countries during a major part of her formative years. Often forgetting English in the process but never French (always spoken at home), she would become fluent in both tongues, a distinct advantage both to her and—as it turned out later—to me.

As her father's international commitments declined and her scholastic endeavors increased, through high school and into college, Andrée gradually became "Americanized." Her habits, behavior, speech, and dress reflected local custom. In almost every way, she had been assimilated, culturally, socially, linguistically. But there was something indefinable about her that subtly and mysteriously remained Parisian.

This quality—along with her poise, charm, beauty, intelligence, and vitality—she retained throughout life. We celebrated the 61st anniversary of our wedding with a trip to Benbow, the spectacular resort, near Mount Shasta, where Andrée's parents had taken her nearly three quarters of a century before.

We had a wonderful time there, and on the trip itself. Andrée was happy, vivacious, and affectionate as always. I thoroughly enjoyed the fun, wondering—as always—how I could be so lucky.

Two months after our return, she—a nonsmoker—was in the hospital. With lung cancer.

Days and weeks and months, after her death, I drew breath and little else. Aimless and inconsolable, I passed the time in a state of shock and disbelief.

My son, Richard, and brother-in-law, Jack (Charles Henri) Bonno, equally distressed, similarly bereaved, tried to bring me back to life. They insisted I should acquire a computer, Andrée alone having been our domestic digital expert. I demurred. They pushed. And, at length, I relented.

When I slumbered on, despite the computer, Jack suggested one day that I could and should produce an autobiography. Easy and worthwhile, he ventured, for someone who had known so many interesting and famous people.

Meanwhile, my erstwhile colleague in history at San Diego State University, Professor William Hanchett, had been pressing me. "Get off your duff, damn it. Write that book on higher education!"

Encouraging. Even intriguing. Pointless, too; except perhaps as a command to awaken a semi-somnambulant mind to constructive consideration of the puzzle that life seemed to have become.

By *constructive*, I mean that when answers to puzzles fail to materialize, finding the right questions can serve as an acceptable beginning. Once exposed to writing, or the idea of my writing, I could not avoid thinking about it. The more I thought, the more my mind became involved in the actual concept and the key questions implied: the ins and outs, pros and cons, and whats, whys, and hows.

Questions such as these are not too difficult, excepting only *why*. Why never ceased giving me pause. A question asking more questions, it cries out, "Where is the meaning in life?" "In *your* life?" "Is there a meaning?" "If so, has it changed with Andrée's death?" "If there is no meaning, how will writing a book produce one?" And "Will such a book have a theme, a thesis?"

A theme? Well, yes, many themes. It's an analysis of higher education, its achievements and failures, as seen by a lifelong participant. It's intimately concerned with a career, a marriage, and with the critical evaluation of a number of important persons in public and professional life.

But a thesis? No. And without one, it seemed there'd be no book and probably little reason to write one. Little reason, that is, until I saw the thesis *staring me right in the face.*

In reviewing the record, I have constantly been reminded that decisions taken, and offers contemplated, accepted, or declined, were invariably reached jointly.

More than that, Andrée's wise counsel and carefully reasoned pragmatism rescued me from many potential missteps, and never failed to guide me effectively.

She opened doors for me over and over again. My professional development could easily have followed an entirely different course. I can—and do—document instances when her advice, and even her presence, significantly influenced my career choices. A book without her would be a book devoid of critical essentials.

And as for *The Education of a University President*, take out Andrée's role in my learning process and you're left with the intellectual equivalent of the four-year-old "trike tike" you can find on page 7 of the following work.

C.R. Webb
Santa Rosa, California

PART ONE

Chapter One

THE TRICYCLE TERRORIST

◆ ═══════════════════════════════════

*Early childhood, including a physical confrontation
with the Sacramento Northern Railway, directly resulting in
corrective action by the city of Oakland.*

ℬorn in 1902, Albert Krueger was too young to fight in World War I,
known as the Great War (1914–1918). But he was old enough to be aware
of its carnage and—as he began medical training—to be acutely aware of its
aftermath, influenza. Scientists have estimated that this frightful pandemic,
abetted by pneumonia, carried off up to 100 million souls worldwide by the
time of its peak in late 1919.

Surely, Krueger also encountered early on the disconcerting statistic that
more American soldiers and sailors had died of influenza and pneumonia
than were killed by enemy action in the war just ended.

It is reasonable to conclude, however, that he probably failed at the
time to notice reports of my birth, on a bright and comfortable October 4,
1919, at Alta Bates Hospital in Berkeley, California. (No matter! Our paths
would cross during World War II in US Naval Medical Research Unit #1,

working on influenza and bubonic plague. There, my commanding officer would be none other than Albert Paul Krueger, MD, PhD, Captain, United States Navy.)

Most of the world was also becoming bright and comfortable by the end of 1919. People were healthier, thanks to the gradual subsidence of influenza, although its devastating global presence would not soon be forgotten. (In one year, in fact, it had killed more than the number who died in a century of bubonic plague during the Black Death of the Middle Ages.)

Recovery from the war to end all wars arrived sooner in the United States than abroad. Cheerfully boastful of having shown Europe "how to make the world safe for democracy," the country was all about returning to "normalcy." Business, and such things as Prohibition, bootlegging, rum-running, gangsters, and automobiles, prevailed in the Jazz Age.

My father hated jazz. But he had nothing against bootleggers, whose interest in fast cars did not go unnoticed, as his business grew lustily. He sold new-fangled contraptions. No longer referred to as horseless carriages, they sported the optimistic name *automobile,* a vehicle not dependably mobile and anything but automatic.

His was a world of new Velies, Jewetts, and Paiges, as well as a motley procession of tattered "trade-ins" graced by names such as Essex and Pierce and Franklin and Oakland and Star and—of course—Moon. The list was endless, as were his days, or so it seemed to his family. *We* endured, while *he* gradually built a steady clientele who regularly returned to the WEBB MOTOR COMPANY on Shattuck Avenue to ogle and, often, to buy the latest models.

My world was a bit smaller and, I contend, less hectic, though my mother—barely finding time to exercise her newly won right to vote—might have disagreed. We lived in a modest house on Carlotta Avenue in North Berkeley. Fortunately, I have retained few detailed recollections of those days.

But when I was about 18 months old, we moved to Webster Street. There—I clearly recall—we were less than half a mile from Berkeley's already famous Hotel Claremont.

At Webster Street, moreover, I learned that I had a four-year-old sister and a six-year-old brother. This amazed me, since hitherto I had had no knowledge of such beings. I quickly reined in my surprise and vexation over their presence, finding they could perform wondrous tricks like tying shoes, drinking from a glass, pushing a baby carriage, and even carrying me during locomotion crises.

These were normal parts of learning and getting along, I suppose. I was pretty much a normal kid. Normal, that is, except for a few eccentricities. A sort of precocious idiot, I sometimes did mindless things, said strange things, even *after* learning to speak. "No," my sister pleasantly observed, "*especially* after you learned to speak."

Mindless things? For a three-year-old? Come on. Still, I must confess an incident or two. The first, occurring at Webster Street, was more a matter of perception than dullness, an example of how an innocent mind can err. Wildly err.

Overhearing one day a metaphysical discussion among my parents and others, I burst forth with the confident announcement that I knew God and in fact had seen Her (yes, *Her*. Dull perhaps, but prescient). My parents listened carefully and patiently, though they were unable to hide their astonishment.

So, to convince them, I described God. Curiously, I see Her now. She was tall (like everyone then) and was standing on a small stool. Her hair was long, dark but graying. I still recall the blue-green robe, stretching to Her ankles. Could there be any mistake? Clearly, this was God, because I saw Her.

Either my parents said nothing to me or I refused to hear them. Gradually, probably years later, I reasoned that they immediately knew I was referring to someone who was my godmother or the godmother of one of my siblings.

And the stool? Well, I suppose God can stand on a stool if She wants to.

This episode merely tells a tale of infantile innocence, no earthshaking moment in the annals of childhood cluelessness. Soon, however, I would be graduating to a much higher level.

The scene changes to Hearn Street in Oakland, where we moved about a year later. Hearn Street! A name to remember. Actually, to forget, for its days were numbered. Only a block long, it ran from Chabot Road southward to Shafter Avenue, a street with few distinguishing features other than tracks belonging to the Sacramento Northern Railroad Company.

It was wonderfully exciting to one small, wide-eyed boy to see and hear those magically moving and snorting creatures as they mysteriously appeared at the end of Hearn Street. But when they kept on going, I was left sullen and dismayed astride my tricycle as the phantom, ever smaller, faded.

Accordingly, on a certain day that must have lived in my mother's memory for the rest of her life, I resolved to assert myself.

The tricycle terrorist is the one on the left.

Seeing a freight train slowly grinding eastward on the Shafter right-of-way, we nonchalantly positioned ourselves—trike and I—in the middle of the tracks, directly in the path of the approaching caravan.

Deliberately—whistles blowing, wheels clanking, engineers shouting—the train slowed. Irate trainmen burst forth, intent on removing this insane or inept infant from their way and—as soon as possible—from their jaundiced sight.

Eyes fixed on the train, slowly, ponderously, approaching, perhaps 50 feet away, I was filled at first with awe of the beast and curiosity over the blue-clad, gesticulating trainmen running toward me.

I don't recall experiencing anxiety at the time, at least not until it may have occurred to me that trouble lay ahead, either directly, on the spot, or worse, later at home.

Who punished me, infuriated engineers, frightened parents, or both, I do not remember. The point is not who punished me. Rather, it's that a wandering waif, long, long ago, single-handedly altered the map of Oakland, California. No longer would it display the name of a thoroughfare known as Hearn Street.

While the actual scene of the crime, altered somewhat, still remains, it should be noted that city authorities took corrective measures immediately. Access to Shafter Avenue was summarily blocked, and Hearn Street officially became Chabot Court, just a few days after my salient sally onto the Sacramento Northern Railroad Company tracks.

With this reconstruction and renaming caused by a willful trike-tyke, the story of my civic rearrangements comes to an end. Still, the record should show that it was the first and, quite possibly, my most far-reaching contribution to the public weal.

Perhaps not the most wayward. After all, I was only four. At that age, the opportunities for future mayhem are endless.

Mayhem and molesting freight trains require correctional action. Yet, how chastise a four-year-old? And how mete out appropriate punishment for an offense so lacking in precedent?

The answer to that conundrum came shortly after the Shafter Avenue caper, when I was enrolled in kindergarten at the Chabot Elementary School. Chabot was where the first taste of academic life proved not to be to my liking. Indeed, one semester there, fumbling, floundering, and foundering, was one semester too many. I didn't like the place, nor the teachers, nor what I considered regimentation.

*Marcelle Bonno and daughter, in the mid-1920s, on
one of the first of Andrée's many transatlantic voyages.*

Though the experience at Chabot School was anything but divine, I
eventually decided, worldly action lacking, that the choice of punishment
must have come from Above. Only Eternal Wisdom could render judgment so precisely calculated to fit my indefinably heinous crime on Shafter
Avenue.

Fortunately, one semester at Chabot was the full extent of the divine punishment. Moving from Oakland back to Berkeley, closer to my father's business, I found John Muir Elementary School a welcome change, congenial, pleasant, and more complicated.

Our new house in Berkeley (2726 Elmwood Avenue) was bigger, and better located, a great improvement over Chabot Court even though there were no freight trains for me to flag down. But streetcars could still be seen nearby on College Avenue, an extension of Broadway, the main north–south thoroughfare in Oakland.

Intersecting nearby with Ashby Avenue, College Avenue continues north a mile or so to Bancroft Way where—as its name implies—it ends at the University of California. Thus students, who happened to live in Oakland, could board a street car at 7:30 in the morning with every expectation of arriving in time for eight o'clock classes at Cal. In reverse order, my mother could follow the same route south to shop at H. C. Capwell's or other department stores in Oakland.

That College/Ashby intersection was all of 200 yards from our home When we lived there, cars could reach us by following Ashby eastward to a point where it divides, Elmwood to the right, Ashby on the left.

With the postwar increase in automobile congestion, however, Berkeley's city planners simplified traffic patterns by blocking the entrance to Elmwood Avenue, making it directly accessible only by foot, while confining through-traffic to Ashby Avenue.

No problem. Not for me. Walking from home involved passing two or three houses to reach the area where Ashby and Elmwood join and then, half a block to the College/Ashby intersection, a simple jaunt even for a five-year-old.

But what wonders that short trip revealed. Standing ready to cross, on the southeast corner of the intersection, my hand clasped tightly in my mother's, I could see the long, low American Trust Building to the right and across Ashby. On the left, we passed a busy barbershop where I would be shorn many times but never, as I recall, without a watchful maternal presence.

Then, with my mother's usual admonishment, "Look both ways," we'd cross College Avenue to the delights of the other world: a drugstore with all its magical details and, just two doors down, the marvel of all marvels, a moving picture palace.

Surely, I had emerged from my Chabot Court cocoon and fluttered into the storied realm of Kublai Khan.

In later years, exploring this enchanted neighborhood, I'd find pastry shops, candy stores, shoe stores, dairies, and hardware, haberdashery, and toy stores. Still later, gasoline stations sprung up and, on Ashby, a block west of College, a public library blossomed, where new worlds would emerge. Just one block farther west, moreover, lay Alta Bates Hospital, where I was born.

All these delights, however, were exceeded one glorious day when my father, usually too busy to shop, came home with a surprise. He had discovered an honest-to-goodness new factory on the west side of College Avenue about a half block north of Ashby. He held a large round can filled, as he explained, with the factory's only product, Golden Bear cookies. I probably had experienced heavenly delights before (after all, according to my mother, the first word I learned to spell was c-a-n-d-y), but the actual sensation, this time, was rapture, rapture I shared with two siblings.

My mother and I, 1925.

Those were very good cookies indeed. We bought and devoured many more of them before the company went out of business. I may have resolved in those precious months that I would someday become a Golden Bear. But that's enough about cookies, however delectable.

Beyond such delights of another time, one may reflect wistfully on current conditions, comparing our bustling, sprawling hodgepodge of industrial complexity with that municipal organization of my childhood days that combined business and industrial pursuits with comfortable residential amenities.

The Elmwood district of Berkeley attained such a state, a complete, merchandising community, lacking only a large department store, surrounded by an upscale residential area. A relic of the recent past, that structure has essentially disappeared from our society, only partially replaced by the ubiquitous malls and shopping centers that presently dominate the urban landscape.

Life on Elmwood Avenue was not all Golden Bear cookies. I recall a malodorous episode when the neighborhood bully caught me struggling with my first pair of roller skates one far-from-memorable day.

Gleefully regarding the wobbly scene, he decided to join the fun, scooped up a handful of horse manure, and triumphantly thrust it inside my collar and down my neck.

Let this pungent episode serve as a reminder that my father was an automobile dealer. His merchandise shared the streets with conveyances of earlier generations. We regularly heard the steady clop-clop of hooves on pavement and the junkman's high-pitched cry, "Rags." Horse-drawn vendors of ice, fruits, vegetables, and all sorts of knickknacks were heard, seen, and smelled, and their wares purchased, on a daily basis.

In this cozy, semirural environment, one rude and manure-unchallenged neighbor could smugly saunter off in his own cloud of glory while I retreated in ignominious discomfiture. It was not the last time I cried my way home for a bath and clean clothes.

Nor would it be typical. Life was generally carefree and happy, especially since each passing year saw more motorized transportation, fewer horse-drawn vendors, and less manure. My memories are full of football, baseball, and other games played in the relatively quiet streets. And, of course, there were birthday parties, with ice cream and cookies and candy. Friends brought laughter and shouting, screaming and whispering, and marvelous toys, balloons, airplanes—some propelled by rubber bands—and gadgets galore.

The best present was a football. Not just any old football, but a genuine, varsity football from the University of California team.

My father had remained active in the Cal Alumni Association and the "Big C" Society well after his time "on the mound." In fact, annually, he assembled and pitched for a team of big- and minor-league athletes that competed against the Cal varsity baseball team, usually the first game of the spring.

Pitching successfully well into his fifties, he often heard Coach Clint Evans's frustrated, high-pitched cry to his team, trailing the "Ted Webb All-Stars," "Don't let that old man fool ya!"

He fooled them a lot, but always as friend and alumnus both on the field and in the halls of the University of California; thus, the annual present. His procuring a "game ball" for my birthday, which fell near the season opener, became a yearly ritual as did his taking me to the first or second game despite their coinciding with his busy Saturdays.

It did not matter at all that the treasured "pigskin" was often scuffed up, or that Cal had few winning seasons. I was overjoyed at the prospect of witnessing the first game which, unlike the tight schedules today, usually featured opponents such as Montana or the University of Idaho, once considered soft touches. Esoteric locales, like Moscow, Idaho, or Missoula, Montana, became commonplace in my vocabulary, while possession of an authentic varsity football enhanced my popularity in the Elmwood neighborhood. Pickup games on Piedmont Avenue could seldom occur if my precious football and I were absent.

That preferred status, however, did not last long. Athletic friends gratefully accepted the use of the Cal ball, helped me wear it out, and found humble but adequate replacements for it. Though lacking the pedigree of mine, these balls were tolerably useable and relatively unscuffed. Discovering that footballs were replaceable, erstwhile friends soon regarded my preferred status as ancient history.

Piedmont playmates being bigger and better, their adjustments came as no surprise to me. It was also apparent that tired varsity footballs and hastily contrived street games were but a temporary distraction. A chance to see Cal football in action seemed to promise permanent significance. Annual trips to Memorial Stadium had captured my imagination and lifelong interest.

Besides, they were magic. A father's magic, that is. With games falling on busy Saturdays, magical planning was a necessity for him. It was my thrill, wonder, and anxiety when my father and another man picked me up a few minutes before kickoff time (never did we arrive early) and drove directly to the stadium.

After some stops at "do-not-enter" checkpoints, a few words here and "proceed with caution" gestures there, our "chauffeur" dropped us off at the gates. A short walk and a brisk climb up stadium rows landed us in our seats barely in time for the opening kickoff which—I was easily persuaded—had been delayed until our arrival.

If the mad march to the stadium fell a little short of sleight-of-hand, our exit—at least—convinced me that my father still had a card or two up his sleeve. Leaving the game a few moments before its end, always a minor annoyance to me, we walked about a hundred yards to find a car magically parked, and facing in the right direction, ready to whisk us away well before the crowd emerged from the stadium.

While guessing that my father had simply planted, or had others plant, that automobile there early in the morning when streets were quiet, I continued to be amazed. I so enjoyed the luxury, the convenience, and the elegant simplicity of the technique that I often thought of it, resolving to repeat the trick if ever the opportunity arose. As luck would have it, almost a quarter century later, in San Diego, the like-thing struck again. More of that later.

An indifferent student but generally a happy camper at John Muir, I learned there that the best period of the day was recess, where I encountered baseball and such things as the differences among right field, left field, and left out. It was also where and when I discovered soccer, a game of nonstop running, wherein one soon learned to stay clear of big Michael Jose and his ankle-seeking boots or suffer the consequences. In sum, recess was where I first noticed how disconcertingly short time can be.

John Muir, of course, taught more than avoiding Mike's boots. Each of the following three examples occurred on or around school grounds. But generally, they show educational side effects, rather than specific knowledge gained through the academic process.

During recess one morning, I ran down an embankment toward a creek where all the boys and a few, very few, girls enjoyed showing off their prowess by leaping across the water. With élan and self-assured confidence, I launched. At that moment another lad, twice my size it seemed, also launched . . . from the other bank.

We collided midstream. If it had been a foreign-language class, or a baptism ceremony, my flight would have been successful, for it was total immersion.

Andrée dances on the slopes of North Berkeley, in 1932.

Still at it in 2002, on a caboose near Dunsmuir in Northern California.

Tearfully, and soaking wet, I somehow found the tricycle and sobbed my way homeward. Here, in fact, was a lesson. Though not from the classroom, it provided palpable instruction in the science of applied physics:

A near-irresistible force meets a far-from-immovable body.

Years later, I received another lesson, one on humor and human relations in general and on my father in particular. I had acquired an old baseball glove, a parental castoff, no doubt. In class, a girl sitting behind me asked to see my leather jewel. I readily complied. And that's when Vesuvius began to rumble.

My classmate refused to let go of the glove. I tugged. She held. I grasped. She remained unrelenting. Exasperated, I tore it from her hand, just as I heard the teacher gasp,

"Richard! Give me that mitt."

Oh! If today I had the insouciance, animal spirit, and energy of an uninhibited ten-year-old. So . . . How did I respond? Right!

I gave her the mitt. From the rear of the classroom, my prized possession described a graceful arc. Sailing across the intervening space in the sort of flight perfected by generations of ballplayers, it landed elegantly upon the blackboard in front of which the unamused teacher had been standing.

No excusing my mistake. Provoked or not, it warranted punishment. It humiliated the teacher in front of her class and justified her seeking redress, at the very least, in the form of punishment of the miscreant. Therefore, she made a telephone call. And that was her mistake.

Dinner table talk that night seemed to follow the usual pattern, no innuendos, no startling announcements, relatively quiet, and suddenly too quiet. My father was looking at me, "Gotta call today from an irate teacher!"

Though the tone of his voice was calm enough, his manner made it clear that he was irate too.

"Kids throwing things at teachers! That's bad. So bad, she felt she had to contact the parents. Had to call my office! She was really angry. Went on and on, adding to my anger over the incident, until finally, she said, 'You know, Mr. Webb, if I hadn't ducked at the last second, that mitt would have hit me right in the face.'"

The quote brought a smile to my father's face. Noted for his control as a pitcher in college baseball, he had to confess that the teacher's deploring the accuracy of my toss made him say to himself, "That's my boy!" We all laughed, because it was clear that the quote helped him transfer what was left of his annoyance with me to this humorless and self-centered person whom he had quietly dismissed with words to the effect that he would speak to me. I suspect that he did not tell her he would also laugh with me.

That episode, both frightening and uplifting, taught me a lot about my lineage. The contretemps and its happy ending reinforced my growing awareness of fair play, reciprocal relations, judgment, humor, and equations of form and substance, significant matters of which my father was a studious observer.

The third lesson is both the most important and the simplest to relate. It involves arithmetic and a small boy in a strange place, namely, school. We were taught arithmetic in the second and third grades. I enjoyed it. It was easy. It was logical. But it proved too easy. I can't say I got bored, but my mind wandered.

Not out to lunch, I may have been at recess, as mathematics progressed beyond simple addition, subtraction, multiplication, and division. I wasn't paying attention. Got behind. Way behind. I became academically disadvantaged. It was easy to conclude, therefore, that I was not very bright, a self-assessment that would persist through junior high school until learning in high school that I had an above-average IQ. This tendency is mentioned in passing because teachers and counselors now understand that it's not an uncommon phenomenon. Some students simply "drop out" from boredom and inattention, not from lack of intellect.

From bad times with skates and mischievous neighbors to scary times on tricycles, to good times with birthday parties, Cal footballs, Golden Bear cookies, and games in neighborhood streets and yards, the semi-idyllic days and carefree haunts of Elmwood Avenue were gradually playing out. I was growing up.

Five or six years old when we arrived, now seven, now eight, nine, ten, eleven, tricycles having given way to a bicycle, and books beginning to vie with movies and games, I fancied myself ready for new adventures, new challenges.

The first significant challenge had come in the form of music lessons. My parents, who often spoke of my singing songs I had heard before knowing how to speak, felt I should have formal instruction in music, but they were reluctant to push me since I had not shown much interest. After a year or two of pro-and-con discussion, they "persuaded" me to take piano lessons. I was eight or nine, a little fearful, somewhat short of enthusiastic, a bit too late to become a child prodigy, but full of curiosity. In any event, I went along with the experiment, going regularly, once a week, to my piano lessons.

Regularly? Well, yes. Dutifully? OK. Cheerfully? Maybe. Enthusiastically? No. Still, I continued the practice two years or so. Practice is the operative word here: my progress was erratic, the result of poor practice habits, according to my teacher.

Poor? If she only knew. Those practice habits were not poor. They were nonexistent. Using ears more than my eyes, I could fool her most of the time,

*Andrée at nine years, overcoat
needed in early spring, 1932.*

*C.R., in the backyard of 2726
Elmwood Avenue, about 1928.*

though probably not as much as I thought. I even improved some, though more, I was convinced, from maternal aid than from my teacher's effort.

Whatever the cause, teacher and pupil eventually parted, the one exhausted by her recalcitrant charge, the other happy to escape an instructor whom he considered inept and whose skills, he knew as a fact, were inferior to those of his classically trained mother.

Another housing move, in the fall of 1931, conveniently sealed the separation. Also, in this second year of the Great Depression, my parents could easily have been persuaded that expensive piano lessons that I considered a waste of time were simply a waste. ◆

Chapter 2

THE SAGE OF MARYSVILLE

◆ ══════════════════════════

Teenaged growth, touching on the life and influence of the
outstanding jurist Eugene P. McDaniel.

ℰarly on a September morning in 1931, I rode my bike to a new school, Frances E. Willard Junior High School, on Stuart Street at Telegraph Avenue. Independently mobile and adventuresome, I was ready for change. Big change. John Muir Elementary School—with its splashing creek, teacher-seeking leather missiles, towering sequoia and calamity-bound tricycles—was now behind me. And on the same morning that Willard Junior High beckoned, moving vans appeared at 2726 Elmwood Avenue, which would no longer serve as our family home.

After the final school bell rang, and with printed directions in hand, I set off to navigate from new school to new home. Bicycling eastward from Willard to the Claremont Hotel area and the famous Berkeley Tennis Club, I sweated half a mile up Tunnel Road to Roble Road. A right turn there and another at Roble Court, and I was home, at last: Number 18, my address for the next decade.

Laboriously bicycling up Tunnel Road that warm September afternoon, my 11-year-old self may well have been groaning at the prospect of future struggles with that unforgiving incline. Thoughts of future perspiration on a daily basis were easily put aside, however, when I thought back to a minor calamity that had clouded our last few days at Elmwood Avenue: we had had a fire. Though efficiently and quickly quelled, it was very stressful on my family, nonetheless, and I had been disturbed by the lingering smell. In one day, my family exited smoky, stinking shingles and settled into clean, fresh-smelling quarters. A blissfully satisfying experience.

*Andrée in authentic local Brittany peasant costume, 1932
(from a French commercial postcard).*

The new home at Roble Court had Spanish architecture and a tile roof, but the comforting transfer from wood shingles to tile roof dealt merely with externals. The essence of the move was that it marked closure on my carefree Elmwood days. More than that, coinciding as it did with my 12th birthday, the move signaled the end of childhood in many ways. A time of exploration, trial, and error, it overflowed with harbingers of life ahead.

The house itself, built in 1922, was modest compared with other homes in the area. I thought it was beautiful. My sister was happy with her room and the adjoining bathroom and shower that she shared with my brother and me. He and I enjoyed a room to ourselves as well as a glorious sleeping porch with a blue tile floor, marvelously sliding glass windows, and a magnificent view of San Francisco Bay.

My father was grateful, and considered us lucky, to have a roof over our heads during the Depression, with unemployment close to 25 percent. He was especially pleased to have found a home in a quiet neighborhood in the Oakland/Berkeley hills, some three miles farther inland from our previous house. The area provided a better climate for my mother, who had been suffering from respiratory complaints. She was relieved by the drier air and overjoyed with the beautiful garden and tile patio.

She also was happier when she had an automobile at her disposal, considering our new location. Shortly after we moved in, however my father was down to three cars ready for sale, one of which he had to use to commute to work. When the automobile business improved a little, my mother would have a car at her disposal. But only temporarily, however, until it was time for the car to go back on the lot to be sold. We all laughed with her over her mock complaint, "Every time I'm just getting to know and like an automobile, he sells it."

Times were indeed tough. But we seldom went hungry, though I can still hear Mom saying to my brother, sister, and me, "Just fill up on bread and butter." Butter? Yes, butter. It was cheap in the thirties. The famous phrase "Guns AND Butter"—trumpeting an economy that could afford both—would come much later. Later, when some of the Depression-era stringency abated, Mom could manage an occasional treat for us. Even so, she assuaged some feelings of guilt about it with a pleasant admonition and its incongruous tag, "Help yourself, but hide the evidence."

My father was simply not into extravagance, and that fact takes us back to butter. It was cheap, alright. All over the United States it was cheap. And, where we lived, it was *dirt cheap*. We got our butter from a Mr. Heimboldt, a gentleman dairyman who lived around the corner, just three minutes away by foot. Not only did he sell milk, and cream and cheese, he delivered them all, at practically give-away prices. We never *ordered* cream; it was included, "Free!," at the top of the milk.

Delivering several quarts of milk every other day, Mr. Heimboldt kept thirsty teenagers in dairy heaven, and all with raw milk. I sometimes wonder if my longevity (so far) might be the result of his raw milk. Given all the hamburgers, fries, and other "bad things" I've consumed since then, Heimboldt's milk deserves high honors at the very least. For sure he was a godsend to my mother, struggling to keep me filled—especially when she had no transportation—and to my father, trying to make ends meet.

Even with a productive dairy farm so near, we experienced no disagreeable smells, flies, or other reminders of Mr. Heimboldt's avocation. We lived during a time and within an area blessed by an ecological wonderland of perfect balance. Thus, window screens were not needed to keep bugs at bay. Insects respectfully remained outside, except for an occasional fly whose unwanted entrance invariably elicited the weary reaction from my mother, "How did that nasty fly get in here?" But that was Berkeley in the thirties: fewer people, less garbage, insects that knew their place, houses without screens, and people who seldom locked their homes and never locked their automobiles.

Marysville, California, where my maternal grandparents lived, some 50 miles northeast of Sacramento, may have been less open than Berkeley. Rural Marysville had a great number of unemployed or itinerant farmworkers, often simply called tramps, who roamed the streets looking for handouts.

My grandparents—Judge Eugene P. McDaniel and Mary Addella Peacock McDaniel—lived in a large house at 612 H Street, about three-fourths of a mile northwest of the city's business district.

An attractive park near their house was part of the route for itinerant hoboes: from railroad tracks to town to the well-known backdoor of my grandparents. Graciously, my grandmother filled the stomachs, and often the coffers, of unemployed or underemployed porters, switchmen, steam-tenders, and gandy dancers. Then, with words of moral support, she cheerfully sent them off to their various callings including, for some, the blessings of life in a side-door Pullman car. My grandmother continued to fearlessly feed the hoboes who came to her door, even when they showed up in mysteriously increased numbers, a result of the widespread practice during the Depression of tramps secretly marking houses where they could expect a generous welcome.

The park near my grandparents' home was more than a place for itinerants to reconnoiter and arrange refueling ventures. It also served as a favorite gathering spot for children of all ages and, for everyone, the locale for band concerts on summer evenings and Sunday afternoons. Scarcely 100 yards away from my grandparents' home, that park became my auxiliary playground. Very large to me at first, the size of the park grew smaller summer to summer. Gradually, I aged enough to be left in Marysville for longer periods without troubling my grandparents.

During long summer days, I encountered waves of new stimuli, new friends, and new attitudes, as well as new household arrangements and very different topics of dinner conversation. Perhaps most challenging was interacting daily with a host of cousins, aunts, and uncles.

I was surprised, somewhat, in detecting a subtle change in my mother's demeanor once we were with my grandparents, more deferential, as if— in her parents' home—she were a child again. Also, I noticed the slightly altered attitude of my father. He seemed no longer in charge of conversation and behavioral protocol. One of the most self-assured of men, my father appeared to slide into a mode of deference, courteously assenting to all suggestions and most observations—assuredly difficult for a Republican guest in a household of Democrats.

Simply put, to me Marysville was another world. Stimulating, exciting, but very different, it was a world of hunting dogs and guns, horse racing and breeding, taxidermy, carpentry, the law, crime stories, courtroom drama, English literature, and Chinese immigrants.

Judge Eugene P. McDaniel

My grandfather was Mr. Marysville. Judge Marysville, actually. He was a man who, in 30 years on the bench, had a decision overturned only once. (That appellate court judgment, in turn, was reversed by the California Supreme Court, thus sustaining his original ruling.)

On another occasion, one of the McDaniel opinions reached the Supreme Court of the United States, where Justice Oliver Wendell Holmes declared it "a classic." Such praise for his work was commonplace. Erudite and logical, his rulings were highly regarded throughout the state. His legal skills were so sought-after that he served as a substitute on the superior court bench of all but four counties in California, often repeatedly, as in Los Angeles. He was also a talented public speaker in constant demand.

He was renowned in many areas, not just the law. One was horse racing and breeding. He was also the son of another famous man, Richard S. McDaniel, an outstanding physician. My great-grandparents, Dr. and Mrs. McDaniel, lived on the top floor of a building at the northwest corner of Fifth and D Streets, Marysville. His medical office occupied the bottom floor, where their son, my grandfather, was born on the first day of May, 1862.

Not so well known: when Eugene McDaniel retired from the bench, at age 75 years, he resumed his law practice on the top floor of a similar building close by. As a teenager, I visited him in that office. And many years later, I spotted that same building, possibly both buildings, in the company of my son, Charles Richard Webb, III, an artist. In a satisfying reprise, my son's pen name is now Richard McDaniel.

Marysville's "Chinatown" was only a few blocks away from both buildings. One of the largest Chinese settlements in Northern California, its growth coincided with the tenure of the Judge. Maybe not cause and effect, but surely no coincidence. Earlier treatment of "coolies" in California had not faded from memory. Too often, a "fair shake" was a forlorn hope, within and without the law. As district attorney for 10 years before his judicial appointment, Eugene McDaniel earned a reputation for fair treatment of all, including but not limited to minorities. The Chinese knew this. And they respected him, liked him, and felt beholden to him, so much so that it could be embarrassing. Not always remembering that he had no favorites and used the law to ensure a level playing field for all, they'd produce enormous quantities of candy and other delicacies at Christmastime and mountains of firecrackers around July 4th. During that holiday, fireworks filled the air and H Street. Next-door rascal, Paul Rock, brought out his German shepherd, Lady, to join the fun. Her idea of fun was to bite the exploding firecrackers, often in midair. When she succeeded, she'd whimper away, only to return to the fray in seconds.

In private life, the Judge generally avoided handing down decisions. He was the observer and the quiet instructor, a role he liked to assume with me as, for example, in the board game checkers. Invariably winning, he would gently point out my errors, following up the correction with the advice, "It's simple. Give away one piece, take back two. Give two pieces, take back three." If he explained *how* to do that, I did not understand. But one day, when he nonchalantly countered my proud *triple jump* with a game-ending *quadruple jump,* I got the message.

Nonjudgmental, never arbitrary, he ruled by persuasion and common sense. Measured and elegant, his words were witty, sometimes archaic, frequently arcane, always nonthreatening, and, well, . . . judicious.

Mary Peacock McDaniel shared some of these qualities, although persuasion was not her strong suit. When it came to cuisine, kitchen etiquette, or raising children and grandchildren, she was forthright and quietly authoritative. She was the first one to say to me, "Don't take the 'lazy man's load!'" Though precise meaning of those words may have escaped me, I soon learned from the context what she was talking about. But the lessons didn't stop with her and my grandfather. There were her brothers, my great-uncles. And my mother's brothers too!

Much did the four men teach me, but seldom through direct instruction or admonition. They taught by action, bromide, quotation, and demonstration, using many "methods" while casually ignoring the pupil.

Looking first at the great-uncles, George and Will, we find them sharing a large house with their mother, next door to their sister's family. On an ample plot, which easily accommodated outbuildings, there was room for stables, gardening sheds, and equipment storage. A mini-plantation, it supported steady activity with a stream of gardeners, cleaners, and carpenters, tending fruit-bearing trees, exotic flower beds, and vegetable patches.

And yes, there were live peacocks there. That a flock of peacocks boarded with my Peacock family had once amazed and delighted me. My childish joy at their presence turned to relief when they were later removed, presumably because of the noise.

Reaching the Peacock home involved walking a few steps from the screen-enclosed porch that backed the McDaniel house, descending a short flight of wooden stairs, turning right, and crossing a small garden. While my grandparents transited this walk daily in 30 to 45 seconds, it presented an obstacle course for me. Adventures too: weeds and flowers and plants and snails and slugs and lizards and ants and bees and ladybugs and dragonflies and hummingbirds, and, of course, peacocks, confronted me on every side.

I soon learned to leave the peacocks alone and was repeatedly warned to treat Great-Uncle Will the same way when he was practicing archery, which he did on a narrow and slightly elevated pathway extending about 100 feet alongside the Peacock house. Launched from a site near the front porch, his arrows usually found the mark, a straw-filled target close to the kitchen entrance. That was too close, some thought, to a small building across the walk from the kitchen, where my Great-Uncle George, Will's brother, spent most of his time. Still, Uncle Will managed to put on great shows for admirers and to scare the daylights out of the unwary. My fears abated in time, as did my natural timidity, in the presence of these eccentric gentlemen.

Uncle Will turned out to be friendly, talkative, and willing to demonstrate the intricacies of archery, even though I was not yet strong enough to pull the bowstring all the way back. He was also a stamp collector, and although I was too young to appreciate his huge, complex, and colorful stamp collection, he was still pleased to show it to me. The collection was very valuable, too, as my cousin Lowell McDaniel would tell me with exasperation much later, upon learning what happened to the stamps: Paul Rock, who for some time had assiduously cultivated Will and his hobby, wound up inheriting the collection in its entirety.

Uncle George was smaller than Uncle Will, as well as more reserved, withdrawn, and—it seemed to me—secluded. I have memories of Will in various places in and out of the house: in the garden and on his archery run or in the kitchen tinkering with his stamp collection or listening endlessly to the radio. But George? I recall him in only one spot, his taxidermy shop, the small building mentioned earlier—which in earlier times was probably a garage or more likely a stable—just across the way from the kitchen door.

Hardly large enough to stable three or four horses, that tiny studio was stuffed, so to speak, with a grand collection of animals displaying, in varying degrees, the art of taxidermy and exuding an odor both mystifying and overpowering. It was an entirely new world to me.

Fascinated and, at the same time, disturbed by the smells and the rather distant presence of this little man bent over his workbench, I never entered without a vague sense of foreboding. George treated me well enough and explained his esoteric art in language equally esoteric. But in a kindly way, he would soon convey the message that the pressing demands of the hour dictated a return to his scientific labors rather than prolonged explanations of their intricacies to awestruck nephews.

Politely dismissed, I was more than ready to leave the arcane and redis-cover the familiar, a set of activities more down-to-earth. Less intellectual, busier, noisier, and a generation nearer, this haven was the carpentry shop of my mother's brothers, George (yes, a second Uncle George) and Gene McDaniel, all of a hundred feet away from Great-Uncle George's stuffed animals.

The yard behind the McDaniel house led to a fenced dog run and then to an alley lined with garages and other small buildings. In one of these build-ings, within hailing distance of their parents' home, the brothers had set up shop. There, all sorts of wonders were performed by all sorts of whirring, grinding, rending machines making melodies I had seldom heard before. These sounds were music to young ears, in sweet sensual harmony with the olfactory transition from feathers and formaldehyde to the heavenly scents of fresh-sawed cedar and pine of Uncle Gene and Uncle George's domain.

That carpentry shop was sheer enchantment. Like the taxidermy studio, it also had its mysteries. But they were explained in action rather than by dry and distant discourse. Nondescript pieces of lumber, deftly fetched from scattered bins, barrels, and nondescript piles, rapidly became household items. Tables and chairs would appear, followed by shelving, moldings, end pieces, picture frames, sidings, posts, planks, and any number of small objects for which—neither then nor now—could I find a name.

Elton McDaniel, George's son, was often there to explain the fine points. Six months to the day my junior, he was at least six years ahead of me in knowledge of the world, his world at least. The sure and instant transforma-tion of lumber into furniture, which I saw as magic, he dismissed as simple craftsmanship, explaining the more sophisticated techniques as mere "tricks of the trade."

If these words make Elton appear condescending, or George and Gene just journeymen, such is not my intention. Elton (George Elton McDaniel Jr.) admired his father, from whom he learned the "tricks of the trade" and much more. His father was an elegant gentleman, a competent musician, skilled contractor, and highly regarded businessman of whom it was said, and not too hyperbolically, that "he built Marysville."

Elton and I were pals. Summer pals mostly, but we always kept in touch and, because of the nearness in age, were usually paired off in various ways such as having a separate table at family dinners. We constantly played together, and Elton, though younger, was always the host in Marysville. He showed me the town. To my parents' horror, he also showed me the local billiard hall and who knows what else.

He tried to show me how to walk a hunting dog twice my size. He even attempted to teach me how to ride his pony—bareback, no less—with disastrous results. Elton was simply precocious. Or at least precocious compared to me. Growing up in a small town where everyone knew and respected his father and famous grandfather, he may have learned early that more was expected of him.

Marysville was not my childhood life, however. It was barely my summer life. As long as it seemed then, it seldom lasted more than a month. But it was a concentrated existence, a practical learning experience. And hot. Heat I'd never encountered in Berkeley. Heat that made a lifesaver of the city's new swimming pool, proudly referred to as the *natatorium*.

The heat in Marysville was so intense that there were afternoons just too hot to swim. Too hot, that is, even to think of the sweltering trip to and from the natatorium. Those were days for lying down to listen to a radio broadcast of the Oakland Oaks, often playing the San Francisco Seals (in the old Pacific Coast League) and blissfully falling asleep sometime around the third or fourth inning, only to wake up (game over) soaking wet with perspiration.

And nights? Hot. Insufferably hot *inside*. Dinner must have been a challenge to those who prepared it. Once in a while it could be a challenge for diners too, even for "small fry." On warm nights, we'd sit out on the enclosed porch, ubiquitous electric fans oscillating, windows open, flies ignored. Eating silently and hurriedly, we could make a chore out of the usual, pleasant repast. I just sat there, looking forward to evening beyond the oppressive confinement of the house, a time of sitting on the front porch gradually cooling down while we conversed and twirled our fiery punks in defiance of the relentless mosquitoes.

Before we could escape, however, there was the clean-up hour. Then, if we were lucky, the Judge would produce his Velie cabriolet, a four-door convertible with black leather interior, canvas top, and isinglass "windows." My siblings and I would slide in, luxuriating in the texture and smell of the leather seats. Then—our genial chauffeur in command—the majestic phaeton smoothly conveyed us to the "Ghost Tree," a few miles out of town, for root beer floats, peanuts, and other goodies. Sometimes we would stop instead at a local creamery for fresh-churned ice cream, a grand delicacy in the days before bulk packaging. On those occasions, we never failed to bring home my grandmother's favorite flavor, strawberry.

Treats and sunset would give way to porch-sitting time and to the long and cooling summer twilight. When twilight brought hosts of crepuscular insects, Elton and I mounted a counterattack with our glowing punks, wielding them gleefully while our elders, seemingly oblivious to the menace buzzing around them, talked away, and listlessly flicked their Japanese fans at the persistent mosquitoes.

Well before the hot days and stifling nights of summer ended, my father drove again to Marysville to collect his family. I was always a little blue, returning home after an exotic sojourn in a pleasantly foreign environment. But, eventually, I came to enjoy this annual rite of transition, since it presaged a new school year, renewed friendships, and—just as important, it seemed—an escape from the unrelenting heat.

Escape was instantaneous, usually as we approached the Carquinez Bridge, where the blessed fog began to roll in. Driving down the old route from Sacramento in earlier days, before the bridge was built, we'd hit the fog near the Vallejo cutoff. On either route, unbearable without air-conditioning, the valley heat dominated three seasons of every year. What a relief, at last, to reach the Bay Area fog, the cool caress that became my friend in early childhood and has remained so ever since.

Growing up in Berkeley and Marysville consumed about a decade, from child to teenager. Thus, when I returned to the Bay Area in late summer, 1934, it was high time to be thinking of high school and the vastly different social environment that lay ahead. I would soon discover that my schooling was about to change dramatically. ◆

Chapter 3

"UNI"

◆ ══

University High School, Oakland, California, and the stolid "Ms. Typewriter," whose sophisticated pragmatism demonstrated the art of good teaching.

 $\mathcal{T}$ he common term "middle school" is preferable in my judgment to "junior high school," primarily because the phrase "junior high school" can be misleading. It tells little of what lies ahead, and much that is wrong, whereas "middle school" is precise. It reveals only what is ascertainable, the chronological gap between schools.

Willard Junior High School did a reasonably good job in helping scores of teenagers manage the transition. Any failure to prepare its students adequately for high school was a fault of nature, not of Willard's staff. Its instructors, for the most part, were excellent. I remember with pleasure the teaching skills, for example, of Miss Visaide in Latin, Miss Kellogg in music, and the Mayne sisters, Minnie in math and Bessie in English.

Then there was Mr. Beardsly, a historian dubbed Old Beerbelly by students who derided him because of his obesity and unkempt attire. One

C.R. at Willard Middle School, in 2009.

morning, classroom instruction was interrupted by an explosive crash caused by some 30 textbooks and notebooks from 30 desks dropping simultaneously to the floor. The expected moment of silence and Mr. Beardsly's cold stare that followed this deliberate and grossly disrespectful prank gave way to a quiet and unexpected lecture on mass behavior.

Eloquently and extemporaneously, Mr. Beardsly delivered a speech on Adolf Hitler, illustrating the ways in which the Nazis made use of mass rallies, rabble-rousing distortions, dissembling, and outright lies to persuade the ill-informed and manipulate the gullible. One of the uses of history, he explained, is to teach people to see through such techniques. Not only was his analogy relevant to the book cascade, but it also held us students spellbound for 15 minutes right into the lunch hour. The nickname Old Beerbelly disappeared from students' vocabulary that day.

If Mr. Beardsly's 15-minute ad-lib had been a mini-portrait of what I learned at Willard, the transition to high school might have been easier. But it portrayed no such thing. It was only a small part of the total picture. It made a strong impression on most of us, but its effect was cumulative, and not fully recognized until later in our academic careers. Nor am I implying that Mr. Beardsly was a better teacher than others at Willard. He just had a great moment, one that would not be surpassed by any teacher I encountered in high school.

While transfer from elementary to middle school is modest and hardly noticed by some, the next step is huge, its enormity easy to miscalculate.

University High School was located on what was once known as Grove Street, in Oakland, two miles southwest of Berkeley's Claremont Hotel. When I attended, a few hardy souls walked to Uni—as it was called—from their homes close to the hotel. The rest of us took the train.

My typical school day began with a brisk walk. From Roble Court to Tunnel Road, past tennis club and hotel, I covered about a thousand yards to the train. While as a rule it was a fairly easy 10-minute walk, oversleeping—not uncommon among teenagers—inevitably brought on early morning nightmares.

I usually reached the halfway mark to my destination, the train, at a spot some 200 yards past The Uplands, a street that intersects Tunnel Road from the south. This point was the first place on my walk from which I could actually see the Key Route train sitting there next to the tennis courts, connected to the Claremont Hotel by a covered, wooden-shingled stairway.

Key Route train sitting there? Well, if it was not, I had missed it. And also, if the train was already moving as I reached the halfway mark, I knew that I would miss it. But I soon learned that if I began running when it still lay motionless in the dock, I had a good chance of catching the train, provided it didn't begin moving just as I began sprinting. Ultimately, the task of getting Key and Kid in sync boiled down to legs, luck, time, timing, and alarm clocks.

Time, and holding to it, were big at Uni. To me, everything was big there. Though only a little larger than Willard and John Muir combined, the school seemed enormous. Taking up a city block, it presented an imposing facade to newcomers. Once inside, we discovered that a great amount of walking its long halls lay ahead, and time between classes was limited, allowing no room for dawdling.

The attitude, moreover, appeared large too. There was something in the air that seemed to say, "OK, kids, you've had your fun and games, now get ready for the Big Show. This is high school."

A subjective reaction on my part? Probably, but at the same time there *was* a prevailing "attitude." The school got good press and had good word-of mouth rapport with the community as well as a well-publicized connection with the University of California. Its very name, University High School, sent a message.

Nevertheless, intimidating as the word "University" may have been in the title, its impact was secondary to the words "High School." We former middle schoolers were *all* intimidated, whether we transferred to Uni or Berkeley High. Both were very good schools, virtually unrivaled in the East Bay area, except by Piedmont High School.

Both Uni and Berkeley High were beneficiaries of reflected prestige from their connections with the University of California. While Uni enjoyed a sort of "family" relationship through official association with the School of Education at Cal, Berkeley High School profited from its close location, about a half mile away. Its teachers were in contact with the university and its professors, with ready access to Cal's libraries and other research facilities. Berkeley High's students also benefited from a location in the heart of the city's business district, only a few steps away from the well-stocked Berkeley Public Library.

Having attended only one of these high schools, I shall not try to compare them. They were both top-notch institutions but were widely different. Some have said that Berkeley High was more rigorous, and some have insisted that Uni was more innovative.

My recollection is that a sense of innovation and creative teaching dominated Uni's educational philosophy. The teaching staff put great emphasis on *active* learning and, especially, learning by doing. They consciously rejected any procedure that required *active* teachers to dole out information to *passive* students. They constantly sought new ways to motivate students through active learning.

Uni teachers were generally successful in these efforts. That, however, does not mean that their innovations always worked. A rather dubious example of curricular innovation greeted me my first year at University High School in the shape of two courses, one entitled Social Living, the other, Personal Management. The two courses were overlapping, ambiguous, and vague. The ideas behind them were admirable and their goals meaningful, yet I doubt that they advanced students' academic or social skills. I do recall that "active learning" in Social Living came at personal expense.

One day, the teacher, much to my dismay, asked a girl and me to come to the front of the room. We were to show the class how to dance. Seeing our facial responses to her words, the teacher must have sensed our "active" panic.

Upon learning my fate, I stood there frozen, motionless and red-faced, until I was prompted to put an arm around the girl, who now was also blushing. By this time, as the snickering in the room grew louder, the three

Andrée on the campus of the University of California, June 1935, with her proud father, Professor G. D. Bonno.

of us stood there awkwardly: two hoping for exit and the teacher, no doubt, actively seeking it. Gracefully recovering her sangfroid, our intrepid instructor put my hands in the right places and dismissed us with some well-chosen words about dance steps and ballroom etiquette.

It was a genuine, if misguided, effort to show students how to confront social situations on the dance floor as a preview of the complex interrelationships of grown-up life. It could have backfired. Had she chosen the very insecure or disturbed, long-lasting psychological damage might have resulted. For my partner and me, there was a little temporary embarrassment; but for our teacher, I suspect, it was not an experiment she would attempt again soon. Credit is due her, nonetheless, for innovating and being ready to assume risk. Better a good idea gone awry than overcaution.

Instructors in chemistry, physics, music, English, and Spanish were all good at Uni. One of the best there was a biologist whose teaching I enjoyed greatly despite her saying to me one day, "You'll never amount to anything, young man. You're just a dreamer."

She was right. I was a dreamer. Fortunately, I haven't changed. Eventually, I would find that some dreamers fail while others excel. It all depends on why they dream, what they dream, when they dream, and whether they are awake at the time. Some bright students dream because the pace of instruction is too slow. Bored, they dream and fall behind. If too far behind, they drop out.

Forgetting dreamers and dropouts, we return for a moment to *active learning,* which takes us to a very special teacher at Uni. She taught the course from which I learned most, retained most, and derived the greatest long-run benefit. It was a short course, one semester, one hour per day, but it was intense and challenging.

Her specialty was typewriting, and the way she presented it was compelling. Few, if any of us, had ever experienced such concentrated, sequential, and systematic learning. True, the subject matter lent itself to the way it was taught, as did the teacher's personality. Gifted, patient, unrelenting, and tough, Ms. Typewriter (for that is how I think of her) would brook neither resistance nor objection to her methods, which began with denying us our desire: We were forbidden to use the glistening machines sitting there, silently singing siren songs inviting our eager hands to touch. No! No. We were directed instead to study charts and diagrams. Active learning? And I'm looking at pictures and graphs? The history of typewriters and how they're made? "Gimme a break!"

It got worse. Our grousing and grumbling grew each day as we did finger exercises and studied diagrams until one morning she turned the class in a new direction. Reminding us that learning to type was all about our fingers and our minds, she informed us that we would now begin "typing."

Subdued cheers turned to sullen silence when we were told to "type" in accordance with charts in the manual; fingers only, *on our desks.* So we followed diagrams that showed where the fingers should go, as our teacher walked around the room to guide us.

Once satisfied that we were all "on the same page," she directed us to "copy" sentences in our instruction manual and to "retype" them if—heaven forbid—we made any errors. While not all of us appreciated her sense of humor, we did as we were told.

Though saying we were on the *honor system,* she had the uncanny ability to detect mistypes and was pleased to correct the usual culprits. The wayward were encouraged to practice the drill at every opportunity outside of class.

The day after starting this exercise, we did it again. And again the next day. And the next. More days of this peculiar game followed. Then a strange thing occurred on the Key Route, the train many of us rode to Uni and back: We were "typing" letters to each other with our fingers, on our notebooks, on our seats, on the chair tops of our seats, on each other, and wherever we could find a place to put digits to work. We were even reciting sentences back and forth to one another to determine who could "type" the fastest, the *slowest* among us self-righteously insisting that he was the most accurate. The peculiar game was turning out to be fun and ended up with our laughingly admitting that dear old Ms. Typewriter, damn old Ms. Typewriter, knew how to play the game too, her game.

When somebody deliberately spilled the beans about *our* game, the teacher smiled and ended *her* game with the words, "It sounds like your fingers are ready."

Handing out material to be copied and directing us to place fingers on keyboards, she walked around the classroom to check our posture and the position of our hands. General instructions followed. We typed. She helped the clumsy or mistaken and admonished peekers, "Look at the copy, not your hands. Let your fingers do the typing!"

After a typing trial of the first paragraph, we were allowed 15 minutes to retype the balance of the handouts and to turn them in at the bell. Few completed this first of many tests within 15 minutes. Those who did made lots of errors. One girl finished in 10 minutes and departed, eliciting remarks by fellow students that her machine's end-of-line bell sounded like an alarm clock.

By the time the semester ended, all of us in this quintessential example of *active learning* had become reasonably good typists, not a peeker among us. We learned by doing, and we learned so well that most of us probably *never* forgot. I never forgot, or at least my fingers never forgot. Nor did I forget the obvious lesson here, that we learn by doing. Or as my son, Richard, reminded me, in the words of Aristotle, "That which we learn to do, we learn by doing."

Old Ms. Typewriter made typists out of us all, and in the process gave us much more, simply in the way she taught. I am grateful for those extras. Still, I am most thankful for the skills learned from her basic discipline. If it weren't for Ms. Typewriter, I might now be using *the Columbus System* (Discover and Land) to type this manuscript.

Like Ms. Typewriter, most teachers at Uni were interested in students as individuals—much more, it seemed to me, than at Willard Junior High, where *impersonal* was the order of the day. Uni teachers were consistently alert to students' extracurricular concerns and challenges, eager to help or guide where indicated. Teachers' benign interference frequently steered teenagers away from trouble or, correspondingly, helped pave the way to achievement through recognition of hidden talents.

This institutional attitude touched even me on several occasions. I recall, for example, certain teachers suggesting I run for junior class president. I ran, was elected, and served (but I never again ran for office). A more dramatic example in my senior year involved a school performance. Edmond Solara, a budding genius and probably a Uni alumnus, wrote us a beautiful operetta. To this day, his haunting melodies saunter through my head. Our music teacher recommended me for the lead role and, more than that, persuaded me to accept the part when offered. I anticipated the months of memorizing lines, learning songs, and rehearsing the staging, singing, acting, and general performance.

Ah, yes. I had anticipated all this. But there was something I was not fully prepared for: the gorgeous Beatrice Miller. Tall and blonde and attractive beyond description, she was Edmond Solara's girlfriend and *my* leading lady. Both Edmond and Beatrice were mature, well beyond high school age. Ed was an accomplished musician and Beatrice had a beautiful voice.

And I—sweet 16 and seldom been kissed—was there to hold her hand onstage, sing love songs to her, embrace her, and at last—before a packed house, with Edmond and, naturally, my mother and father in the audience—to perform the *coup de grace,* planting a kiss upon her luscious lips.

I learned a lot that night in the auditorium at Uni, "learned by doing." I discovered that I could stand onstage in an austere and expansive auditorium before several hundred students, faculty, and friends and not give in to sheer panic. It was close, however, since I was apprehensive, anxious, maybe even terrified. Would I forget my lines? Not hear the prompter? Suffer a fit of amnesia kissing Beatrice on stage?

My near panic at the operetta became a sort of catalyst to reflections on the significance of graduation from University High School. These apprehensions, offstage, became mixed with larger concerns. Flight from the cocoon of high school to a larger and more sophisticated environment would involve questions such as, Should I go to work for the Webb Motor Company? Or go to college? Or both? Or neither?

I'd soon learn that forging answers to questions such as these was a bit more complicated than kissing a glamorous young woman onstage. In addition, looking back, I see a clearer picture of the role Uni played in preparing me for new adventures.

The school and, particularly, its teachers, took deliberate aim at preparing students to resolve problems sensibly, to base decisions on evidence, and to be mindfully aware of the possible consequences of any action. They constantly sought ways to help students develop confidence in their ability to resolve academic and social conflicts effectively.

The biology teacher who chided me for dreaming may not seem to fit this mold. She may have been trying to shock me into better performance. Whatever her reasoning, I'm sure she was trying to help. And the music teacher who cast me into a sea of operatic tempests surely was attempting to encourage, lend me confidence, and raise my sights. University High School gets an A for effort. I don't know enough about my fellow students, but for me it's easy: where I have enjoyed some success, Uni deserves much of the credit. As for failures, I'll take the blame. ◆

Chapter 4

SATHER TOWER

◆ ═══════════════

Matriculation at the University of California, with observations
on several of its extraordinary professors.

$\mathscr{A}$ny success University High School may have had in preparing students for the grand transition to college, gainful employment, or the great unknown (travel, drift, and "self-discovery") was not evident to me at the time. I had prepared for college, and my parents expected it. But uncertainty was in the air.

The Depression lingered. Several friends had to forgo college to help support their families. My brother and sister, already in college, knew that staying there was problematic, given the vagaries of the automobile business. I worked at the Webb Motor Company, my father's business, throughout the summer of 1934. That, and some free weekends of basketball and baseball at local playgrounds, helped me avoid deep thoughts on the subject of Higher Education.

The end of summer brought clarification. Already admitted to the University of California, I was confronted with one more hurdle: the dreaded

Subject A exam, a comprehensive writing test required of all entering students. It should have been easy for me, since English and athletics were my best subjects in high school. Yet my anxiety persisted because failing the test resulted in automatic enrollment in a course routinely referred to as "Dumbbell English."

Well I recall entering the huge examination room, already crowded with nervous students, noisy and restless. That vision backed up rumors that nothing could be worse than enrollment in Dumbbell English.

Ignoring suggestions of scoffing friends that a course in Dumbbell Swahili or Arabic might be more daunting, I faced and dispatched the beast, clearing the way to slaying other dragons, such as registration, course selection, and first days of classes.

For some students, these activities were preceded by a week of the ancient and barbaric procedure of rushing, an intricate game of social fencing, thrust and counterthrust, between prospective member and fraternity or sorority. This rite of passage carried a load of disappointment and heartbreak, especially in the more sophisticated and often heartless female version. A young woman, after a week or so of complicated negotiations, might or might not receive an invitation to join a sorority. She then might or might not decide to "pledge." If a prospective pledge receives several offers, nonselected sororities may never hear. They're used to that.

The statement above is simplified, just as the process has since been humanized by the partial substitution of electronic communication for slow and, for rushees, tantalizing postal service. The role of fraternal societies has shrunk in the last half century, though there has been a minor resurgence in recent years.

I pledged Alpha Delta Phi at Cal and have never regretted it. The main emphasis, since its beginning in 1832, has been literary. In my day, a major part of every regular meeting was devoted to literary production, each brother being required to deliver an original piece before the membership at least once a semester.

The male rushing process was comparatively easygoing, little more than lunches and an occasional bowling match. It was so low key that pledging negotiations took place at the same time I was going through the formidable registration process.

Surmounting long lines of registration in Edwards Gymnasium and the bewildering process of signing up for classes, I learned that it was not necessary to select a major. But it appeared to be expected. "What are you going to major in?" I heard on every side. History was my chief academic interest, but my sister said, "Everybody majors in history!" My father said, "Learn to think. Logic is what you need." Not lacking for advice, I wavered. History was out. English had appeal. I thought, "learning to think" sounds like a good idea.

My sister, Virginia, and my father at Claremont Country Club, early fifties.

So I majored in philosophy. First semester of freshman year with Lucretius, Plato, Aristotle. Got lost in Plato's cave. Read what Socrates had to say, or ask, only to learn much later that he wrote nothing or, if he did, none remains. Learned from Aristotle that "man is a political animal," but in time found that he meant simply that men "live in the *polis.*" In sum, I learned about The Nature of Things (*De Rerum Naturem*) but little about thinking logically.

The second semester turning abstruse, I switched from philosophy to English, where I reveled in rediscovering old favorites and finding new, like William Congreve, who intoned more than three centuries ago, "Women are like tricks by sleight of hand / Which, to appreciate, one should not try to understand."

I also encountered the famous words of Alexander Pope, "Damn with faint praise," a phrase I remember my mother occasionally uttering with some vehemence. Additionally, I learned the rest of the couplet: "Damn with faint praise, assent with civil leer. / And, without sneering, teach the rest to sneer."

Returning for a moment to the swirling mob of registering students, I recall experiencing a sense of wonderment as I waited in the course-selection line. Here for sure was another world, one that overwhelmed any and all efforts to compare with high school.

Where at Uni, for example, could I choose among offerings in economics? astronomy? astrophysics? biochemistry? political science? jurisprudence? torts? business? business administration? agribusiness? sociology? geography? geology? geophysics? paleontology? psychology? education? physical education? statistics? trigonometry? calculus? oenology? ecology? philosophy? comparative literature? Romance languages? Slavic languages? Far Eastern languages? Arabic? Hebrew? Hindi? linguistics? morphology? zoology?

A bit dazed, I signed up for several courses, anxiously thinking of actually attending these exotically entitled classes. A scary moment, but it was also exciting. At least I recognized the word at the top of my course list, geology. The class was taught by a strutting little popinjay burdened by a disproportionately large name: Norman Ethan Allen Hinds. Intense, dramatic, and spellbinding, he was loved and held in awe by most of his students.

I'm not sure about the *love* part, especially after receiving my first midterm grade. Amazed, however, and admittedly awestruck, I concluded that geology was a winner. Would I become a geology major? Strangely, a philosophy professor, Douglas Strong, would soon push me in that direction.

Freshman literature, another winner, was taught by Guy Montgomery, an engagingly effective little fellow (all BIG MEN, it is odd that so many were small in stature). As forceful as Hinds, Montgomery was less flamboyant but just as persuasive. Students admired him and probably loved his red face and white goatee. Awestruck by Hinds, they were astounded and charmed by Montgomery and his recondite handling of an immense subject. His teaching made me want to remain an English major (though later he influenced me to desert that discipline).

Professor Douglas Strong, a good scholar with impeccable credentials, introduced me to philosophy. Fascinated by Lucretius and engrossed with Plato, I found the course becoming a bore, somehow, as the semester dragged on. Perhaps it was the hour, or the transition from Lucretius, Plato, and Aristotle to Berkeley, Hume, Kant, and Nietzsche that turned me away. These, and Dr. Strong's unemotional, even dry presentation, may have combined in a gathering disavowal of all things "philosophical."

Curiously, years later, when I chaired the History Department at San Diego State, we hired Douglas Strong Jr., a most engaging, charming, and competent scholar, more interesting and entertaining than his father, it seemed—but perhaps by then my understanding and appreciation of merit had matured and mellowed.

Other first semester courses, with one notable exception, were of little interest to me. That exception was Western Civilization, taught by the rather nonexceptional Dr. Franklin Charles Palm, professor of history. Palm broke the mold in many ways. He was fairly large in stature, compared to Hinds and Montgomery. Speaking with a slight lisp in somewhat colorless tones, he also lacked the animation of the other two. Western Civilization met on Mondays, Wednesdays, and Fridays in the largest room in Wheeler Hall. Though dry at times, Palm's lectures nearly filled the cavernous space, with some 250 students enrolled and an average attendance of 175.

Professor Palm was solid, dispassionate, and thorough. Other outstanding scholars in the Modern European History faculty included Robert J. Kerner and Raymond J. Sontag. Kerner was brilliant, didactic, and opinionated. Sontag, whom I would encounter only in upper-division classes, combined the best qualities of Palm and Kerner.

Palm was very popular with students. His Western Civilization, the basic course in European history, was popular too, fulfilling several lower-division requirements for history majors and other disciplines. There were other reasons for Palm's popularity. Some said he was an easy grader. Not true. Neither easy nor hard, he graded carefully, with close attention to the evidence. This I know directly because later, as his teaching assistant, I saw him examine—one by one—midterm and final examination grades, discuss with me each student's performance in quiz-section, and only then assign final grades for the semester. It was a deliberate and prolonged operation. Students knew they got a fair shake.

Nevertheless, there were detractors who declared that Palm was an easy mark, had favorites, and indulged in alcohol. Some delighted in dredging up tales of his early *bon vivant* days, often with Norman Ethan Allen Hinds. A favorite rumor had them appearing in morning classes still attired in their rumpled tuxedoes after a record-breaking debauch the night before.

Somewhere in between, I suspect, lies the truth. Palm was a teacher and, at the same time, a seriously gentle revolutionary in a field where he saw too often the stodgy, remote, absentminded, or simply absent, professor.

No bombs, no rushing to the barricades for Frank Palm. He was content to make war, quietly and by example. His main target? The aloof and aloft, who regarded those at their feet as secondary to their research efforts and scholarly writings.

Because he considered direct interaction with students—as many as possible—to be fundamental, Professor Palm made himself accessible. Students coming to his office in the library were welcomed and encouraged. There, as in his lectures, he preached the all-encompassing need to strive for objectivity in seeking the truth. He also reminded us on many an occasion of the equal importance of suspending judgment when looking for correct answers. Additionally, he stressed the need to look for both sides of any argument. In the process, he encouraged and guided generations of students in following these principles and no doubt changed the thinking habits of many. I know that I was one of the many. Indeed, for years my grandfather had encouraged and my family had expected me to become a lawyer. Did Palm dissuade me from following that profession? I don't know. But I do know that in his emphasis on being accessible to students and in his subtle and indirect attacks on some of the attitudes and excesses often displayed in his profession, he did not lose sight of the ongoing need for rigorous scholarship in academe, to which his many publications amply attest.

I might add, speaking of scholarship, that his common-touch attitude with fellow faculty as well as students, his belief in the significant role of the common man, was reflected in one of his major works, *The Middle Classes: Then and Now,* which was published just prior to my first acquaintance with him.

Professor Palm alerted his students to many historical concepts, some that could easily have been missed along the way. One of these was the disproportionately large role *chance* has played in the drama of human development. Alexander the Great's draught of tainted water; the horse, in 1701, that stumbled on a mole hole, ending the life of King William III; or Hitler's ill-fated decision to invade Russia come to mind.

One could be aware of such relatively commonplace catastrophes and aware of their consequences, but totally unaware of their combinability into a theory of *chance.* This made a great impression on me and my fellow students.

At best, I was vaguely aware of chance, or at least of the "oh, doggone-its" and the "if onlys" on every side. But never had I heard its role so deliberately and clearly laid out. Unknowingly, Palm pushed me toward my father's injunction to learn to think and to learn some of the rules of thoughtful inquiry.

I was finding I needed thoughtful inquiry while struggling with the tumbling kaleidoscope of changing majors. Palm may have shown the way, but I did not follow the road all at once. Philosophy had already fallen by the wayside. English literature would hold me in thrall for several semesters. But then I experienced the writings of the famous anthropologist Alfred L. Kroeber. His examination of Tlingit Indians, in Alaska, neurosurgery in ancient Peru, the mysteries of culture growth, and more, combined to alter my course once again.

Changing to anthropology ended the game of major-tag. I was hooked. Fascinating, novel, valid science, anthropology was a natural development of my interest in geology and paleontology and a close cousin to history in its methods. Moreover, I concluded self-righteously that the switch from English to anthropology was a move from play to work.

I had an additional reason for leaving English. It goes back to Professor Guy Montgomery, who played a part, as briefly mentioned earlier. He was a favorite professor. I wanted to take more work with him. Looking for advanced offerings in English literature, I enrolled—a mere sophomore—in an upper-division course on William Shakespeare.

There were only eight students in the class. I soon found out why. Montgomery had the class studying *Macbeth* for the whole semester using the *variorum* edition, with all the renderings including spelling and wording changes, alternative phrasing, and numerous incidental variations. Two weeks into the course and having covered only the first three pages of *Macbeth*, I withdrew from the class and resolved to withdraw from the major.

Fleeing anthropology was a different matter, though advanced offerings brought similar problems. No microscopic dissections of limited editions were required, but anthropology's emphasis on mathematical analysis and sophisticated measurement techniques cooled my ardor. After a while, I gradually lost interest in repeatedly measuring cephalic indexes, calculating bone dimensions, and checking comparative pigmentation.

A more compelling course of action, however, had to do with the machinations of Adolf Hitler. A rapid deterioration of international relations had brought European history to the fore once again. I still enjoyed anthropology, but history would henceforth be my main academic interest.

Having accumulated sufficient units in each of the three disciplines, I would graduate with an English, History, Anthropology degree. History would become my sole major in graduate school.

By the time I was doing graduate work, however, the United States had become involved in World War II; and during those years, life would be dramatically altered. My revolving ride in majors was part of that change.

I was fortunate to be enrolled at a top-tier university. Signs of strength were everywhere. A great university, with a great library and a teaching staff comprising the very best professors drawn from top-notch institutions all over the world, Cal's reputation for high-quality research, publication, and instruction was unassailable.

Undergraduates came in awe and keen anticipation. They remained if they applied themselves vigorously and continuously to their studies. They learned and absorbed within a rich intellectual atmosphere and an academically permissive culture.

Students were free to harvest the fruits of knowledge wherever the effort might lead. They were also free to slide, wander, fall prey to unproductive pursuits, or simply fail outright. Bailouts were conspicuous by their absence. Good students applied themselves and therefore graduated with superb credentials and an A-1 education.

The major weakness arose from the need, mostly financial, for huge classes taught primarily through lectures. Two hundred or more students at a time—listening for an hour to brilliant lectures in pleasant surroundings and in comfortable seats—had to learn something. But they also lost much in the process. Even the brightest, the most attentive, might occasionally let their minds wander or succumb to *Morpheus*'s stealthy approach.

Yet because of need and tradition, lectures were the system. And in a variety of ways, the system worked. Industrious students turned lectures into active learning by diligently taking notes. Professors routinely augmented lectures by assigning collateral reading enforced with rigorous written tests.

Moreover, administration of larger lecture classes was accomplished at Cal, and elsewhere, through mandatory quiz-sections that usually met once a week and were conducted by graduate teaching assistants who reported to the lecturer. Quiz-sections became a solution to some of the lecture short-comings. They gave undergraduates a chance for direct interaction with knowledgeable young teachers. They provided active teacher-training for the graduate instructors, like an intern program. They also were helpful at exam time, both to students and to the professor in charge, since teaching assistants often did grading, and more. On more than one occasion I would benefit from these quiz-sections, both as an undergraduate and as a teaching assistant (more on that later). As an undergraduate, I was just trying to learn how to learn. I was aware, for example, of great teaching (dull teaching as well); but there was little coherence in my thoughts about who was doing it and why, nor about the relationship of class size to the professor's performance or scholarship to his ability to teach.

Indeed, I'm not altogether sure that as an underclassman I learned how to learn at Cal. Not directly, at least. It was a gradual development, coming from observation, reflection, and interaction with other students, an important aspect of the learning process. Students learn from one another and learn how to learn.

Another area that helped me learn how to learn was extracurricular activities at Cal. Joining with others in groups and teams helped me mature in ways that had a distinct bearing on my future development. Floating more or less academically, the first year or so, I easily became involved with other floaters. I soon joined the University Choir. Freshman baseball followed in the spring of 1938, and joining a jazz band completed the overreach.

The choir thrilled me. It also dumbfounded me when its leader—*pianissimo* being called for—dampened our enthusiasm by telling us to lower our voices. "Softly, softly," he coaxed, "like singing in the library."

There was less harmony but lots of fun—and long hours—on the baseball field where, recalling the illustrious career of my father, I decided that I, too, was a pitcher. Two developments thwarted that fantasy. First, my physical skills fell short. Second was Mike Koll. A gifted pitcher, Mike starred the freshman season and would carry the varsity for three ensuing years. Me a backup? Forget about it. Mike didn't need a backup. Still, during the season of 1938, I diligently attended practice every afternoon for three or more hours.

My friend Tom Haven possessed a large collection of jazz records to which he and I listened at every chance. One day he greeted me by saying, "How would you like to play a dance gig?" When, I responded doubtfully, he added, "It's a trio job, $5 per man, two and a half hours." That was Big Money in 1938! I accepted at once and resolved to brush up on the piano, which I had resumed playing as a senior in high school. We enlisted Dick Duhring, a talented saxophonist, and Tom Stanton, a trumpet player and guitarist who later achieved fame as a band leader in Europe and the United States. Tom Haven played drums, having taught himself by practicing with wire brushes on a telephone book in time to his records. Luther Nichols soon joined us. Trained on drums by Johnny Valiotis (later famous in Santa Rosa, California, as entertainer and chef Johnny Otis), Lute seamlessly fit in, alternating gigs with Haven, who would become increasingly involved in campus politics.

Less harmonious than the choir and not having quite as much fun as shagging baseballs, we played well enough at a fraternity dance to be invited back. Before long, we played a succession of fraternity gigs and nondescript barn dances, all of little significance. There was one gig, however, that requires some explanation, because it bears strangely on events occurring many years later.

That event took place at Cal's old student union building, Henry Morse Stephens Hall (known as Stephens Union). In those days it housed various offices of the Alumni Association and the Student Association (ASUC). A beautiful building constructed in 1921, its huge upstairs meeting room was a very popular gathering spot, both formal and informal.

Popular with the large contingent of foreign-born students, Stephens Union was a favorite hangout of Chinese scholars, whose governing group, in the spring of 1938, decided that it was *the* place for their annual formal dance. Four of them came to Roble Court one night to audition us. After we played for 10 or 15 minutes, all four got up as one and, without a word spoken, departed. A few days later, much to our surprise, one of them phoned me, inviting us to play.

More surprises. We showed up at Stephens Union at 8:30 PM on the appointed night to be ready for the 9:00 downbeat. Nobody there. At 9:30 the hall was still vacant.

Did we have the wrong night? Wrong place? Not Stephens Union?! Impossible. At 10:00 PM a young man walks in and busies himself with some papers at the far end of the hall. Then mysteriously disappears. When another enters at 10:15, we're on him fast:

"*What's the deal?!*"

"Party here."

"*Tonight?*"

"Yeah."

"*We were told to start at 9 PM!*"

"Chinee time!"

Laughing at his cool joke, he leaves us smoldering while two couples amble in; then another. Now, at 11:00, several more Chinese students enter, and as the band starts up again, a few couples venture to dance. By 11:30, the hall is jammed, the band's relaxed, and the joint is jumpin'. They hardly stop dancing until 1:10 AM, when the band folds. We're pooped; they ought to be. A marvelous evening, unenchanting at the beginning, instructive overall.

This droll dance was all part of the learning process which, for me, included a near flunkout. My double-wicked candle had been burning brightly with extracurricular activities, primarily baseball and music. Baseball practice snatched long hours from my days and left me too exhausted to study much at night.

On academic probation for the fall semester, 1938, I did not have the benefit of grade inflation, which infected higher education years later. Hitting the books and soon erasing the probation stigma, I also easily decided not to try out for varsity baseball the following spring. So ended my blooming baseball career, or so I thought, having no way of knowing that some 30 years hence I would become a college baseball coach.

Returning to Stephens Union for a moment, I should mention that, while other formal events were frequently held there, the Chinese Students dance was somewhat atypical. Formality was there, to be sure. But predominantly, it was an informal, popular meeting place, a casual, most-any-hour gathering spot where students—black, white, Chinese, Japanese—would wander in and out or stay to read, talk, and whisper. A lot of us went there to play the piano or—more often—listen to others play.

On one occasion, when the Benny Goodman quartet—Goodman, Wilson, Hampton, and Krupa—were on campus, we were lucky enough to hear the great drummer and vibraphonist Lionel Hampton perform in Stephens Union under the most extraordinary circumstances. (More on that in chapter 20.) ◆

Chapter 5

"FRANCE IS NOT VICHY!"

◆ ═══════════════════

War clouds. Professor Gabriel D. Bonno, Chairman of Cal's French Department, delivers a public lecture, both eloquent and stirring. No less stirring, in some eyes, is the vision of his daughter, Andrée.

Relegating baseball to spectator status helped me form more consistent study habits. Not a scholar yet but a student learning what a college education was all about, I was becoming more aware of what was inside those walls. I had found time to see the library and its infinite resources, the maintenance and clerical staffs, professors, and administrators all in a different light.

The administrators I already knew about, since Robert Gordon Sproul, president of the University of California, lived directly across the street from my family on Elmwood Avenue. He and my father were good friends, and his children and I were playmates.

But languishing in lower-division courses, I often regarded professors—those famous author/scholar/lecturer professors—as aliens from outer space. I caught glimpses of them in classes in huge, impersonal lecture halls. Some—like Hines (geology), Montgomery (English), Olsen and Kroeber (anthropology), and Palm (history)—scintillated, inspired, or entertained.

Upper-division and graduate classes were better. Professors seemed suddenly human. They were intent on finding ways to interact effectively with students, regardless of class size. Such a one was Raymond J. Sontag, professor of Modern European History. A senior when I first heard him, I could not take any more of his courses, since time had run out with Adolf Hitler's impact on global geography. Encountering Sontag so late emphasized the end of my college days and their coinciding with the rapid approach of war. In a few months I'd be called to active duty. With the passage of time and imminence of war, courses in recent European history took on new meanings, and that is one of the reasons Sontag enters my narrative at this point and not earlier. The other reason is that he belongs to a category of teachers that I like to think of as *super-professors* and of whom I will present one other to join him in a moment.

But first, a word about Dr. Sontag, who customarily offered a logically developed lecture to a class of about 65 students. Filling about a half hour, it would cover a variety of nineteenth- or twentieth-century topics such as the Franco-Prussian War, the Dreyfus Case, Social Darwinism, or the long-term causes of World War I. Seamlessly, Sontag's presentation would end with a call for questions from the class. Queries invariably produced an ad-lib answer as precise, direct, and polished as the lecture that preceded it. We all hung on his phrases, mentally applauding the choice of words, the clean and measured rhetorical style, and the total absence of cliché, bombast, or hyperbole. It didn't seem to matter whether a single question elicited a response that consumed the balance of the hour or that many questions brought forth many answers. All responses, regardless of length, were essentially the same in thoroughness and precision.

Though flawless, Sontag's teaching skills were not unique. Upper-division and graduate students were well served by any number of dedicated professors. I have already mentioned the dramatic flair of Professor Hines, the subtle wit of Montgomery, the sparkling certitude of Kerner, and the dispassionate scholarship of Palm. Sontag combined the talents of these and other capable instructors, including one whom I have not mentioned but whose talents are excelled by none of the academicians touted above: another super-professor, Gabriel Dominique Bonno, professor of French Literature at the University of California.

Professor Bonno at his study, 1943.

As with Professor Palm, I eventually got to know Dr. Bonno quite well. But, unlike my experience with Palm, I did not take a number of his classes. In fact, I had no formal work with him and only one intensive course on the study of French, in preparation for the graduate language-requirement test.

I did, however, have the opportunity to hear some of his formal lectures and, much later, to meet several of his advanced students. Invariably, their recollections of him were filled with expressions of admiration and affection.

Gabriel Bonno was a handsome man and slight of build, but well proportioned, another medium-sized "big man," one might say. He had a well-modulated voice and a sparkling French accent. When he spoke, people listened. Charmed by his intensity and enthralled by his impeccably correct English, they were captured by his unassailable logic and elevated by his sense of humor. In a word, he was brilliant, witty, solid: a born educator, a dedicated teacher, a world-famous scholar, and a family man.

Early in his career he had acquired all the credentials to attract the University of California and other prestigious centers of learning. His research and writing had already received scholarly attention on both sides of the Atlantic, even before the American Philosophical Society published his exhaustive treatise, *La constitution britannique devant l'opinion française de Montesquieu a Bonàparte* (1931).

During the last days of the Roarin' Twenties, Gabriel Bonno arrived at a crossroads. Almost simultaneously, he received two professorial offers. One was from the University of Pennsylvania, the other from the University of California.

Penn was—still is—a top-notch institution, more widely known at that time than most West Coast colleges. The American Philosophical Society's location in Philadelphia had given Bonno convenient access to the library of the University of Pennsylvania as well as an opportunity to make friends among its scholars.

The area had many attractions for him. An academic and intellectual center, it was close to the roots of American civilization, to its history, culture, and politics. His wife, Marcelle, who spoke little English, naturally favored Pennsylvania because of its proximity to France. For her, California was way out in what she referred to as "Indian territory." All these factors had Gabriel Bonno leaning toward the East, a posture that may also have been influenced by Penn's higher salary offer. Weighing the pros and cons as he studied the various attractions of the two universities, Bonno knew that academic prestige, proximity to great libraries, and the area's concentration of outstanding educational and cultural institutions all favored Pennsylvania.

Thus, at the moment of decision, when logic clearly pointed eastward, he chose the West. Strange? Not really. Logic has many eyes; and what one man sees, another denies.

California's attractions are legion. The cosmopolitan character of San Francisco, moreover, and its significant French population could hardly have gone unnoticed. And Cal, even in 1929, had a strong reputation, a brilliant faculty, and—already—an excellent library.

He made his decision. While hindsight tells us it was a wise one, it could easily have gone the other way, causing the University of California to lose a distinguished scholar who would, in time, chair its French Department with distinction for many years.

Besides, I cannot help thinking that if he had decided to accept the offer from the University of Pennsylvania, I would never have met his daughter, *Andrée*.

Not that I would meet her right away. First, she had to run an obstacle course to gain admission to Cal. Admissions officials, in their wisdom, decreed that she enroll in the Extension Division for a semester to offset deficiencies they perceived in her Franco-American college-preparatory training. Next, much to the righteous indignation of her father, she was required to pay out-of-state tuition, a goodly sum in those days compared to the negligible amount paid by state resident students. (The most I ever paid was $26 a semester.)

Her father, a full-time professor in full-time residency for most of the preceding decade, quite logically asked, "Exactly what is your definition of in-state residency?" This was a rhetorical question, however, since, officially, foreign-born and nonresident were treated as synonymous.

A moot point, true, but since his original decision was the sine qua non of my future life and career, I find it relevant for two reasons. First, in fairness to the administration of the University of California in the thirties, it could be said that Bonno might also have experienced bureaucratic annoyances at Penn. Universities anywhere can be stodgy and hidebound at times. For all we know, his original decision in favor of Cal might have been based, in part, on conjectures of greater academic freedom there.

Second, while his decision was a great stroke of luck for me, it was not the only stroke of luck. *Chance* in History? Let me tell you about Chance in History as it touched Andrée and me:

At Willard Junior High School, my homeroom desk was second from the front on the far-left row, nearest to the window. A girl named Jean Porter had the misfortune of sitting at the desk directly in front of me. She was gangly, tall, and rather homely—a perfect foil for a rude 12-year-old boy who delighted in teasing her. Jean survived the yearlong ordeal of sharing homeroom with me with a blend of good humor, some exasperation, and frequent outbursts of anger. Eventually, Jean forgave her tormentor. More to the point, however, she soon grew out of the awkward age and blossomed by the time she reached college.

Blossomed? More than that, Jean became a campus beauty. As such, and with a good personality, she attracted the attention of all the best sororities during the rushing season. She pledged Pi Beta Phi, one of the three or four most prestigious sororities at Cal at that time.

Jean had a younger sister, Muriel. When Muriel matriculated at Cal two years later, Jean smoothed Muriel's way through rushing and pledging Pi Beta Phi. No glamour girl like her sister, Muriel was perky, gregarious, and cheerful, making friends easily, even as a child.

As a child, Muriel attended Hillside Elementary School in North Berkeley. In 6th grade an event occurred that would influence the rest of her days. As she would write many decades later, "I remember so well Andrée's arriving in my classroom . . . were we 9 or 10? She was presented as a new student and there she was, adorable in her straw hat with navy ribbons down the back!"

Muriel and Andrée became fast friends for life almost from that day on. Muriel quickly recognized that her new friend, having divided her early years almost equally between France and America, knew little of our customs and perhaps less of the English language. Actually, she picked up English easily when here but forgot it while living abroad.

In a word, Muriel took Andrée under her wing, taught her the latest slang, latest games, latest tricks, best haunts, and best among their peers either to befriend or avoid. They enjoyed a happy childhood together, sharing schools on their way to college where, as one might guess, they became sorority sisters. Andrée's "Big Sister" in Pi Beta Phi would become none other than Muriel's older sister, Jean.

So what's the big deal? Surely I'd have met Andrée through my knowing so well her sorority "big sister," Jean. Not so fast! Jean and I circled in different orbits. I had scarcely seen her since our days at Willard. She went to Berkeley High, I to University High, and our paths at Cal simply did not cross. Yes, it might have happened, but not likely. I needed another lucky day.

The lucky day came one bright autumn morning on the sweeping steps in front of Wheeler Auditorium. Long and only slightly elevated, the wide steps were a major congregating area for students between classes. The steps also provided men a prime location from which to ogle coeds walking on a nearby sidewalk, especially on sunny days. Late one morning, waiting for an eleven o'clock class to convene, I was standing on the steps talking to Tom Haven. Yes, that same Tom Haven who had inveigled me into the dance band business at $5 per gig. Tom abruptly stopped talking to look up, smile, and wave at Carol Goeppert. Carol, his future wife, waved back as did a raven-haired beauty accompanying her.

"Who's that with her?" I asked.

"Oh, one of the Pi Phi pledges," he replied casually.

"I've got to meet her," said I, and not one bit casually. "Does she have a name?"

Tom showed little interest in what I *had* to do. But good friend that he was, he called me after a few days to say that the coed's name was Andrée Bonno, that she had been born in France, that she was very popular and nearly as charming as she was good-looking despite no longer sporting a French accent, and, according to Carol, she might be amenable to meeting me, since I was a good friend of Tom Haven.

I hardly knew just how lucky that day was, that culmination of a concatenation of contingencies that improbably appeared before me on the steps of Wheeler Hall.

It seemed like eons until Andrée and I met a week or so later. We went to a Cal basketball game with Tom and Carol. I'm sure it was a very important game, but I don't know why. I'm sure we were playing against a very good team, but I don't know who. We must have won, but I don't know why, unless it's because I felt good that night. I don't know why I felt good that night, since I was sure that I had made a poor impression on Andrée at and after the game.

Poor impression is a bit of an understatement. From the steps outside Wheeler Auditorium, she looked like other attractive women on campus, pleasant to behold but not specially to rave about. But seeing her at close range simply launched me onto a course of readjusting any notions I had hitherto held of physical beauty. All the clichés come to mind. They all apply. They all fall short.

I had never seen a face quite like hers, either in sculptured grace and harmony or in expression and sparkling animation. The night of the basketball game, I was overwhelmed by this vision, by her quietly alert charm and grace. Was I struck dumb? Like Socrates at his trial? Well, in a way, yes. But a bit more like, *struck stupid.* There I was. Back on Shafter Avenue. And there was the train, Tom the engineer, Carol a passenger. And Andrée, a gorgeous bystander, quietly observing, as I sat there—wrapped in wonderment—on my tricycle.

"On my tricycle"? A far-fetched stretch from 4 years old to 20? Perhaps, but at 4, I helped change names of city streets, while at 20 I'm tongue-tied in awe before this wisp of a lass almost three years my junior.

I'll concede some exaggeration here, but very little of how I might have felt at the time. And certainly, while more than a "wisp," she was slight of build, five feet, five inches tall, and struggling for several years to surpass 99 pounds. "For the record," it should be added that she would not attain the full measure of her physical beauty for another five or ten years.

Despite my self-perceived poor impression, I managed to see her again. And again, as gradually our mutual attraction grew. Weeks passed, and 1940 gave way to 1941. By spring we had become *best friends* on campus, soon making tentative matrimonial plans. Optimistic plans, as it turned out, since Andrée's parents quickly registered opposition, firm and passionate, to the idea of any long-term commitment between me and their daughter. At one point, they even forbade us to see each other, an arrangement of which we were not especially fond.

Twenty-first century readers may find the idea strange: forbidding a young couple from seeing one another. Granted, but first, we must consider the circumstances. Professor Bonno had called me to his office and gently informed me that he and Mrs. Bonno were of the opinion that Andrée was too young to be seeing just one boy since about six months still remained until her 18th birthday.

To this reasonable comment, he added, "You have to consider that she has not lived long in this country. That fact contributes to her lack of experience, and therefore further accentuates the effects of her youth."

Following this inescapable logic, he suggested that a "moratorium" in our relationship would probably be good for both of us. Never once did he use the word *forbid.* He appealed to me on the basis of reason and *my* regard for his daughter, in effect leaving me no choice.

I walked out of his office enlightened and depressed, a sad high: the high part lay in the knowledge that I had just met a likeable and persuasive man, a great man, indeed, who sent me forth with the gift of an unpleasant truth.

At the very time he was instructing me on ethics, student life, and the logic of human relations, Gabriel Bonno was immersed in and overwrought by the unfolding tragedy of conditions in France.

France, the world of Louis XIV, Lafayette, and Napoleon, had become by 1941, the world of Marshal Pétain. Pétain, the "Hero of Verdun" in 1916, was now the senile and incompetent leader of Vichy France, pitifully overseeing the inept and corrupt government after the defeat by the German *Wehrmacht* in the summer of 1940.

While the British, virtually alone, fought on, General Charles de Gaulle and the Free French struggled to preserve some semblance of order in the ravished countryside. The beleaguered French people existed under frightful conditions, including famine, lawlessness, Nazi officialdom, and every kind of scarcity.

The French press kept Andrée generally aware of these hardships, as did radio and the primitive television of the day. More direct news from grandparents and other relatives in France surely came to her, though filtered by her ever-watchful parents. I know that she was worried about her grandparents, of whom she often spoke.

Professor and Mrs. Bonno sought out as much information as they could. It came from many sources, some of which were official in nature. For example, they were in close touch with the French Consulate in San Francisco, where they had many friends. Professor Bonno, a recipient of the *Legion d'honneur,* the highest award of the French government, was a semiofficial member of the Administration of France and as such received a yearly stipend for life.

Naturally, the Bonno family did all they could to ease the pains and pangs of compatriots in Vichy France who were suffering the indignities of life in an occupied land amid scarcity of food, clothing, and life's smallest amenities. Wherever, whenever, and however possible, they sent financial aid. And Marcelle Bonno, as I later discovered, spent days in the post office sending care packages and nights wrapping more gifts for the next day's postal assault. On Saturdays, too, she often dragooned her ready-and-willing daughter into care-package duty as well.

The flow of relief packages from Berkeley to Paris to Bordeaux, site of the Pétain government, gradually increased. Largely symbolic, it nevertheless coincided with the clandestine struggle of the "Free French" against their oppressors.

The care packages, whatever their effect, were tied spiritually to a great effort abroad. At home Andrée, Gabriel, and Marcelle Bonno fought in their way, and fought hard, for the Mother Country.

Additionally, Andrée took up her own fight: she convinced her parents that the "moratorium" should end. As I joined the team, slowly at first, we witnessed the unfolding of wartime events together. From the fall of France and the creation of the Vichy regime to the crucial Battle of Britain and Hitler's great mistake (invading Russia), we saw it all, lived it all, together. (Well, not quite all, since I was in the Pacific for the planned invasion of Japan.)

The Vichy regime was feeble, corrupt, incompetent, despicable. More than that, it was an embarrassment and a source of humiliation for millions of French citizens. It did, however, help provide me the opportunity to see and hear a marvelous performance.

It was in Wheeler Hall—not the Auditorium from whose steps I first saw Andrée—but at the rear, directly across from the Charles Franklin Doe Library, in a small lecture room with a seating capacity of fewer than 100, a little too small for the occasion. It was packed.

I went with Andrée and her mother. The speaker was Gabriel Bonno. The subject was the political situation in France, which meant that the history, role, and accomplishments of the Vichy government and of its personnel were to be analyzed, dissected, and judged. Unmercifully, I might add.

Quietly and dispassionately, he spoke of the fall of France before the German Panzer divisions, the swift breaching of the Maginot Line, on which the French army had overdepended, and the flight of the French government to Bordeaux. Referring briefly to the choice of Marshal Henri-Philippe Pétain as head of a provisional government, he condemned the creation—"from bad to worse"—of the Vichy regime under Pétain's successor, the corrupt, treacherous, and dictatorial Nazi-collaborator Pierre Laval.

At the mention of Laval's name, Bonno's demeanor changed a little. Always eloquent but not always dispassionate, he allowed his voice to rise as he excoriated Laval, enumerating his crimes and Vichy's failures. Then, pausing for a brief moment's gaze at his emotion-tense audience, he turned—eyes flashing—to deliver in carefully measured cadence his eight-word peroration: "FRANCE IS NOT VICHY; VICHY IS NOT FRANCE!"

If I were given to clichés, I might say, "There wasn't a dry eye in the house." But I'm not, so I won't say it. Yet I'd wager that the room was full of moist eyes when he finished. Though it was a long time ago, I'm pretty sure my own eyes were not dry. Maybe that doesn't count since, after all, I may have already suspected that he would be my father-in-law.

It was a grand speech. And, future father-in-law or not, I was proud of Professor Bonno and, yes, a bit in awe. For his daughter, my feelings might be expressed with words other than *awe*. She was certainly awe-fully pretty. ◆

Andrée in the spring of 1943,
at the time of her engagement announcement.

Chapter 6

THE RECESSION DESTROYS GRAHAM

◆ ══════════════════════════════════

Brief discussion of the automobile business and its role during the
Great Depression.

As the war dragged on, and I got to know Andrée better, I discovered
many other outstanding qualities: exceptional intelligence, a quick wit and
ready sense of humor, a sharp understanding, and a thoroughly disconcerting ability to read me like a book. "Well," she'd tease, "at least like a comic
strip."

Both busy, we saw each other often but seldom for very long. With the
"thaw" at home, the "often" part gradually increased. Also, having never
learned to drive, Andrée's parents would greatly appreciate, later on, having
a son-in-law as chauffeur.

More immediately, their daughter loved to travel by automobile. She
retained this love all her life, partly because of early privations and initially,
I like to think, as a way to be alone with me. When I could borrow an automobile, we took short trips to exotic places like Richmond and Pinole and
Hercules.

Later, I bought a 1937 six-cylinder Graham sedan from my father for $300 at $50 down and seemingly endless payments of $25 per month. Called the Small Six, plainer than the definition of plain, it had no radio and, worse, no heater. You'd think with Andrée aboard I'd have little need for a radio and less for a heater.

While such was indeed the case, I recall shivering during one New Year's Eve, probably 1940, when even a small blanket would have helped and, without which, we were simply unable to see the New Year in, the alternative being fast freeze.

Aside from that episode, the Graham served us well. Trips were many, short, mechanically uneventful, and relatively inexpensive at less than 50¢ per gallon. Dependable and affordable, the very bottom of the line, the Small Six was cheap, unadorned, frill-less, and thrill-less.

Graham's chapter in automotive history is an interesting one. Innovative; as brilliant as it was innovative; and as brief as it was brilliant, Graham was the product of several marriages. When Jewett and Velie went out of business, in the early twenties, my father secured the Paige franchise.

Paige was a solid and serviceable automobile, reasonably priced while not especially glamorous. Its appeal and, apparently, its future prospects were dramatically augmented in the mid-twenties when Paige merged with a group of mechanical geniuses doing business as the Graham Brothers.

The Graham-Paige, as it would now become, was an almost immediate success. The Graham Brothers introduced new design and innovative engineering, such as four-wheel hydraulic brakes. They repositioned rear shock absorbers outside the springs to provide more lateral stability, a feature that combined with new body configuration to prompt the advertisement, "Wider than it's high."

In 1929, for a publicity stunt sponsored by the *Oakland Post-Enquirer,* my father drove a Graham-Paige roadster and a frightened news-editor (the official observer) up dirt roads to the Mount Diablo summit to shatter the existing time record to the top. He received a prize for this stunt, a monster silver-plated trophy cup, which my nephew, Eugene McDaniel Webb Jr., still displays.

The feat may not have been the best advertising, especially for an automobile manufacturer that stressed safety as one of its major characteristics. But it helped validate Graham-Paige's claims to advanced engineering and exemplary performance. Another example of Graham-Paige success was its steadily mounting sales figures.

On October 18, 1929, driving a 1929 Graham-Paige roadster, my father, Charles R. "Ted" Webb, broke all records for elapsed time up Mt. Diablo. His mark, 23 minutes, 3⅗ seconds, earned him the perpetual trophy. The official Oakland Post-Enquirer *observer (and passenger), Forest Pridmore, sits fearfully beside the determined driver.*

C.R.'s father, Ted, is second from the left, holding cup with his left hand.

From the beginning of their merger, the Graham Brothers dominated Paige. Graham-Paige would be controlled by the Grahams largely through the engineering innovations mentioned above. Ironically, the marked success of Graham-Paige provided both the justification and the economic aid to help Graham buy out Paige. Thus, the merger ended in 1930, setting the stage for a revolution in automotive design and the introduction of a spectacular new model the following year.

In 1931, on a rainy Christmas Eve, my father came home with a surprise. With a conspiratorial look, he motioned to my brother and me, gesturing toward the garage. Our sister, Virginia, tagged along, naturally expecting some grand toy.

It was grand, all right: a new automobile, both strange and beautiful. Never had we seen a design like that. The usual boxlike sedan with which we were all familiar had been superseded by graceful, flowing lines. To add to the glamour, it was glistening with raindrops that seemed to bead rather than flatten out on top the hood.

Totally awed, we heard strange words, *streamlined* and *iridescent.* The car was a beautiful light blue, a blue I'd never seen before, and certainly never on an automobile. The paint was a new development made from fish skin pigment. We may well have been the first teenagers ever to see the 1932 Graham Blue Streak.

The next day, we were all up early—even earlier than the usual Christmas morning, when kids seem to hear the first cock's crow right after their parents twisted the last corkscrew. The big package in the garage added hugely to our excitement, which was hardly dampened by the rain that had continued through the night.

With a little more than ordinary efficiency, accompanied by more than the usual amounts of clamor, my mother and father piled passengers, presents, and luggage into the car, and we were off before eight AM, heading for Marysville, some two hours away, for a family Christmas celebration. We all marveled at the quiet smoothness of the Blue Streak with its straight eight-cylinder engine and aerodynamic design.

I sat there enjoying the slippery silence and beaded raindrops on the hood. Virginia was entranced by the view through the enlarged windows. My mother commented on the enhanced interior space and neatness, a result of the outboard trunk being incorporated as an integral part of the body. Gene had questions about design, such as "How about the Chrysler

Airflow? Wasn't that a forerunner?" Dad responded, "Yes, in a sense, but mostly no. Basically, it was just an upside-down bathtub."

We drove through the underpass marking the main entrance to Marysville, and my mother, as she always did at that point, recited Walter Scott's words from "The Lay of the Last Minstrel":

> Breathes there the man with soul so dead,
> Who never, to himself, has said,
> This is my own, my native land!

At that moment, I saw a large, outdoor clock, reading 9:45.

We're here? So soon? It seemed much shorter than usual. Time went faster because we were enjoying the ride? Or did the car just *go* faster? And much more quietly?

I would have answers to those questions a year or two later when my grandfather spent a summer in Los Angeles serving on the California Appellate Court. My father, who, by the way, was a fast driver, provided the transportation in one of the successors to the Blue Streak. Rolling along at a good clip—somewhere between Fresno and Bakersfield—we were all surprised and amused to hear my grandmother's voice from the backseat, "Oh, Ted, can't you drive a bit faster?"

Those cars were exceptionally quiet and deceptively fast. Their revolutionary design, powerful, high-revving engines, and unquestioned quality promised success in the market for years to come. Determined to exploit those qualities, my father worked hard, soon becoming the Northern California distributor for Graham.

Graham's popularity soared. By 1937, it had captured third place in California sales, just behind Chevrolet and Ford, and outselling Buick. The six-cylinder baby of the Graham family, the same model as the used Small Six I bought later, was a hot item. It sold new for about $600.

But "my" Six was not the only thing that 1937 brought. That year, the Graham factory was crippled by a lengthy strike. Production halted. Dealers simply could not get automobiles to sell. Spreading labor problems, combined with stringent fiscal restraints and rising interest rates throughout the nation, helped bring on the Recession of 1937. On the cusp of bankruptcy for the rest of the year, Graham never fully recovered.

The strike was finally settled, later in the year. But, as my father observed, "the pardon came too late." He was forced out of his huge store in San Francisco, on Van Ness Avenue, at close to a million-dollar loss. Big money in those days.

Still looking for *their* pardon, the Graham Brothers were able to secure new financing after the labor disputes subsided. They managed to produce a sharply attractive new model in 1938 (introduced in late 1937), the car automotive writers described as appearing to *be in motion when it stood still.* "Shark Nose," they called it. With its rakishly tilted front end, it soon caught the collective eye of automobile enthusiasts throughout the land.

"Sharknose," as the press immediately dubbed the model on which our wedding car was based, a 1939 Graham Supercharger Sport Sedan.

When it became generally known that the 1938 Graham produced outstanding performance to go with its good looks, expectations rose for both the automotive industry and the Graham franchise. My father reacted typically, determining to keep the Oakland dealership operating and putting my brother, Gene, in charge of the Berkeley store.

Initial sales were brisk but soon fell off as the recession continued unabated. Unemployment increased (19% in 1938) while the number of customers decreased.

Sales slumped, inventories swelled, and lingering costs of the strike and of engineering the new model multiplied. The Graham Brothers, seeking economic salvation, entered into negotiations with other struggling manufacturers, particularly Packard and Studebaker.

Graham—after a merger with Packard and the purchase of Studebaker's innovative production dies—produced the handsome but short-lived 1941 Graham Hollywood, soon only a collector's item. World War II ended the recession, helped put the quietus on Studebaker and Graham, and underwrote Packard's survival as a manufacturer of engines—such as those for Rolls-Royce—and as a major contributor to the Allied war effort.

Recession and the war's effect on my father were far-reaching as well, both changing his operations dramatically. Like the recession's contribution to the closure of the San Francisco store, the double dip of 1938—a sort of recession within a recession—threatened a similar fate for Oakland's showroom. Another change: Graham's maneuvers with Studebaker and Packard set the stage for my father to acquire, after the war, a new dealer franchise with Nash (forerunner of American Motors).

Meanwhile, since the war years had brought a cessation of all commercial manufacture of automobiles, my father, temporarily, was no longer a *new* car dealer. He remained in business "for the duration" as a moderately successful purveyor of "previously owned" automobiles, and it was in this capacity that he sold me the 1937 Graham Small Six in 1939 or 1940.

Let us recall: when my father became Northern California distributor for Graham, he expanded operations from a sole locale at 2471 Shattuck Avenue, Berkeley, to large, multistoried sites on Broadway, in Oakland, and on Van Ness Avenue, in San Francisco. Events in 1937 killed Van Ness, while 1938 took aim on Broadway. But before the shooting started, the scene changed.

First, my brother, manager of the Berkeley store, decided he was going back to school to study medicine. Second, my father, struggling financially to keep the Oakland store, came to the conclusion that I should drop out of Cal and go to work for him. This scheme I could take or leave. I wanted to help my father, but at the same time, I was sophomorically convinced, just barely a junior, that I already knew everything anyway.

Brother Gene, as always, had a somewhat different slant on matters. His stance in this instance may well have been conditioned by his tendency to assume there was a right way and his father's way to perform any task—an assumption of which his father was well aware. Gene was fond of his father, and a very good son, but occasionally would go too far as when, on assuming the management of the Berkeley store, he placed a large sign on the office wall—his wall, but actually the stately office of his father: *The Customer is always wrong!*

Seeing this sign, Dad blew his top, as Gene knew he would. Making Gene take it down, he simultaneously turned aside as if concealing a smile and laughing to himself.

Gene could smile and laugh and make others laugh. Few could tell a story better than he. But he could be serious, very serious, and my dropping out of college was no laughing matter. Nor was his determination to return to college. In any event, he would have none of the proposed arrangement.

So Gene and I talked and we talked, and I was easily convinced. Gene was persuasive. Starting college as an engineering major, he had dropped out, bored after a few semesters. The experience had made him even more persuasive. Furthermore, I knew he was right.

Accordingly, on a fine summer morning in 1939, we drove to Oakland to confront "the boss" and, in one of the upstairs sales offices, presented our case. Father was adamant at first, but we pressed our arguments. Gene, using the acumen and highly skilled sales technique that his highly skilled father had taught him, seemed to be turning the flank. Awed by his arguments, I remained silent, fixed on the paternal admonition, "Salesmanship is the art of *studied* reticence."

About an hour after our arrival at the Oakland office, we were on our way. The "arrangement" had been cancelled. "Signed and delivered," we would both be back in school together in the fall.

It was a minor triumph of siblings working together for a just cause, but in retrospect I believe we won the argument because Dad wanted us to win. It's even possible that the discussion among the three of us may have helped him resolve his major business problem. Indeed, not too many months later, he closed the Oakland store and returned to his former sales rooms in Berkeley, where he remained until retirement.

That story ends there. But it really doesn't. One more element of luck: Had Gene and I not gone to Oakland that morning, I would not have attended Cal the following semester and quite possibly would never have completed my formal education. *And* I would never have met Andrée. ◆

Chapter 7

THE GREAT LATRINE ESCAPE

◆ ═══════════════════════════════

American involvement in European affairs in the months before Pearl Harbor. Comments on the "old-time" Navy.

The fall of 1939 found me back in college, ready for upper-division offerings. More interesting and demanding than earlier courses, they were highly disciplined and detailed. Autumn hauled my brother back to the books, too, and witnessed our father's happy retreat to 2471 Shattuck Avenue. There, at the original location of his automobile dealership, life became less stressful for him and those around him. But not less stressful for those living elsewhere in the world.

After the Munich fiasco in 1938 and the subsequent fall of Czechoslovakia, tension in Europe had been steadily mounting. The Russo-German Ten-Year Nonaggression Pact, signed August 23, 1939, paved the way for Hitler to invade Poland on the first day of September. England and France then declared war on Germany after two days of futile negotiation.

Not trusting his new partner, Stalin also invaded Poland (September 17, 1939). Thus—partitioned three times in the eighteenth century and briefly resurrected by the Treaty of Versailles at the end of World War I—Poland was split up once again, humiliated as well as partitioned.

While the Nazi blitzkrieg paused to regroup and the British and French girded their loins, the year drearily played out with threats, posturing, and occasional military thrusts, such as the Russian invasion of Finland and a series of provocative German moves toward Norway and Sweden.

The press sneeringly dismissed this period as *sitzkrieg*. But it was a time of nervousness, rumors, and feverish preparations for war, an outcome that increasingly seemed inevitable.

My *sitzkrieg* was mostly in the Cal library. Interest in recent European events was beginning to prevail over purely academic studies, and I was falling captive to a recently encountered lass from *La Belle France:* a lass, alas, whose mother country would soon endure agony while I would dare to dream of ecstasy.

From seeing her, near Wheeler Steps, and after the first date, I became "acquainted" with Andrée rapidly. Met the gal and I was hers? Maybe not that fast. I don't believe in "love at first sight." First recognition, perhaps. Let's just say, that by the end of the year, I recognized her.

Recognized Andrée well enough for her parents to take alarm. Previously a straight-A student, Andrée soon let her grade-point average slide. And I became *persona non grata* in the Bonno household. This was the beginning of the *sitzkrieg*, about the time when Andrée's parents established our "moratorium."

My grades had also fallen. But the fall-off was short-lived for both of us. As disappointed in her grades as were her parents, Andrée quickly made adjustments. She managed her time (and mine) so efficiently that we could see each other nearly as much as before. With her help, such as giving me tips on study habits, my grades got modestly better. By contrast, Andrée's improvement was spectacular, even though she had a tougher road to follow, still contending with the distractions and breadth of lower-division requirements.

It was easier for me in the upper division. Since my studies were confined almost entirely to European History, they closely corresponded to the course of world events.

World events, meanwhile, had become front page news, *the* topic of conversation at town cocktail parties, faculty meetings, and student "bull sessions" everywhere. Adolf Hitler's threatening speeches, territorial demands, and reborn military machine had combined to set the nerves of European rulers on edge. Not ready to fight—yet—they resolved to bring *Der Führer* to the negotiation table in frantic attempts to avert war. The result—previously mentioned—was the Munich Pact in September, 1938, which temporarily avoided war in Europe by sacrificing Czechoslovakia, all but assuring war—world war—in the long run.

Prime Minister Neville Chamberlain returned to the United Kingdom, announcing to cheering crowds the attainment of "Peace in our Time." Winston Churchill and a scattering of others knew that "our time" was destined to be very short. Validating their fears in the following months, Hitler ruthlessly exploited the terms of the Munich Pact. Thus, the word *appeasement* entered the worldwide vocabulary.

Eventually, *Munich* and *appeasement* would become virtually synonymous while at the same time, their meaning was escaping global memory.

One person who would not forget *Munich* was Albert Paul Krueger, who had no love for Hitler. Dr. Krueger was a professor of bacteriology at the University of California. As a United States Navy medical officer, he had been closely involved in research on the great influenza pandemic that engulfed the world in 1919.

As international affairs deteriorated in the late thirties, Dr. Krueger envisioned the possibility of another universal influenza outbreak and forcefully advocated preparation for it on a massive scale. The Navy took note of his ideas and, about a year after the Munich Pact, created US Naval Medical Research Unit #1, under the command of A. P. Krueger, MD, PhD, Commander, USN.

The unit initially comprised some fifteen or twenty members—eight to ten officers and seven or eight enlisted men—drawn from faculty and students from various disciplines within the sciences. As a pre-med major at the university, my brother was studying biology—including a course from Dr. Krueger—and he became part of that incipient group. He somehow got me into it as well.

Gene's getting me into the unit must have been a feat of persuasion, *big time*, considering that I was most definitely not a science student. Ironically, I would serve with the Naval Research Unit on active duty, whereas Gene never did because of a medical school deferment that continued until later in the war.

We organized and were properly inducted into the unit in the fall of 1939. It was hardly a memorable event. I was enlisted as a pharmacist's mate 3rd class, a rating that would seemingly qualify me, two years later, for emergency duty evaluating urine specimens in San Francisco on December 8, 1941.

After our induction ceremonies, a year or two of suspended animation followed while the war in Europe rumbled and spread, growing ever more intense. The Selective Training and Service Act, passed in the summer of 1940, paved the way for an expanded US military capability. Moreover, passage of the Lend-Lease Act, early in 1941, heralded the strong possibility of our direct involvement, attracting the attention of young and old alike.

Clamorous exchanges erupted on every side, in every quarter:

"It's Europe's war. Let *them* fight it!"

"Don't be naïve, buddy! If Europe falls, we're next. For God's sake! Haven't you read *Mein Kampf*?"

Outbursts like these were not unique and not just among college students. They started as conversations, soon became discussions, and ended up as arguments. Usually heated, they seemed invariably to end up with my being relegated to the "naïve" position, I who had actually read *Mein Kampf*.

Naïve or not, only a few units short of graduation, I received ORDERS in June, 1941. Leaving no room for argument, the letter from the US Navy delivered terse instructions to report July 8 for active duty at the Receiving Ship, Treasure Island, California.

There I remained for several weeks, driving in each morning in my tattered 1933 Graham rag top to arrive before 8:00 and—believe me—depart each night promptly at 4:30 by the same conveyance. The only exception fell on Saturdays, when I was shooed out of the building at noon with stern injunctions to return the following Monday morning and not one wit sooner.

This was the *Old Navy*. Definitely the pre–Pearl Harbor Navy.

Life at the Receiving Ship was simple. Pleasant nights ("at liberty") followed boring days involving a tightly disorganized routine. The operational scheme was a pattern of crisp orders and tentative moves, according to fixed plans that—apparently—only the Navy could understand.

Each day produced new actions within a framework that seldom varied. Early on, we were issued full complements of Navy gear and clothing—dress uniforms and work uniforms complete down to the shoes, leggings, compasses, and pickaxes.

Still another day would bring instructions to stencil our names on all the gear. Constantly filling out papers and completing various routine tasks, we suffered the "aid" of primitive loudspeakers delivering incessant announcements, commands, instructions, and admonitions, "Now hear this . . ."

The whole operation was run by yeomen, 1st, 2nd, and 3rd class, with an occasional chief yeoman. These clerks handled the books, typewriters, records, and accounts. They didn't know quite what to make of me. In a contingent of raw, enlisted recruits, I fit because, and only because, I, too, was raw.

Raw, but a senior in college? And with the advanced rating of a pharmacist's mate, 3rd class? A pharmacist's mate, moreover, who knew nothing about pharmacy and still less about hospital duties? (Please note: rated a full step above a hospital corpsman in the Navy, I was an exalted "know-nothing.")

After a while, when the yeomen knew me better, they became amused rather than perplexed. They even snickered at me from time to time. One day, they guffawed. "Hey, Mac! Where'd ja get them leggins?" His Rawness, they discovered, had stenciled his leggings on the *outside*, thus rendering them officially useless while affording the yeomanry many a chuckle.

One morning, however, I witnessed a very important operation that they discharged flawlessly. It was definitely more pleasant than being guffawed at. Two weeks had elapsed since I'd arrived. We were lined up at a number of tables, two yeomen at each, a long sheet of paper in front of one of them. In front of the other were stacks of five dollar bills and one dollar bills. Glory be! Payday! I should have known.

By the time I got to my table, the stacks of bills around the hall were much lower. But we all got paid, one yeoman carefully counting out the money, the other observing first and then checking off names. Two fives and four ones for me? Fourteen dollars? Never in my life had I received so much money for so little work.

That was the big moment at the Receiving Ship, at least so far. It seemed like the second moment—departure from Treasure Island—would never come.

I had hoped for orders to Naval Medical Research Unit #1. Another payday would pass, however, with only a few assurances from Dr. Chesbro, second in command to Dr. Krueger. When orders finally arrived, they directed me to Mare Island Naval Shipyard—specifically to the naval hospital there. How could I possibly muster the chutzpa and medical know-how to avoid being denounced, or worse, court-martialed as a fraud?

Just as downcast as I was miscast, I actually experienced, in my misery, a strong sense of relief upon discovering that my main duty at the hospital would be cleaning latrines. What a reprieve! A reminder, I thought, of Henry VIII's commuting Sir Thomas More's sentence from hanging to being dispatched more honorably by the executioner's axe. A few weeks of cleaning latrines, however, had me thinking I'd prefer to *hang* with the court-martial. But one day, two high-ranking naval officers walked into the area of my work station.

"Those damn idiots! Knocked one of our best typewriters off the goddamned counter. Smashed it to smithereens. Now they're only two decent ones left."

"Doesn't really matter, Captain. We don't have a typist. Jones is in sick bay and Richardson retires next week."

"Un-retire him, Commander. We have a thousand reports to get out, all due yesterday."

"I doubt if we could do that, sir. Richardson's replacement has been authorized. Being transferred from Quonset. Here, only after leave and travel time. If we try to stop . . ."

"Forget it, Commander, We're up that goddamned creek without a goddamned paddle. Gonna be hell to pay."

Having overheard most of this eloquent discourse, I rashly surmised that I might be able to supply the accursed paddle they were up the accursed creek without.

Leaping from the urinal, I confronted the startled officers as they were walking away from my work station: "By your leave, sir. I know how to type."

The captain stopped. Turning around, he looked at me steadily, his eyes as luminous as the four gold captain-stripes on his sleeve. Was he judging *my* effrontery or weighing it against *his* plight? That eternity—all of three seconds—between hanging and court-martial finally ended when I heard him growl, "Clean up and be in my office in five minutes." "Ah," thought I, "*only* court-martial."

Since I actually did know how to type, and since—thanks to old Ms. Typewriter at University High—I could type reasonably well, I was "hired."

Swish! Fake pharmacist's mate becomes fake yeoman. And never again would I clean a Navy latrine.

That was break number one.

The second break would come about a month later, when I received orders to report to Naval Medical Research Unit #1 at the Life Sciences Building of the University of California. ✦

Chapter 8

"I DON'T GET IT!"

◆ ════════════

Life on the University of California campus, complicated by the "shadow of war."

*A*mazingly, as with the Receiving Ship, I was allowed to keep my car at Mare Island, a convenience that allowed me to make the relatively short trip to Berkeley several times during the month I remained stationed there. On those occasions, driving over the Carquinez Bridge and past small towns like Crockett, Rodeo, Pinole, and Richmond, I had time to reflect on Navy life as I had experienced it so far.

The high-powered, efficient fighting machine of World War II had not yet materialized. I saw only an easygoing organization that followed rather strict rules of daily deportment. The more trivial the offense, it seemed, the stricter the punishment. For instance, rules of dress, proper uniforms properly worn, punctuality, and saluting (especially to senior officers) and saluting properly were the norm. Adherence to the local requirements of duty stations and proper respect for naval customs, personnel, and the flag were all strictly enforced.

But let a sailor be guilty of short periods of absence without leave, a capital offense in wartime, and chances are he'd get only a reprimand if he had a decent excuse. This strict attention to minor rules, within a framework of general tolerance, had been more pronounced at Treasure Island, where few duties were required.

Mare Island differed to a degree, particularly at the hospital, where work was more demanding, specialized, and critical. The same general tolerance prevailed, provided the important work got done, done well, and in a timely fashion. If a corpsman's uniform was a bit short of perfection, nobody cared so long as he performed capably.

Also, while I learned little at the Receiving Ship, there was much that I learned at the naval hospital before becoming an "acting yeoman." Cleaning latrines had not taken my whole day. Duties awaited me in the hospital wards, some directly helping patients. Much of my ward time was spent interacting with hospital corpsmen whom I outranked, despite knowing less than they did.

They taught me such rudimentary techniques as taking blood pressure and pulse, performing urinalysis, and, I should not fail to mention, conducting *short-arm inspections*.

This quaint terminology is the Navy's way of describing the practice of checking sailors' genitalia upon their return from liberty to make sure they had not contracted venereal diseases.

I learned some routine medical procedures from hospital corpsmen as well as lessons in practical diplomacy. But once I fell heir to "active yeoman" duties, my quasi medical career at Mare Island ended. "Yeoman-ship" became a full-time job, casting me into a learning environment of a different sort.

In the Captain's quarters, I gradually discovered how to interact with a feisty, frosty commanding officer. In doing so, I necessarily became involved with high-level correspondence. The documents I typed were often delicate and almost always concerned with sensitive information about personnel movement, ship construction, hospital needs, and 12th Naval District plans, highly secret, for new buildings at Mare Island. Every day, while typing, I saw all the details. In the process, I acquired much information about naval development and also learned to keep my mouth shut.

Though not exactly my cup of tea, my assignments had been pretty good thus far, considering that the Receiving Ship sent me home nights and weekends. Even Mare Island had allowed a reasonable degree of freedom.

On several weekends, for example, I was able to drive to Berkeley to see family and friends, and, of course, Andrée.

I certainly had no complaints. Still, it was a separation, and a more definite one than the "moratorium" Andrée's parents had tried on us. Results of both separations being the same, however, each of us was eager to see the conclusion of my hospital functions. By the time the Mare Island tour of duty ended, we had become fast friends but maybe not inseparable . . . yet.

Within 48 hours, our separation time would end. Officially dismissed from Mare Island, transfer orders in hand and a spring in my step, I located the dusty Graham ragtop on a crowded, dirty parking lot. Dutifully, it started right up, and so we headed south without delay, my thoughts on "home" and, particularly, its inhabitants.

As we passed the sleepy little town of Richmond, with its faint smell of gasoline refineries, my reverie on Andrée grudgingly gave way to thoughts of the new assignment. Its location would make it possible to see her more often, to renew old friendships, and to be with family again. Moreover—critical to a college senior a whisper shy of graduation—it landed me in the very backyard of the University of California.

Turning onto University Avenue—with the Campanile, Cal's ubiquitous landmark, already visible about a mile away due east—I quickly realized that all my thoughts had been of what I could do as the *result* of relocation rather than to what tomorrow, on the job itself, would bring.

Eight AM "tomorrow" brought me into the awesome presence of Commander Krueger, his executive officer, and an enlisted man. Dr. Krueger did most of the talking, explaining that the delay in bringing about my reassignment was mainly a consequence of nondelivery of an essential piece of equipment: a 1942 Ford Station Wagon. I learned the military "fact" that a vehicle could not be assigned without a driver and a driver could not be assigned without a vehicle, and delay was in procuring a new car. Though it was still 1941, the naval establishment in Washington insisted on a new model. As it turned out, that 1942 automobile was not only the last Ford but also the last of *any* make until 1945.

I didn't care all that much, since I hugely preferred being neither chicken nor egg to being either a fake yeoman or a fake pharmacist's mate.

In short, I learned that I would become official driver as well as chauffeur to Commander Krueger and other dignitaries. I would also be responsible for keeping the car shipshape, which meant spotlessly clean, inside and out, and in good running order. As a result, I spent most Saturday mornings washing and, occasionally, polishing the station wagon or tuning the engine. Though menial, they were jobs I liked: outside, unsupervised, and usually concluding with "liberty" for the rest of the weekend.

In addition to driving, I had other duties, which varied according to Dr. Krueger's and the unit's needs. Though the work inside was different— all experimental lab activities, glassware and instrument cleanup, medical instruction, and training—still, it was Navy. Daily routine was Navy. Navy regulations were strictly adhered to, especially when the unit grew larger and an old-line chief pharmacist's mate was placed in charge of office management.

He supervised enlisted personnel, established a system of records and accounts, and generally served as a resource officer for esoteric customs and procedures of the traditional Navy. Duty hours were strictly Navy: 0800 to 1630 weekdays, 0800 to 1230 on Saturdays.

In a word, the Research Unit was officially a part of the Navy and, like many naval activities, strict yet informal. But where the prewar Navy could be both strict and easygoing, the Research Unit was relaxed but not easygoing. The unit played by the book while working hard, a team of professionals with a specific task to complete. No matter the similarities and differences with regular Navy culture, however, it all was about to change.

On December 7, 1941, a Sunday morning, several former classmates and I were playing touch football at John Muir Elementary School. Brother Gene, briefly home on his way to McGill Medical School, suddenly appeared at the playground gate. "Andrée just phoned," he shouted, "she heard on the radio that the Japanese have attacked Pearl Harbor!"

No more football. Ever. Not, at least, with any of us playing that morning. Later that day, I received a telegram ordering me to report to an address in San Francisco at 0800, 8 December 1941.

Next day, I found myself at a makeshift enlistment center, a clamoring throng of men pushing this way and that, most of them trying to get through doors guarded by armed military personnel. Chaos outside, Navy order prevailed inside. Tables were set up everywhere in a large room, civilians lined up in front of them, sailors behind. Questions flying. Answers earthbound. Meanwhile, other sailors were directing other civilians to other rooms.

I'd hardly entered the big room—not even presenting my formal ID or uttering "reporting for duty, sir"—when a sailor spotted the pharmacist's mate 3rd class insignia on my arm. Immediately and wordlessly, he escorted me to another room, where World War II began for me.

Paper cups to the fore! My duties started with urine. For a day or two, until emergency measures subsided somewhat, I did urinalysis and operated the sphygmomanometer, skills I had acquired at Mare Island Naval Hospital. After that, it was back to driving the Ford station wagon for the higher-ups.

Reflecting on the pressure cooker of the enlistment center in the days following Pearl Harbor, I was greatly impressed by the cool efficiency with which the Navy moved that operation along. A witness to history, I viewed these crisis maneuvers as a symbol of an easygoing Navy responding instantly and effectively to challenge, which foreshadowed coming exploits at sea such as the resounding victory at Midway scarcely six months after Pearl Harbor.

One can regard the attack on Pearl Harbor as the treacherous stroke that awakened a sleeping giant, and in many ways it was. Certainly, it marked the end of pacifist activism prevailing in many quarters, particularly on college campuses. I know! I was there.

But it wasn't an overnight phenomenon. The "spit and polish" US Navy didn't suddenly become a preeminent fighting machine in the short time between Pearl Harbor and the Battle of Midway.

At least as early as the naval disarmament treaty of 1923, US military officials had been keeping close watch on the expanding Japanese Navy. It was also in the 1920s that our "Battleship Navy" began the transition to aircraft carriers.

More recently—despite protests of isolationist groups—the country as a whole had been gearing up against involvement in the European war. Reacting to the threat of a Nazi triumph abroad, Congress passed and Roosevelt signed the so-called Lend-Lease Act nine months before the attack on Pearl Harbor.

Lend-Lease provided Britain the materiel aid she so badly needed. It also may have ensnared us in the European war, by leading to the shipboard meeting among Churchill, Roosevelt, and their military advisors in August, 1941. Beyond that, its provisions for transfer of armaments and materiel helped galvanize the American economy into expanding production both for domestic consumption and for military needs as they might arise.

Clearly, the mistakes of December 7th aside, we were not entirely unprepared. And while the Japanese may have miscalculated the depth of our resolve, the attack on Pearl Harbor accomplished their goal, to protect their eastern flank so they could extend and consolidate Japanese conquests in Southeast Asia and secure their oil supply. So the Japanese destroyed our Pacific Fleet . . . almost.

They sunk five battleships, put another three out of action, and disabled or sunk any number of auxiliary vessels. But they were unlucky. They put no aircraft carriers out of action, because the carriers were all on a task force exercise well away from Pearl at the time. Otherwise, the Battle of Midway would probably not have happened. No carriers, no highly skilled naval aviators, no torpedoes.

But the Battle of Midway did happen. And it is ironic that the Japanese at Midway lost so many of *their* carriers (to torpedoes launched by pilots of American carriers) that they relinquished sea control, in effect, for the duration. The war in the Pacific had become a war of aircraft carriers, showing that the American Navy had been prepared in many underlying ways. War also changed the Old Navy . . . and the American people too.

I couldn't help noticing this change. One could see it on every side. I even recall, early on, driving the station wagon along the East Shore Highway, now Interstate 80, on the way to Castro Valley, thinking "wartime America!" There seemed to be a new hustle and bustle everywhere, no doubt much of it the usual freeway frenzy, but also a pronounced increase in military traffic, several convoys, a number of drab, dark green automobiles filled—no doubt—with high-ranking officials.

I felt part of it as well. After all, I was on an official, secret mission to buy, of all things, eggs. Not a dozen or two, however. Cartons of fertile eggs.

I knew what the eggs were for and a little about how they were injected, how used. But I wasn't sure as to what end, other than gathering important information about influenza, including its causes, treatment, and containment in the event of an epidemic. All I knew for sure was that my commanding officer sent me out periodically to obtain hundreds of eggs to sustain our research.

For the most part, my daily activities did not change, although I did find myself spending more time driving Dr. Krueger to conferences and official meetings. He always sat up in the front seat and talked to me, mostly monologues on a variety of subjects. After the declaration of war on December 8th, we had a new topic of conversation; however, he became a bit more circumspect and the silences more prolonged. His silences clearly indicated that he knew much that he was not at liberty to share.

Conversations inside the building were different. I seldom saw Dr. Krueger, his office being on the first floor of the Life Sciences Building, the rest of us on the third floor. Necessarily thrown in with other enlisted men, I engaged primarily in small talk. Prior to December 7th, most conversations were about personnel changes. One or two of the men had been shipped out. Others, who remained, were vaguely concerned.

Vague disappeared, quite literally overnight, with the outbreak of war. Although the rate of transfers did not increase, all talk was now about the war—how long would it last and who would be shipped out next. Thinking that I might have some insights or information from driving "the boss," the men confided in me.

One day, driving Dr. Krueger to a meeting, I mustered the gall to inform him of the concerns of some of the comparatively recent additions to his enlisted crew. He reassured me that nobody was going to be shipped out. "Nobody, that is," he added, "provided he performs creditably, follows the rules, and works hard."

He uttered these words within the general framework of the work of the unit, its development, and its relationship to the war effort. Rather than transfers *out*, he implied, transfers *in* were likely. Later, I realized he was confident that no one was likely to be transferred into or out of US Naval Medical Research Unit #1 without his say-so.

I knew that something was in the wind. But months would pass before it blew in. Life and work went on with few changes. For some, the war became an abstraction. For most, however, it was uppermost and ever present. Scarcity, rationing, long lines, transportation delays, car repair problems, automobile scarcity, friends departing overseas or to training camps, radio and newspaper reports—all combined to keep our minds on the war.

For me, life remained both the same and different. After a decade living with my parents at Roble Court, I moved. My mother was not well, and my father had no trouble convincing me that it would be easier on her if I started looking for new quarters.

I found an upstairs room in a home on Le Conte Avenue—that steep hill running up from Hearst Avenue, next to the university, to the impressive grounds of the Pacific School of Religion on the west and the Alpha Delta Phi fraternity, where I had been a member as an undergraduate, on the east. My room was modest, with a semiprivate bathroom down the hall. It had no space for visitors but was adequate to my needs and conveniently close to work. Its location eliminated commuting time and expense. It also gave me easy and time-saving access to the University of California library at night, the only time, along with weekends, that I could make use of it.

Living near the university conferred other benefits, among which was proximity to Andrée's house on Hilgard Avenue, a mile or less away. But she and I saw each other less frequently than one might expect. War had altered our perspective in many ways. We had become more conscious of "unfinished business" lying ahead and standing in the way of long-range planning.

For example, I knew that the Navy assignment provided the magical chance to complete my degree work. Andrée, likewise, was determined to finish hers and to do so in a manner fitting her scholastic capability and her parents' expectations. Our mutual resolve meant that nights and most weekends were library time.

There were exceptions, of course. We got together regularly, often briefly. We always had fun and good talk, both serious and frivolous. But I soon discovered I was biting off an outsized morsel. Educators were not obliged to arrange class schedules in conformance with the duty assignments of naval personnel. Nor did naval officers in wartime care to rearrange schedules of enlisted men to further their off-duty pursuits.

Naval regulations, however, and duty schedules were helpful in figuring out what courses I could take. I usually had an hour for lunch, and I was stationed just a five-minute walk from Wheeler Hall. Free at 1630 most afternoons, I often found weekends clear from 1230 Saturday until 0800 Monday.

I also managed to accumulate some "bonus points" by driving Dr. Krueger and others to meetings or airports at odd hours, which bolstered my requests for some flexibility.

Thus, even with my military duties, I managed to take classes at Cal. One memorable course was taught by Dr. Benjamin Kurtz, a highly regarded professor of English literature, once a week from 4:00 to 6:00 PM

A venerable scholar whom students referred to as "Mr. Chips" (from the novel by James Hilton), Dr. Kurtz graciously admitted me to English Lit 406, a course limited to graduate students. He expressed little concern over my undergrad status or that my attendance would be uneven or that I'd often be late to class. It was an enjoyable and informative course with only six students enrolled and taught in a casual manner full of witty comments on all things human.

Professors Kurtz and Palm (professor of history, whom we have seen before) regularly encouraged and supported me. Kurtz followed my graduate work, even advising me on the thesis and, when his book on Charles Mills Gayley was published, in 1943, fondly autographed my copy. Palm helped immensely on the thesis, both in seminar and in individual study courses, one by himself and the other by Lawrence Harper, professor of American history.

My case must have been unique. Sailors, especially in wartime, do not find themselves on university campuses in seminars and individual study courses.

Though difficult at times, the schoolwork proved relatively easy compared to the academic challenges I had anticipated. Thus, by the summer of 1942, I had ground out sufficient credits to attain a combined undergraduate degree—a bachelor of arts in History, English, and Anthropology.

Having completed this modest step, I managed to find the time to prepare for and pass the examinations for promotion to pharmacist's mate 2nd class.

In the process, I began to realize that I was hooked. Why stop with a bachelor's degree? In graduate work, one concentrates on independent study courses, seminars, and writing a thesis. Seminars are taught at night. *Voila!* So just like that, I enrolled in the graduate division.

Seminars and independent study courses from Professors Palm and Harper would eventually clear the way to tackling the thesis. But in the meantime, seminars were demanding and time-consuming. We analyzed various aspects of history, drew conclusions, and presented results in detailed research papers. Fellow graduate students, in attendance, were customarily invited to make critical comments on these papers, under the professor's watchful eye. Scary, but fun.

Independent study courses are like small seminars, rigorous, demanding, and intense, usually involving a professor and only one student and covering a single area. The student will prepare a scholarly paper or present results of his research to the professor more directly and in whatever form the professor requires.

More fun, and a lot scarier, was the thesis. First, find a solid topic. Seminars provide some help at this stage. Next, develop a preliminary bibliography, a search that involves consulting a bibliography and, often, even a bibliography of bibliographies. (There are enough of these strange animals to support a few bibliographies of bibliographies of bibliographies.) Finally, complete the research, prepare a general plan, a preliminary outline, and start writing—always being aware that it is not uncommon to have to interrupt writing to redo some of the research.

I did all these things, including the interruptions. Enjoyed much of it. Panicked at regular intervals. Did a score of rewrites and restarts. Produced a thesis, *The Pact of Paris, 1928.*

Submitted it. Learned of its approval. And, miraculously, was awarded a master's of arts degree in history in February, 1944, about a year and a half after my first graduate seminar.

Although those 18 months seemed to drag at times, they mostly passed rapidly, crowded with action and midnight oil. Thesis work was all-consuming, of course, but other matters intruded.

I became a teaching assistant, *in my spare time,* for Palm's lecture course in Western Civilization. There went my noon hours! Weekends and nights were for research, seminars, and thesis, but I somehow found time to play in a band. I recall a dance one Saturday night when a guy wandered up to the piano and said, "I don't get it!"

"You don't get what?"

"Well. You're in the Navy, aren't you?"

"Yes".

"I don't get it! Aren't you Dr. Palm's TA?"

"Yes."

"And you go around with that beautiful Bonno girl!"

"Of course! She's my fiancée."

"And now, you're playing in a dance band! I just don't get it!"

As he sauntered off, mumbling his odd refrain, I thought of other things he might not get, such as seminars, research, and the thesis. Yes, I was spread thin, but never to the neglect of naval duties. In fact, about the time of "Mr. I-don't-get-it's" interrogation, I was promoted to the rating of pharmacist's mate 1st class, just a step, albeit a big step, below chief petty officer. ◆

Chapter 9

TOP SECRET: SATHER TOWER REVISITED

◆ ══════════════════════════════════════

Shortly after the attack on Pearl Harbor, US Naval Medical Research Unit #1, under Professor Albert Paul Krueger, MD, PhD, Captain, US Navy, changes its emphasis from influenza to bubonic plague.

Chief petty officers, it has been said more than once, "run the Navy." They know where all the nuts and bolts are and what to do with them. They show subordinates how to get the job done; that is, show, browbeat, wheedle, persuade, or simply order them to do so. In the enlisted world, chiefs enjoy great respect and even greater authority.

Correspondingly, petty officers 1st class enjoy a sort of reflected prestige sitting, as they do, so close to the center of enlisted personnel power. But at Naval Medical Unit #1, there was no "top dog" among the enlisted men. There were no chiefs—no chief *pharmacist's mate,* that is.

As mentioned earlier, there were two enlisted classifications in the unit: (1) three or four original members, biology majors mostly, well qualified but a little short of a college degree and (2) newcomers, hospital corpsmen, with little Navy training and no college.

I fell somewhere in the middle of the two groups, a bit closer to the more highly qualified group since I was an original member. But with the promotion to pharmacist's mate 1st class, I became even further removed from the newcomers. Moreover, I now held the same rate as the most qualified enlisted men in the unit. They had all reached "their top." Navy rules were clear: sea duty was required before one could be considered for advancement to chief petty officer.

There was some grumbling among those denied advancement on such technical grounds, even though they had known the rule since the beginning. I, of course, could not grumble because my promotion to pharmacist's mate 1st class had been so recent.

Soon enough, grumbling subsided because of general satisfaction with the duty and devotion to the research, the nature of which was about to change . . . dramatically.

A few months before I started graduate work at Cal, Dr. Krueger was called back to Washington, DC. After a few days we learned that he had been promoted from commander to captain. Because the next rank is admiral, promotion to captain is a huge jump, arguably a grander step than hopping from 2nd to 1st class pharmacist's mate.

On his return, we discovered that the big promotion was only a part, the minor part, of the Washington diversion. Early in the morning of his return, we were convened in a quiet and solemn session in one of the larger rooms upstairs (topside, I should have said, it being the Navy). I was surprised at being included, given the subject. After a few general remarks, including the war, atmosphere, and weather in Washington, Captain Krueger officially informed the assemblage that we would no longer be working on influenza. We would forthwith concentrate on bubonic plague. We'd been cleared *SECRET* at the outset. Now all of us, enlisted and commissioned alike, had to be cleared *TOP SECRET*. Security, always tight, had now taken on a new meaning at US Naval Medical Research Unit #1.

Following revelations of the new mission, days were filled with visits from, and interviews with, federal security agents. It seemed we spent equal time completing the myriad forms they supplied. These lengthy forms left nothing to chance, finding facts that some men said they had not even known about themselves.

Our reassignment of duties, the unit's jokesters complained, was not to conduct research on *Pasteurella pestis* but rather to contend with this palpable paperwork plague now infecting the unit.

Still, security activities added to the general excitement over a new enterprise. They also served as a reminder that Navy security—wartime security—was only part of an equation to which the specific content of biological research had now been added. No fleas on us, thank you.

As matters settled down and new routines evolved, we gradually became aware of the enormity of our new assignment. There were subtle changes required of us. Necessarily, we became more isolated from the community. We had to be very circumspect in social contexts, careful of our speech and behavior, a bit withdrawn but not aloof. In the process, members of the unit drew closer together. Walls between officers and enlisted men came down, frequently leading to friendships that crossed well-established lines.

We could no longer view our activities as a sort of long-term and academic exploration of possible calamities, such as influenza pandemics, that might occur. Rather, we all clearly recognized that we had become directly involved with actual wartime contingencies.

Our government and military leaders were not contemplating biological warfare, but they were very much aware that other countries might be. It was all serious business, and we were definitely in it, *TOP SECRET* and all. The security agents who had cleared us with such painstaking thoroughness knew how definitely we were in it. They had to be sure that there would be not only no "leaks," but also no biological accidents.

So how much rubbed off on me? Plenty. And it all blended with other parts of my life. I was maturing, changing, learning. Reordering my life, and adding college degrees, was part of it, as was my developing relationship with Andrée.

Her transcendent physical beauty and Parisian charm, as I discovered early on, were not her only remarkable attributes. Like her father, she had a keen sense of humor, and, also like her father, she could be very serious. Believe me, we had many serious conversations. Serious *talk* can sometimes be too serious, boring. Serious *conversations* are seldom boring. They get somewhere, have substance, coherence, balance, judicious shadings, even humor.

Studious and discerning, Andrée helped me mightily in my master's thesis preparation. She read the manuscript, thoughtfully reviewed the sentence and paragraph structure, rendered invaluable comment on historical content, tactfully suggested alterations, and, infallibly, detected typos and word transpositions. (I am happy to have noted recently that I did not forget to give her well-deserved credit in the introduction to the thesis.)

For the rest of her life, I asked her to read and critique everything I wrote. Such benefits no longer existing, I persist without my best editor. Would that she were here to correct the deficiency. But if she were, I would not be writing.

Of course, not all our conversations were serious. We talked about everything, even the frivolous. We talked constantly about the war, the Navy, everything but what the unit was working on. (I never divulged—to her, my family, or anyone—the subject of our research, not even after we were married, not until long after our war work was declassified.)

Gradually, I had become aware of the growing incongruity of my position in the unit. In many ways, I just did not fit. Even from the beginning I was a sort of anomaly, overrated as a 3rd class petty officer driving a station wagon for Dr. Krueger, a responsibility for which even a hospital corpsman might be overrated.

This anomaly grew with two promotions, but not as much as at the other end of the enlisted spectrum where I, as a pharmacist's mate 3rd class, was least qualified yet would acquire an advanced degree at Cal. Master's degree or not, I was still underqualified for medical research, especially after *Pasteurella pestis* entered the picture.

On the other hand, as pharmacist's mate 1st class, I was elevated well above the majority of newcomers to the unit, a growing group of enlisted men, many of whom had had more naval experience than I. In some ways, they had better qualifications as well, mine being largely of the paper sort.

These considerations did not weigh too heavily on my mental balance sheet, nor did I have much time to think of them while taking seminars and writing a thesis. But Andrée and I talked about them in spurts, the long spurts falling on weekends and occasionally involving automobile trips in the surrounding countryside.

One of the short spurts I remember fondly—all of five to ten minutes in duration—occurred regularly at about 12:50 pm on the broad pathway connecting the Life Sciences Building with Wheeler Hall, Charles Franklin Doe Library, the Campanile, and the east end of the University of California campus. Once and sometimes twice a week, I would be returning to the unit from one of my noon teaching assistant classes. Andrée had a class in the Life Sciences Building that was dismissed at about the same time.

As she walked eastward and I westward, we spotted each other almost simultaneously. She looked straight ahead, and aside, then back to smile and wave. I reciprocated—sort of—shuffled a bit, not sure how to comport myself while traversing that great distance, narrowing so slowly.

Andrée gazed eastward, her eyes fixed on the roadway to Sather Tower, the iconic Campanile that presided then, as it does today, over the lush grounds of the University of California.

As I walked westward, my favorite sight of the moment was this coed, decked out in modest clothing, always stylishly worn. Often suggesting the attire of a laborer, suspenders and all, her garb was rescued from any hint of drabness by a bright gold or Kelly-green upper half.

The Campanile dominated her view. Its omnipresence towered over all, and on that walkway, she always saw it directly behind and over her swain.

Sadly, I fully recognized this fact only late in our lives. At a Cal reunion, we had once received a table prize: a perfect cardboard replica of the Campanile. Cleaning house one day and looking for things to throw or give away, I spied the tattered remains of our prize. Thoughtlessly, I suggested disposal.

Andrée's response was an immediate and vehement *No.*

I still possess, still treasure that replica. I cry, too, just as every thought of the Campanile and all that it has seen bring tears to my eyes. That walkway, and our meetings there, remind me constantly of the flowering of our "twenty-something" relationship. They also remind me of the thousands of other *couples* who became, or started to become, *one* in the shadow of the Campanile of the University of California.

Those "brief encounters" when we met beneath the nurturing Campanile ever remain in my memory as the crystallizing moments that symbolized a mutual maturing and the gathering resolve to set our course together.

The University of California Campanile.

Despite the war and its sad tidings, it was a time of fulfillment and happy days for us. Wistfully happy, however, as Andrée worried about relatives in France and was often troubled over her parents' similar but more pervasive concerns.

I, too, anguished over bad news from the front as well as the state of my mother's health. Sorrow over "killed in action" reports of friends and acquaintances was a constant companion. Anger came one day, along with grief, when I learned that my good friend Tom Sagamori, whom I had known since 7th grade at Willard, was killed in the bloody struggle in Italy. He had been a member of the Japanese contingent fighting for the Allied cause.

Matters like Tom Sagamori's death deeply concerned me, as well they should have. I never had a chance to talk to Tom about the war in Italy. Did he enlist to escape internment? Or simply as a demonstration of his patriotism? No matter. His death, fighting for his country, disturbed me extraordinarily. Did it also give me guilt feelings? I don't know.

But I do recall a recurring sense of unease. I could not help wondering about living in my hometown and working at the University of California while others fought abroad or had been torn from their Berkeley homes and deposited in southwestern internment camps.

Comfortable with *my* books and the magnificent Cal library and *its* books, my teaching assistantship, and "all that jazz," had I fallen into some sort of cool heaven when hellfire embroiled the rest of the world? Had I been influenced by my highly qualified enlisted associates, grousing about being stuck at the pharmacist's mate 1st class level for lack of sea duty? Or—on the other hand—by their steadfast adherence to the status quo, safe at home, regardless of rate classification?

Whatever the reason—guilt, self-esteem, incongruity—somewhere along the line, perhaps when Tom died, I applied for transfer and direct commission as a naval officer.

Andrée and I had tossed around the pros and cons endlessly. As I would learn later, she would invariably discuss the particulars of major career decisions only as they affected me. Not that she was diffident or self-effacing, but she did so for the sake of common sense and long-term logic. Though dreading the probability of my departure, she could not ignore the exigencies and expectations of wartime America.

The reaction of her parents, who, by this time, had graciously accepted me as a good friend of their daughter and as a prospective son-in-law, was a bit different. At first they studiously avoided direct reference to the situation or any comment on my (our) decision. Over the following months, however, it became clear that they concurred completely in our decision. Not only did they concur, they warmly supported me. Perceptions had gradually been changing for months, both at home and abroad. Care packages were still going to France, but with less urgency as conditions there had improved. A degree of household serenity had returned with the gradual lessening of hostilities in Europe.

A significant and blessed event, moreover, had dramatically changed family life. On April 26, 1942, their only son, Charles Henri Bonno, was born. Andrée was thrilled, after almost 20 years as an only child, to acquire a baby brother. We were all overjoyed, seeing him in good health and good spirits, bright, cheerful, and full of fun.

As Charles Henri grew out of babyhood, events in my life similarly tumbled along, in some semblance of order. The thesis got finished, birthed, delivered, and accepted. Degrees, bachelor's and master's, were conferred, respectively, on Andrée and me in January, 1944. The Bonnos were very proud of Andrée and me for these attainments. My commission as ensign, USN, arrived in March together with orders to report 15 April to Naval Training Center, Tucson, Arizona, precipitating a mad rush of wedding preparations and related activities.

Marcelle Bonno threw herself into the urgent tasks of preparation. She secured church approval and the date, obtaining in the process a dispensation for a wedding during Lent as well as a dispensation for her daughter to marry a non-Catholic. She repeatedly traveled to San Francisco, several times for the sole purpose of procuring an exquisite dinnerware service as a wedding gift to Andrée. She handled all details (wedding dress, church, reception, catering, engraved announcements) flawlessly.

Bride and groom were not idle. Long anticipating *the day*, we had had our share of San Francisco trips, sometimes accompanying Mrs. Bonno to Maiden Lane, more often heading for Ransohoffs Jewelers. There, eventually, we settled on an engagement ring.

Late in April, 1943, we had announced our engagement at a cocktail party given by sorority sister Madeleine Goodrich. At a propitious moment, Madeleine emerged from the kitchen with a trayful of drinks, our names etched on the glasses. *Clever*, to some appreciative sisters, *corny* to others, those glasses served as souvenirs and reminders. And several guests might have looked forward to becoming bridesmaids less than a year later.

Selecting bridesmaids in wartime was not easy, so many sorority sisters having moved. Good friend Muriel Porter was off in Mexico doing archaeo-logical digs, but Muriel's elder sister, Jean Porter Thompson, was available to serve as matron of honor. She was joined by Mimi Smith and Mary Starbird as bridesmaids.

Nor was finding ushers any less difficult: Luther Nichols was at sea with the Merchant Marine, Tom Haven was a naval officer in the Aleutians, Charles Young was in the Army, and Hal Sams had been killed in a Marine Corps training accident. Nearly every live body my age was duty bound.

But three fraternity brothers, younger and still in college, showed up: Irving Diamond (later president of Marin College), Ian Wishart, and Mar-shall Robinson. Having completed his MD degree at McGill University, my brother, Gene, was interning at Franklin Hospital in San Francisco and, fortunately, was able to attend the wedding as my best man.

Andrée quite naturally shared in many of her mother's tasks, the most pressing being the selecting and fitting of the wedding dress. She also joined me in some tasks, one of the more exacting but most pleasant involving selecting, purchasing, altering, and fitting new uniforms. No slapdash, one-size-fits-all process at the commissioned officer level—not then, at least. We had to go to a local haberdashery shop and custom-order a blue dress uniform and a khaki uniform. Khaki was the day-to-day outfit. Chino would do. But *we* decided on a dress khaki uniform. Never regretted it, since it was a great semi-dress uniform, and, anyway, I soon learned that chino pants and shirt were the real work attire, usually with tie and almost never with the jacket.

One significant part of my preparation left no role for the bride. This was catechism. Marriage arrangements worked out with the Church required that the groom undergo a training program with a priest covering Catholic beliefs, tradition, laws, liturgy, and practice. At Newman Hall (on the UC campus), where the wedding would be held, I met regularly with a kindly father who patiently guided me through the catechism.

As an arbitrarily enforced learning experience, I might have resented the process. But somehow, I did not and, accordingly, gained significantly from the immersion. The ritual was easy to understand since my only theological awareness derived from the Episcopal Church, which had many liturgical similarities. Of tradition, too, I had some awareness through history courses, although Reformation studies were often tinted with Protestant coloring.

Everyone was helping by this time: the priest, the haberdasher, the jew-eler, the seamstress, the thesis typist, Navy unit enlisted men and officers, my father, my brother, my ever-supportive sister, even *Tue Gee*.

Who was Tue Gee? Kong Tue Gee was a man who worked in my father's shop. He also lived with us for many years while I was growing up and had his own room and bath at Roble Court. My mother taught him how to cook, and a good cook he became. My family had fallen in love with Andrée somewhere in the magnitude of 10 seconds after I fell in love with her. Tue Gee, being a member of the family, also fell under her spell, and particularly loved to cook for her.

Often, in the years leading up to our wedding, Andrée was invited to join us for dinner. Brother Gene, having learned some French at San Rafael Military Academy, liked to engage her in conversation in her native tongue. Andrée usually answered in her impeccable English, undoubtedly not wanting to embarrass him with the proper pronunciation of her equally impeccable French.

Her reticence caused Gene some disappointment. But his disappointment (ours, too) turned to delight when on occasion her mother would telephone. At the table, eavesdroppers all, we'd nod and smile and quietly chortle over the rapid-fire exchange emanating from the adjoining room where Andrée was on the phone. At the end of her conversation, as if on cue, we would just barely be able to submerge our appreciative laughter as the all-French barrage abruptly came to an end with the marvelously incongruous words, "OK, Maman!"

While I knew that my family were all happy for me to have encountered such a gem, I sometimes wondered if their joy came primarily from the expectation that this paragon would soon become a member of the family. Doesn't matter. They all pitched in. Mother and father made it a point to become acquainted with the Bonno family. Dad provided necessary transportation and automotive backup for the wedding and also arranged to pick up bride and family and bring them to the church on the appointed day.

Of somewhat more dubious support, on the night before the wedding, brother and father kindly took me to Bill's, a well-known bar and favorite of my parents. Bill's was located on College Avenue in the Rockridge section of Oakland. A sort of traditional send-off and certainly no harm intended, the evening left me a little hungover on our wedding day. *Quel dommage!*

A more significant "hangover" was the honeymoon transportation. One other matter that "Mr. I-don't-get-it" didn't get (or know about) was that on many weekends in '42 and '43, when I had time off from the Navy, I worked for my father who, after 1941, had no new cars to sell. I scouted the scarce market looking for clean and mechanically sound cars to buy. I traveled to many automobile auctions and regularly searched the "want ads."

Two fathers and a stubborn wedding gown:
Professor Bonno, the seamstress's apprentice.

One Sunday in the fall of 1943, I found a gorgeous 1939 Graham Super-charger sport sedan. A black beauty, though a little rough around the edges and needing new upholstery, it was in serviceable condition. One of the last of the stylish Grahams, it was the one that automotive writers described as "looking to be in motion when standing still" with its rakishly tilted front end.

I bought it for $600. Gene, devoting rare days off from interning, helped me fix it up, new leatherette upholstery and all. It would be our wedding car and our exhilaratingly scary cross-country transportation months later.

But first, the Rite of Matrimony: preparations and last-minute adjustments came off without a hitch. The marriage license had been secured well ahead of time, March 13, 1944, to be exact. Announcements and invitations went out in timely fashion, photographers and caterers for the reception showed up promptly and performed ably. Seemingly endless wedding dress alterations resulted in a fitting conjunction of bride and gown.

The ring was not forgotten. Father of the groom escorted bride and family to the church in carefully measured cadence, precisely synchronized with the beginning of the service. Groom was a bit uptight, but best man expertly calmed him down. Father Thomas F. Ryder conducted the ceremony splendidly.

And while the audience murmured appreciatively, the radiant bride reigned supreme, the cynosure of all eyes.

As the crowd was ushered out, celebrants could savor the ceremony and admire the quiet beauty of Newman Hall in its flowerless austerity during the Lenten Season.

Though understandably anxious to get away, bride and groom thoroughly enjoyed the reception, their friends, and family. Quantitatively speaking, we enjoyed cake and champagne less, hardly having a moment to partake thereof. We were busy with other things: talking to wedding guests, posing continually for eager photographers, and busy *not* drinking champagne. At some point, Andrée flew the coop to change into her going-away outfit. When she reappeared, finally and spectacularly, she was smartly decked out in a gray flannel business suit and a striking black hat, with a single gardenia adorning her lapel.

More pictures, more oohs and aahs, a little more champagne, a lot more cheering and congratulatory send-offs, and we were aboard the Graham Supercharger sedan, multicolored ribbons, signs, and tin cans adorning its hide. Rice in our hair and joy in our hearts, we were on our way.

The day had been a delight, but strenuous and, as contemporary slang had it, "we were bushed." Nervous energy saw us across the Bay Bridge to San Francisco without mishap, where we arrived at the Mark Hopkins Hotel. Did *my* hands tremble just a little bit while *I* deliberately and carefully signed the register as Ensign and Mrs. Charles R. Webb Jr.?

Hungry after not eating at our reception, we went on a brisk walk

Wedding photos, March 29, 1944 (clockwise):
at the front door of the Bonno home at 483 Boynton Avenue, Berkeley;
the bride and groom at work; bridesmaids Mary Starbird and
Mimi Smith and matron of honor Jean Porter Thompson.

Andrée and I at the wedding reception, she in her "getaway" attire.

down Nob Hill to enjoy the cuisine of a high-class French restaurant. Then, exhausted by the climb back *up* Nob Hill, we joyfully survived the rest of the evening. And thus, on the evening of March 29, 1944, the two of us became one.

Still a little tired the next day, we checked out of the Mark Hopkins Hotel and assaulted Golden Gate Park. We sampled attractions such as the Japanese Tea Garden, the de Young Museum, and Stow Lake, where we rented a rowboat to while away an hour. That evening, we left for the easy drive to Santa Cruz.

Santa Cruz proved delightful. Far from Carmel's colorful frenzy, it was peaceful, unassuming, and quietly active, with some of its establishments having experienced wartime closure. Andrée and I found it restful; so benignly restful in fact, following the excitement of the last two days, that we slept almost until noon on the morning of March 31st.

That afternoon we leisurely visited amusement parks, those still open, and lollygagged around the beaches. It was cold, but who cares?

We spent the next morning in similar pursuits. But by noon we were anxious to put Santa Cruz and its gentle *insouciance* behind us. No fooling! It was relaxed and pleasantly comfortable. Still, we had things to do, and time was short.

I had orders to be in Arizona prior to 15 April 1944, so at this juncture, according to plan, Andrée and I returned to Berkeley. One of the men I served with, one of the most capable officers in the Naval Reserve Unit, the highly respected Lieutenant (jg) Sherman Watkins, became a very good friend. He and his wife thoughtfully arranged to be away from home during the last week before my departure for Arizona. They generously gave Andrée and me the keys to their lovely house in North Berkeley.

By late morning, April 2nd, Andrée and I were comfortably ensconced in the Watkins' home. Everything was shipshape—freshly laundered linens, towels, tablecloths, and suchlike. We found a note offering us every best wish and telling us where to find essentials and what numbers to call in event of need. In the refrigerator, *another* note told us what to do with the bottle of champagne to which the note was attached.

With such ample provision for our needs, we were able to address tasks such as writing thank-you letters; acquiring "supplies" and backup clothing for Arizona; seeing associates, friends, and their families; and making sure that all personal bills and accounts had been properly discharged.

I checked with the University of California to make sure I was departing in good standing. I also visited Naval Medical Research Unit #1 to extend my respect and appreciation to its personnel and particularly to its commanding officer. Finally, I arranged transportation to and around Arizona.

The comfortable accommodations of the Watkins' home, so convenient to the University of California, helped us enormously in not only completing necessary tasks but also bringing Andrée and me a week of joy and fulfillment.

Andrée helped me in my predeparture tasks while also attending to a load of chores of her own and her mother's. Additionally, she assumed much of the responsibility for taking care of her 11-month-old brother, who certainly had the right to be hugely out of sorts over all the commotion. But, I must say, he has never complained about it to me. ♦

Chapter 10

"YOU'RE ON REPORT!"

◆ ══════════════════════

The brig, *Naval Training Station, Tucson, Arizona. Beginning four months of training of direct-commissioned officers scheduled for combat duty.*

My father drove Andrée and me to San Francisco on an April morning, so I could catch a train to Los Angeles en route to Arizona. Andrée, who had not yet learned to drive, prevailed on him two weeks later to repeat that performance. But this time, it would be *she* who was leaving for Arizona, a move that would have unforeseen consequences.

I arrived in Tucson after the two-leg journey: a scenic and comfortable trip from San Francisco to LA and a scraggly, dusty, and drab one from LA to Tucson. An equally drab Hotel Congress, downtown, provided lodging until reporting time, 0700 15 April 1944, at the US Naval Training Station on the campus of the University of Arizona.

No verdant fields, spacious vistas, and elegant architecture, the University of Arizona was plain in 1944, plain, dry, and dusty. The University of California it was not. Nothing to suggest the relatively attractive campus it

In my khaki dress uniform during World War II.

would later become, it contained only three major buildings (four, if you count the temporary classroom structure).

Most prepossessing of these was the University Administration Building, a large, three-story edifice of ancient lineage and fittingly drab perspective. Stone-faced and austere, it projected the perfect personality for housing a group of naval reservists on a mission. Temporary "toe-the-line" specialists, they co-opted the building as their headquarters for indoctrinating newly commissioned officers just a trifle greener than they.

The other two buildings were an all-purpose conglomeration serving as theater, hospital, and high-grade storage and Bear Down Gym, by far the most important building to us. Originally the university's gymnasium, Bear Down, was large enough to house 800 "indoctrinates," all commissioned officers.

Bear Down was everything. Bear Down was "everywhere." We lived there. We heard reveille there and, at night, the spirited tattoo and wistful taps. We shaved and showered there, urinated and defecated there. Slept (most of us) there. We even studied (some of us) there.

Reveille was at 0600. Or was it 0540? If you asked an officer/recruit, "What time is reveille?" you might get the answer, "Immediately after taps." If you asked me, you'd hear, "An instant after falling asleep."

Tattoo was played at 2140, taps at 2200. There was a firm rule regarding taps: after taps, no one could leave his bed, for any reason, before 2220. The intent was to give people a 20-minute chance to fall asleep before commotion began. The rule had come about because immediately after taps some recruits had been taking a trip to the well-lit lavatory to study.

The problem for me was that at 2200, many men clattered past me on their way to their nightly "study hall" in the bathroom. I just could not get to sleep before the overachievers' exodus. Often the noise caught me coming *and* going, exodus and return. The men's return could be worse, in fact, because it was staggered, everyone returning to his bunk at a different time. The problem was aggravated by my performing with the other buglers at 2140 and 2200, so I was always late getting back to my bunk.

My lack of sleep fed on itself. Tired as I was from persistent insomnia, I still lay awake night after night, increasingly worried. Growing ever more weary, I finally "solved" the problem. It was easy: I simply fell asleep in classrooms.

Afternoon following hot afternoon, I fought to keep my eyes open in stifling classrooms, dozing off and arousing jerkily under an instructor's watchful eye. I began to realize that court-martial might be lying in wait, just around the corner—and all because of sleep, or my lack thereof.

Cashiered from the Service? Sent home in disgrace? Was that about to be my fate? It certainly would be, unless I could dream up an exit from Bear Down. But in no shape to *dream up* anything, I needed help. That help came from a most unexpected quarter: a surly lieutenant commander in the naval reserve.

The situation was bleak and the setting—Bear Down—intolerable. But it wasn't *all* bad. There was some freedom at the end of the day and on weekends. Bear Down could get festive after the dinner hour and before tattoo. Jokes and improvised entertainment were staples. Celebrities among us were generous in sharing their time and talents. For instance, Dennis Day, a performer on *The Jack Benny Show*, sang for us many times and also recounted amusing stories from his days on the show.

Some of us were permitted to form a jazz band, which performed casually and also would put on a big show for the entire base toward the end of our stay. Additionally, there was enough time to enable me to call Andrée almost every night. Those telephone calls would lead to her decision to come to Tucson, a decision that provoked no opposition from me.

Despite the heat, already high in mid-April, she had no trouble getting around Tucson with public transportation and in finding lodging, first in the Hotel Congress and not long after in a private home with two elderly and kindly women.

One night, during post-dinner "free time," she met me on the base. After a short walk, we sat down on a bench next to a pond adjoining the entranceway to the Administration Building. And there, right there, Andrée met for the first time—and also the last time—Lt. Commander Surly.

He had come in from the street, walking briskly. I rose from the bench, saluting him. Without breaking stride and without returning my salute, he passed us, saying, "You're on report!"

As directed next morning, I reported to the Captain's quarters in the University Administration Building, where a clerk politely informed me that my hearing, called a Captain's Mast, was scheduled for 0930 the following day. Not a court-martial, a Captain's Mast is a proceeding to resolve violations.

Whatever the name of the process, it was apparent that it was the first step in cashiering me out of the Navy. But, I wondered, how so fast? And how did that nasty fellow at the pond know that I slept through my classes?

The Captain's Mast answered some of my questions and raised others. There were five or six people in the room, including a stenographer, a few officers, and an enlisted man. No captain ran the Captain's Mast; instead, it was Lt. Commander Surly. My offense was not sleeping during class. Rather, I was charged with being with "a woman" in a restricted area. In my defense, all I could say was that I was not aware it was a restricted area and that the woman was my wife.

One of the officers in the room, apparently a lawyer in civilian life, insisted that there should be some written proof that the area was indeed restricted. The lieutenant commander, outranking the lawyer, put him down abruptly, declaring: "Of course it's restricted, and he was there with *this woman*. That's a clear-cut infraction. The man should be punished severely so that cadets in training will understand the meaning of discipline and understand that when regulations are broken, we cannot use legal technicalities to mitigate or lessen the required punishment."

Rebuffed, the lawyer held his counsel. But I noticed him writing a few words in a notebook as the proceedings ground to a close. Dismissed and ominously informed that the corrective measures would be known later in the day, I was relieved that the proceedings had nothing to do with classroom insomnia, and angry about how they involved *this woman*. I also had developed a slight annoyance with a certain lieutenant commander.

That afternoon, my punishment was issued, and it was severe, thanks to Lt. Commander Surly: I was ordered to the Navy brig, and I was to remain there, excepting time for meals and classes, until graduation day. Thrown in the brig! For sitting with my wife in an unmarked area!

However, when I discovered that the brig was also the hospital, I suspected that incarceration might afford some advantages. Out of 800 young men undergoing rigorous physical training, I reasoned, you're not going to find too many in need of hospitalization. And that's the way it worked out for me. Often I had the brig/hospital to myself; other times, I had only one "co-patient."

That first night away from Bear Down, I slept pretty well, waking up once only because I did not hear the lavatory clatter. From then on, I slept very well, gradually waking up—so to speak—to the fact that this quiet, clean room was indeed "the brig." I figured the chances were fairly good that these delightful "sleeping quarters" would be my prison for the rest of the time in Arizona, some six more weeks.

My resentment over the cavalier treatment and harsh penalty for a questionable infraction soon gave way to a relaxed acceptance bordering on amusement. In fact, it was damned funny to fellow inmates and even some members of the instructional staff.

Then, after several days of imprisonment, it became funnier still. A nasty rumor, claiming there had been *no* infraction, hit the base. Funny became hilarious when, within 48 hours, fresh rumors circulated that the Executive Officer's clerical staff was busily at work typing up a newly created set of regulations. I heard that the regulations devoted a separate section to "restricted areas." This addition was necessary to address the lawyerly lieutenant's objections at the Captain's Mast as well as to justify my sentence.

While vindicated, I still wasn't laughing. Nonetheless, however unjustly treated and judged and sentenced, I wondrously benefited from the official errors. Soon as possible I told Andrée the news. She had been very embarrassed by the incident the other night and indignant over the cavalier treatment I had received. Cast in the brig didn't sound very nice to her, at least not until further word was forthcoming.

The Executive Officer's amendment to the regulations benefited me still further. Almost overnight, I—the perpetrator of heinous crimes—became a celebrity, the *Happy Prisoner*. Dumped on, he's up "smelling like a rose" while the surly "X O," willing to change the rules but not the ruling, gained nothing but universal scorn. Fellow officers could only shrug and smirk, while enlisted men snickered.

The "prisoner" at US Naval Training Station, Tucson, Arizona, 1944.

The instructional staff fit somewhere in between. Mostly enlisted men, they were all regular Navy. They were good teachers and, without exception, knew their subjects to perfection. In the classroom, they were no nonsense, all business. Outside, still business, they tended to be friendly, communicative, and ever ready with answers to questions.

They knew Bear-Downers and we knew them, to a degree. As you might expect, they knew about me and my prior naval career as an enlisted man.

They were astute in recognizing and adjusting to the peculiar positions of their trainees. Regular Navy working with a bunch of reservists, they also were enlisted men instructing commissioned officers.

With tact and sensitivity needed in exchanges between commissioned students and enlisted faculty, some faculty simply kept their distance. The more relaxed instructors talked and listened to students freely. Since those faculty could and did talk to other personnel, word traveled freely on the base. The *Happy Prisoner* became famous and was soon known as simply the Prisoner or the Convict.

As a celebrity, I was treated differently. I was generally expected to be in prison only during sleeping hours. Otherwise, I was as free as all other students. Schooling and feeding were alone explicit in the rules, which otherwise prescribed no restrictions (an odd omission, considering the litigious circumstances).

If I showed up at tattoo, no one was surprised, and no one, even the officer in charge, complained. Likewise to joining a pickup softball game after evening "chow." Nor to playing in the band. (Who'd dare, since I was the only pianist "in residence"?) Nor to appearing at all rehearsals for the big musical, not to mention participating in the actual performance. When weekend liberty was permitted, no one told the criminal he had to stay in jail. And certainly, if "Lt. Commander you're-on-report!" happened to spy Andrée and me in a theater on a Saturday night, do you think he'd chance opening his mouth?

I've wondered about him a little and the *cause célèbre*. Did it bother him? (Probably not.) Was he embarrassed? (Should have been.) Did his fellow officers shun him? Kid him? Ignore him?

And the captain? Did he tease him? Scold him? Transfer him? Look the other way? Resolve never again to let the press of business induce him to have a mere Executive Officer stand in for him at a Captain's Mast? Who knows? I do.

How? Because I was told that the captain was not only "pissed off," he was embarrassed as well. Moreover, it is generally known how he found a subtle, "none of the above" way to put Lt. Commander Surly emphatically and dramatically in his place.

Periodically, as part of the training routine, Bear-Downers marched to a nearby football field for drills and maneuvers as well as for exercise. Ordinarily, the Prisoner marched too, playing with the buglers.

On graduation day, high-ranking dignitaries from Phoenix and Tucson accompanied the captain to that same football field to which we had so often marched. It being the last official act of our school term, everything was done with precision and perfect order, the field decorated, the band in service uniform. Marching to the field, the band arrived in close sequence with several flag-bearing automobiles carrying admirals, captains, and lesser dignitaries who, on a covert signal, emerged as one from their respective vehicles.

Standing there for a brief moment, they were then greeted by the clear, solemn notes from a solitary bugler. It was the *Happy Prisoner* delivering the official welcoming salutation.

I had been driven to the site, bugle and all, well ahead of time to assure my being ready. I waited there some 15 minutes, sweating a little from the heat and a lot from apprehension. Having never played a bugle prior to Bear Down, I was oh, so aware of the need to blow the bugle, not blow the performance.

Basking in the honor while marveling over the circumstances, I wondered who thought of the idea? Certainly not the captain, but surely he had to approve it. Bestowing such an honor on a cadet sentenced by a Captain's Mast? Never! And, as just retribution for a wrongful penalty? In the Navy? As Commandant of NTC, Arizona, only he could have made *that* decision.

"Whatever!" On a beautiful morning in mid-June, band and uniformed brass and honor guard and close to a thousand cadets and visitors congregated on the parade grounds in almost total silence, broken at last by the clear notes of a single bugle officially welcoming all.

The graduation ceremony had thereby begun. The overvindicated bugler was so relieved and amazed by his good fortune that he hardly noticed the rest of the proceedings. Graduation was over, Bear Down and Tucson would soon be left behind. Arizona had been warm in mid-April. By June 15th, it was hot, time to get out of town.

I gathered my gear, hired a taxi, and picked up Andrée—who had been living in an air-conditioned home with nice, older women—within an hour or so of graduation. That afternoon, we caught a train for Los Angeles. It seemed like we had won the same hot and dirty car I had arrived in, except it was dirtier and much hotter.

But we didn't care. It was good to be on our way. We enjoyed talking about the bad and the good of Tucson. And we were anxious to discuss my new orders.

Some days before graduation, cadets had been given a limited choice of future assignments. With a preliminary warning that students seldom received what they wished for, we were told to write down, from a long list of possibilities, our first, second, and third preferences. When orders arrived, I was pleased and surprised to learn that I was going to the Communications School at Harvard University, my first choice.

The favorable assignment was the main subject of conversation on our train to Los Angeles. My reporting date was 1 July 1944.

With just 14 days to cross the country, our mode of transportation undecided, and no lodging, provisions, or restrictions on where we could live, the orders gave Andrée and me plenty to talk about and decisions to make. The first decision was easy: train to Berkeley now.

The second was comparatively easy to make but difficult to implement. No more trains for a while; we would drive to Massachusetts. Drive, that is, if we could secure approval and extra rationing coupons from the Gas Rationing Board.

Upon obtaining approval and extra gas coupons, and making our farewells once more, Andrée and I set off for parts unknown on June 19th. We figured there was plenty of time to traverse the country, even at the wartime-imposed speed limit of 35 miles per hour. ✦

Chapter 11

DID HARRY SAVE MY LIFE?

◆ ══════════════════════════════

Advanced training at Harvard, Coronado, Alameda, Pearl
Harbor, and Maui, preparatory to the invasion of Japan.

*O*ff early in the day, Andrée and I sailed through Sacramento on schedule, conquered the Sierras, and lunched in Reno. Fifty miles short of Lovelock, the right-rear tire blew. Desolate terrain, no vehicles in sight, no habitation or signs of life, I overreacted. Wary of desperados, Japanese escapees, cowboys, or hungry Indians, I fetched an old .22 caliber pistol from the trunk, loaded it, handed it to Andrée to stand guard, and feverishly changed the tire.

We'd lost an hour or so. Not too bad, but the delay changed our plans about spending the night in Elko. Even reaching Winnemucca was an accomplishment. We had traveled over 400 miles on our first day through some difficult terrain, a rate that promised to land us in New England with three or four days to spare.

The next day, we made up lost time by easy sailing to Elko, through Salt Lake City, and into Wyoming. Steady driving and a smoothly running automobile had taken us almost a third of the way. So far, the trip was pleasant enough for us to approach the point of self-congratulations. That was when hubris in the form of Wyoming struck our proud Graham sport sedan.

Some 30 miles east of Evanston, Wyoming, I began to notice that the temperature gauge was creeping up very slightly. Minutes passed, an hour passed, by which time there was no question about its rising elevation.

Not dangerous yet. But, seeing a gas station, we stopped to add water, a stop that caused at least half an hour's delay because of the need for the radiator to cool before I could touch the radiator cap, let alone add water.

"No water needed," a station attendant told me. "Them cars have the best radiators in the business. Your problem's the tail winds in this here part of Wyomin' that make radiators work kinda poor."

So Andrée and I proceeded with some trepidation and much caution, using an old trick I had learned in the automobile business, speeding up, shutting off the engine, coasting as long as terrain and traffic would permit, and repeating the process until the temperature gauge registered moderate temperatures. We'd then cruise at normal speed until the gauge signaled the need to redo the procedure. Thus, we stutter-stepped our way across Wyoming, reaching Laramie in mid-afternoon.

A lovely city, Laramie, seat of the University of Wyoming, though not where we wanted to spend the night. Already behind schedule, we decided to push on. As we left town, however, another dragon rose up before us, blocking the way to Cheyenne. That monster was one huge incline. Steep and long, it was insistent in its unspoken warning: "Don't mess with me. I'm impossible, quite impassable. Turnaround. Go back."

I looked at the gauge, looked at Andrée, looked at the mountain, flipped a mental coin, glanced at the hood of our Graham Supercharger, one hot car. One-hundred-miles-per-hour-hot, that is, forced these last two days to limp along at 50 (read 35, if you like) mph though it had the internal combustion guts to nip over that 8,640-foot crest in one burst.

Were we going to capitulate? Going to turn back? Flip another coin? One more look at Andrée, and I floored it. With a thrust that pinned us against the red leatherette seat cushions, the Supercharger leapt forth, lunging at the dragon, exhaust roaring, whine of supercharger ascending.

Anxiously watching the temperature gauge—holding steady but high—I wondered about visual deception. Was the gauge actually moving? Could it have dropped *down* a notch? Was I hallucinating? Or had I heard our Supercharger say, "No problem"? Hallucinating or not, when the speedometer showed 75 mph, I thought *tires.* Wartime retreads!

Then, two amazing things happened. First, just before I reduced our speed to tire-safe levels, Andrée and I *both* noticed that the gauge had, in fact, gone down. Substantially. This gratifying change had taken place in less than two minutes while we surmounted two-thirds of the hill at full throttle.

Second, as we floated over the summit at about 55 mph, the gauge—back to normal for a few moments—had begun to creep up again. Weird radiator? Always full of water, but ineffective? Shining knight had slain monster, but dragon's teeth remained.

We puzzled over this enigma as we limped into Cheyenne and across Nebraska, inquiring in Ogallala and getting the same answer: "Nothing wrong with that radiator." The answer awaited us in Omaha, where a friendly mechanic got off on the wrong foot by telling me there was nothing "haywire with that radiator." He squared up a little by saying, "Graham makes the best radiators in the business, so we have to find the answer elsewhere." Elsewhere took 45 minutes and a motor tune-up ($2.75). The diagnosis? "Your timing was off. I advanced it, re-gapped the sparkplugs, and replaced points and condenser. You ain't gonna have no more radiator problems." And we didn't. Never again.

Back on the road, Andrée asked whether there was any connection between the mechanical explanation we'd just heard and the dragon-slaying episode on the mountain. "Directly connected," said I, all-knowingly. "If we had told him at the outset about the temporary reprieve at full throttle, he would probably have said 'late timing,' advanced the spark, and sent us happily on our way, while charging us all of 75¢." Andrée demurred, "That's a cute answer, but please tell me in plain English how on earth he could come up with something like that!"

I explained that the Graham, as with other modern cars, was equipped with a device that advances the spark timing when the throttle is opened wide. I *stepped on the gas* in Wyoming to get a running start on the formidable incline confronting us, hoping to reach the top before overheating. The supercharged six-cylinder engine was equal to the challenge, but automatic timing advance provided a major boost.

Early-twentieth-century cars had spark control knobs next to the steering wheel. "Old-timers" knew to advance the spark by hand when they needed extra "oomph" and to retard it if they should happen to overdo the advance, causing the engine to voice its protest with a pinging sound. What some old-timers did not know, myself included, is that spark timing is influenced by altitude. Had I been more aware, we might have escaped that "radiator" trouble.

The Graham had been tuned in Berkeley and, therefore, timing had been set for sea level. Once into and past the Sierras, we therefore suffered from a negative-altitude attitude. With one exception, we traveled, due to late engine-timing, all the way from Reno to Omaha. That one exception was the monster mountain outside Laramie where "flooring it" to surmount the grade automatically advanced the spark.

After Omaha, happily crossing the river into Iowa in our rejuvenated steed, we not-quite-so-happily realized that late spark equated to sluggish gasoline mileage. Wending our retarded way across half the country had taken its toll on our gas-rationing book.

Stopping in Council Bluffs for a refill restored our cheerfulness. Gasoline was much cheaper there. Beyond that, the station attendant refused our proffered coupons, casually remarking, "We don't pay attention to them things. We got plenty gasoline in Iowa."

Two and a half days later, we arrived in Cambridge, still reflecting on this country seen at close hand for 3100 miles, this war with its widely varying reactions state to state, gas rationing *here & there*, radiators, and great engines, precocious, retarded, or both.

We had little time for sightseeing or gawking at the famous places and historic buildings on almost every corner of Cambridge and Boston. First we had to find lodging.

After much searching and stumbling, we found a place on Buckingham Street, half a mile west of Harvard. We rented it jointly with Tucson acquaintances Dorothy and Richard Snodgress, who hailed from Glendale, California. Two couples sharing a three-room apartment in a strange land under straightened circumstances can be trying. While we did have "differences" from time to time, we tolerated each other and remained on good terms for the duration of the Harvard Communications Training Program.

At first Andrée and Dorothy worked and saw the sights together. They shared meal preparation, both wanting to nourish their young and very tired husbands returning from training sessions. So they shopped together and thereby discovered one did not like the other's tastes, in food selection, cooking, and—as it turned out—almost everything else.

Within a few weeks, alternating dinner preparations and dividing chores, they were "on their own" and, although the four of us still ate dinner together, the women could arrange their separate days just as they pleased.

Andrée happily made good use of her forced habit of traveling by foot to walk all around Cambridge. Off early, avoiding heat and humidity, she saw many churches, churchyards, and museums. But her favorite spot, less than a mile away, was Harvard Square. Its quaint stores, colorful garden stalls, and tempting coffee shops crowding Mass. Avenue and Brattle Street provided her a pleasant retreat as well as a picturesque gateway to Harvard Yard, in one direction, or, in the other, just around the corner, the Longfellow House.

I, meanwhile, found that though the programs at Harvard and Tucson were like *day* and *night*, there were some similarities. Both were conducted by capable training staffs, and teaching was competent and thorough. Both had physical drills, both marching and athletic. Both maintained rigorous training schedules. Both were hot, Tucson because it was Tucson, and Harvard because 1944 was of one of the hottest summers on record in the Boston area. Hot and humid.

Essentially, they were different because of different missions. Tucson's was *indoctrination,* Harvard's *naval communications.* Tucson was rudimentary. Harvard was advanced, pedagogic, and sophisticated. Bugles and sick bay at Tucson. Slide rules and Morse code at Harvard. Two months for me at Tucson. Four at Harvard.

Time went fast. Despite the heat, we enjoyed the summer and the distinctly different New England scene and scenery. My training was grueling but interesting, as raw recruits became Navy "communicators."

Amazed to find ourselves mastering Morse code and attaining modest skills in sending and receiving messages, we soon acquired more expertise. Among these were enciphering and deciphering code, celestial navigation, semaphore "conversation," and *secured* telephone communication.

The supreme challenge for me was learning to read and answer messages

All at sea, and a bit less formal.

sent by high-powered spotlights, a challenge to which I responded poorly. Ten words per minute was my maximum, an attainment, were this baseball, that would place me well below the Mendoza Line.

After my classmates and I were able to send and receive various types of naval communications, we needed to be able to deliver the messages to Command, other ships, pilots, or other communicators. Usually we could convey the messages to the intended recipient vocally, in a few words, or via a handwritten note. But not infrequently, typed copy was required. Once again, my naval career may have been influenced by my typing skills—there being no apparent reason why I would be chosen for a fourth month of concentrated training when others in my class finished Harvard Communications School after three months.

That fourth month was a sort of *internship* where our three months of training and learning were put into action: training turned to drilling, learning to application. We applied naval communication skills to a series of imaginary situations, war games, in fact. Intense, deliberately repetitious, interesting, and a bit scary, the "games" made it clear that we were being prepared for some very special exercise.

On graduation, at the end of October, most of us received orders to report to ATB Coronado, California.

Our trip back across the country was smooth and exhilarating in the fresh air of early autumn, the fields redolent with the scents of harvest time. The Graham Supercharger—*and* its engine—were in perfect tune, the temperature gauge reading a steady *normal*. Many easy miles slipped by between fueling stops, gas rationing having ended by then. Our spirits were high, despite the fact that Andrée lost no time in expanding the acronym ATB into its ominous full title, Amphibious Training Base.

ATB Coronado proved to be a delightful place. Were it not for the disconcerting reality of a war-going-on, it could have been paradise for newlyweds. But I was alone.

Residence in the Bachelor Officer Quarters (BOQ) was not too bad, noisy but clean, relatively new, and with good facilities. Besides, it had a well-stocked bar at ultra-cheap prices. "Well-stocked," I should qualify, if you liked Three Feathers whiskey or fake Scotch.

Real Scotch was almost nowhere to be found. Gin might have been acceptable, but I had not yet acquired a taste for martinis. Wine was unacceptable. Beer was available and not bad if you avoided the variety that contemporary wits dismissed as fit only to be "put back in the horse."

On learning the BOQ was crowded and residence there not required, I informed Andrée, who had been living with her parents. She immediately took a train to San Diego and the ferry to Coronado, where I picked her up in a 1933 Dodge coupe I had managed to buy at the outlandish price of $350, much more than it was worth but a good buy considering the market at the time.

As a comparison, expecting momentarily to be shipped overseas from ATB Coronado and Andrée not knowing yet how to drive, I had sold the Graham for $800 (much to the annoyance of my brother, who would gladly have bought it, and at almost any price). In hindsight, selling my Graham was a mistake. I ended up staying in Coronado more than four additional months. Severe automobile shortages would last another three years. The Graham was infinitely better in every way than the Dodge. But we were glad to have any transportation.

I taught Andrée to drive in that Dodge. We drove it to San Diego and around Coronado and several times to Berkeley and San Francisco, where my mother was dying of cancer. We drove it to La Avenida, just about the only decent restaurant in Coronado. We used it, endlessly it seemed, to hunt for a place to live in Coronado.

The crowded conditions at the BOQ were a harbinger. Well, they should have been. The only thing plentiful in wartime Coronado was scarcity, and housing was scarce as a guileless fox.

We hunted to no avail. When two alternatives seemed our only choices—I commute from San Diego (interminable ferry delays) or Andrée return to Berkeley (bummer)—we stumbled on a room for rent. It was a small single room with a shared bath down the hall, a pleasant-enough landlady, and an exorbitant rent. I'll never forget that landlady and, strangely, still recall her name: Beulah Wharf. Very talkative, she had one pet phrase, which she spoke so earnestly and in a voice that sounded filled with tears, "My heart bleeds for all these young people in the military, alone and far from home . . ." Her voice always trailed off at this point. Andrée and I wondered how our $50 could make her *less* sanguine.

Fifty dollars per month! Exorbitant? Not now. Everything's relative. But then, it was big money. Our shared apartment in Cambridge, with all the amenities, had cost less.

During the Great Depression, Bessie Smith sang, "Twenty-five cents? No. No! I wouldn't pay twenty-five cents to go in nowhere!" In 1944, one might sing "Fifty dollars? No. No. I ain't gonna pay fifty dollars to live in no place," despite knowing wartime scarcity controlled the market. Beulah could have charged us more and gotten away with it. We lived with her nearly three months, deemed her lodgings acceptable "under the circumstances," got to know her, and left with no regrets.

Duty at ATB was rigorous, adventurous, and seldom dull. Definitely hands on, it had us constantly in jeeps, landing craft, communication ships, and, occasionally, aircraft.

We conducted daily exercises, telephones at the ready, scurrying around the San Diego backcountry ferreting out mock targets. Locating our "quarry," we transmitted attack information to pilots overhead who, equipped with live ammunition and sophisticated tracking gear, proceeded to find and destroy.

Other times we practiced beach landings. Approach to shore was acceptable, our landing respectable, but debarking was a wild yet disciplined rush—most of us scrambling through the opened bow while the more adventuresome and athletic leapt *over* the sides.

We—commissioned officers, mind you—even took turns navigating, operating, and steering the landing crafts onto the beach. I believe my fellow sailors graded me C+ for my efforts at the helm. My debarking skills, however, would have elicited an F+. Nimble was not my name. The *plus* in that grade merely reflects the fact that I actually did make it from the LCM to the beach.

I had been fairly active playing freshman baseball at Cal, though my back was beginning to hurt toward the end of the season. I checked into Cowell Hospital and was carefully examined and directed to walk more often. It must have been good advice as my back got better and gave me little trouble for several years.

The second week at Naval Communications School, Harvard, I wrenched my back in a basketball game on campus. Navy doctors taped me up from stem to stern. I remained tape-bound for the rest of the Cambridge tour, much to the amusement of fellow cadets and onlookers as we mustered every morning in Harvard Yard.

I could barely walk. When I did, zombie style, my upper body remained grotesquely motionless. At the end of the training program, de-taped at last, I could drive, coast to coast, relatively free of pain. But for years thereafter I walked somewhat gingerly.

Jumping out of landing craft was not going to be my strong suit, a rude development since jumping out of landing craft was exactly what we were primed for in the invasion of Japan. Had any bigwigs noticed my tentative exits, boats to beaches, they would have immediately brought such sorry exhibitions to a halt.

Didn't happen. My stars remained fixed. Course set. Orders arrived, directing me to report in February, 1945, to Air Support Control Command, Naval Air Station, Alameda, California.

Similar orders went to other trainees at ATB, so it seemed clear, as we had often surmised, that early on "our class" was scheduled for the beaches of Japan to help direct the fire of aircraft above. We just hadn't figured out the route. Now it was obvious: we would go from Alameda to a forward base in the Pacific for final preparation and the advance to invasion waters.

With the gradual winding down of the war in Europe, more and more attention was directed to the Far East. The Japanese Empire was shrinking, its conquests and outposts in China and other areas, such as Burma and Indonesia, turned back or under heavy attack. But Japanese military will, determination, and resourcefulness were still strong.

It was evident that a prodigious effort to surmount this force was in the offing and that the war would eventually have to be taken to the Japanese homeland itself. To be involved directly in this effort was both an exciting and a chastening prospect. ATB Coronado involved us, but a little bit at the periphery. Naval Air Station, Alameda, was more immediate.

And Alameda was home. Through-the-Tube-to-Oakland home. Alameda County home. San Francisco Bay Area home. News of friends back from the war (either dead, wounded, or relieved of duty) home. With sadness everywhere, it was also home, for me, to be near family and my mother in her last days.

It was happiness too, to be home with Andrée and her family at a time when Paris had at last been freed, the Nazis driven out. It was a time, a place, of mixed emotions and also a place of waiting at the Naval Air Station, Alameda. We reported each day for little training but much waiting—waiting for daily activities and waiting for the other shoe to drop, shipping-out orders.

Days went by with little or no officially directed activity. We were free to walk around the base, watch air exercises, observe training programs, or even visit the "ship's store." Free to wend and wonder but never to wander far from the reach of headquarters, we were treated as visitors awaiting assignment. Though not "ship's company," we were held accountable both on and off base. Telephone contact, ship to shore, was constant, especially toward the end of our stay when "air supporters" were allowed more frequent liberty.

This casual but firm control continued for the duration of our stay at US Naval Air Station, Alameda. The flexibility did allow me more time with my mother. Since her life was now being counted in days and hours, she asked to spend her remaining moments at home, a plea readily approved by the staff at Franklin Hospital. Back home and, despite sedation, retaining her mental faculties, she was happy to be with her family in Berkeley once more.

Adele McDaniel Webb died February 13, 1945, aged 54, leaving five years of bereavement for her mother, Mary Peacock McDaniel, and 32 years of widowerhood for my father.

I spent the six weeks after her death, before I shipped out, consoling my father, sister, and brother and being consoled by them. Andrée comforted me too, as did her parents, all of them having been fond of Adele.

I was still at the Naval Air Station on March 29, 1945, so Andrée and I were able to spend our first wedding anniversary together and to marvel over what and how much had transpired in that one fast-moving year: the wedding and the Navy brig, the Graham Supercharger's late spark, the Harvard Yard tape-o-rama, ATB landing craft, the lachrymose Beulah Wharf, and Alameda.

We also sorrowed over my mother's untimely death while recognizing it was a blessing that she lived long enough to see us wedded and long enough to know that her sons and daughter were still alive after more than three years of war.

We were thankful that one year found us still together, *and happy* together. On March 29, 1945, we were also painfully aware that our separation was imminent. Indeed, a few days later, my Air Support Control comrades and I were on the high seas bound for parts unknown.

Not entirely unknown. We knew that we were on the Pacific Ocean and that we were sailing west. We also knew we were on a "Jeep carrier," one of those merchant ships converted into small aircraft-carriers, Liberty Ships, as they were also called.

We knew a few other things as well, the biggest being the news received in the captain's office that President Roosevelt had just died.

It was April 12, 1945.

Or, to be precise, it was mid-morning of the 13th before we knew that Franklin Roosevelt had died at Warm Springs, Georgia, in the late afternoon, probably of a stroke. While the significance of his untimely demise was instantly recognized in Washington and abroad, it hit my air-support comrades and me more slowly.

As a group we were sorry to hear the news, both from a human loss standpoint and from concern over the impact on the war effort. Some worried about Truman's capabilities; others surely thought, "What if Wendell Willkie instead of FDR had been elected?" A few must have paused to consider that Henry Wallace, rather than Harry Truman, "might *now* be president of the United States."

All of us had to be wondering whether or not the course of the war, or our part in it, would change. In a few days, however, we learned that our original destination had not been changed. Addressing Congress on April 16th, just three days after assuming office, President Truman announced that he intended to follow through on prosecution of the war in keeping with the plans of Roosevelt, the chiefs of staff, and our allies.

In his excellent work *Truman*, David McCullough recounts the attitudes and perceptions of high dignitaries in assessing the capabilities of the new president: "Among staff holdovers attitudes were changing appreciably, almost by the day, the more they saw of him." Something about the man—plain, unpretentious, direct, self-assured—inspired confidence in those who worked with him. A no-nonsense sort of guy, he got things done.

Nonetheless, as a Republican, I found Truman crude, raw, and disruptive and considered him unequal to the job awaiting him. I even voted for Thomas A. Dewey in 1948, despite some of Truman's notable postwar successes. I was generally middle-of-the-road (my mother a Democrat, father Republican) and favored Dewey on what I perceived as economic grounds.

Today, still registered Republican, I would unhesitatingly vote for a man of Truman's capacity and integrity over any of the presidential candidates whom the Republican Party has produced in recent years. If that statement seems to show a leftward swing on my part, I would submit, to the contrary, that my stance has changed little, while the Republican Party has veered to the right for more years than I care to count. The Party of the Great Emancipator has become embroiled in a struggle to avoid capture by the rigid and bigoted and by religious extremists, anti-science mavens, deniers of global warming, and purveyors of absolute truth—all of whom spout trash bags full of fanciful and fundamentalist nostrums such as *creationism.*

Little concerned with either end of the political spectrum nor, indeed, with President Truman's skill in navigating its straits, we sailors sailed on and sailed on. Endlessly, it seemed. Jeep carriers were not noted for their speed. Ten to twelve knots maximum, they might make eight under ordinary conditions. Later, I would calculate that we had averaged about seven knots on the trip from the mainland.

When finally, in mid-April, we reached the Hawaiian Islands, it seemed like we had been sailing southwest forever. Yet we had hardly left home, judging from the vast extent of the Pacific Ocean. Recently noting its size, Admiral Samuel Locklear III, Commander of the US Pacific Fleet, remarked: "If all the world's landmasses were placed in the Pacific, there would still be room left over for an additional Africa, Canada, United States, and Mexico."

We stayed several days at Pearl Harbor, but, writing Andrée, I could only reveal, "I am in the Hawaiian Islands. When I got here or when I'm leaving (even if I knew) censorship regulations prohibit my saying." When we did leave Oahu, I doubt that many of us knew that we were heading for Maui, or that it was to be our home considerably longer than we might have expected.

Today, we know Maui as the garden spot of the Pacific—or other slogans to that effect—with its resorts and splendid hotels and beautiful beaches and gentle surfs. In the spring of 1945, it had its charms too, with great beaches and unsullied vistas. It was beautiful but barren except for scattered acres of luscious growth and the ubiquitous pineapple plantations.

The Naval Air Station was barren too. It was also gray, dusty, and bleak. Its Bachelor Officer Quarters, though plain, were relatively clean and reasonably comfortable. Hot during the day, not much cooler at night, temperatures were relieved somewhat by cooling breezes that usually sidled in, late in the afternoons.

Conditions were definitely not painful. The bars—one for enlisted men, another for officers—were air-conditioned and amply supplied. They opened at 4:00 PM—1600 hours, I should have said—which reminds me that the old 0540 reveilles of Bear Down days were conspicuous by their absence at Maui, with the exception of pilots and aircraft crews, who were up before dawn. The workday for most other personnel began at 0800. ◆

Chapter 12

WELL, DID HE?

◆ ═══════════════

*Would effective intelligence and negotiations make the "bomb"
irrelevant? Harry's decision saved thousands of lives on both
sides. But was mine saved simply because I reach advanced
theaters too late to see action?*

I'd soon be able to tell Andrée that I had been at Pearl Harbor and was
now stationed at Naval Air Station, Maui. For the rest of the world, and
in correspondence with her, I would remain Ensign C. R. Webb Jr., *Staff,
Comdr Air Support Control Units, Amphibious Forces, US Pacific Fleet, c/o
F.P.O., San Francisco.*

Mercifully, that ponderous handle—along with my rank—would later
be changed to Lt.(jg) C. R. Webb Jr., *Staff C.A.S.C.U., Phibo Pac, F.P.O., San
Francisco.*

No more training stations. Everything—overseas, staff assignment,
paper promotion, amphibious duty—proclaimed loudly and a little ominously that this fledgling cadet and erstwhile ensign was now officially "at
war." My apprehensive father and anxious wife subsumed their concerns

under the banner of staunch patriots supporting the war as well as the individuals involved in its outcome.

Quite naturally in accord with these sentiments, I preferred "Staff, Comdr Air Support Control Units" to NTS Tucson or ATB Coronado; in other words, I preferred to be in the *thick-of-things* rather than *training-and-more-training*. But being in the thick of things had two sides to it: *stand tall* and *crouch*. At Maui, we were much closer to each of these imperatives. After Harvard's Communications School, subsequent training pointed clearly in one direction: the beaches of the Rising Sun.

Even the most optimistic among us foresaw either an Allied victory or a personal *Setting Sun* on those sands. And some ruefully contemplated the distinct possibility of achieving victory at the forfeit of our lives.

While we think of blue as *the* Navy color, gray, especially in wartime, is everywhere. Consider the sea at a distance, the ships plying it, buildings, uniforms, the ever-changing and ever-the-same tides, and even the patterns of warfare: gray at a distance, black and white and, unfortunately, red up close.

Blurring colors make me think of that perennial whimsy on Navy life, "hurry up and wait." Not unique to the Navy, it's a melody most service men and women have sung. It takes the colors black and white and applies them to human conditions, universally covering almost anything where outcome and expectation somehow diverge at 180°. This blurring gives us expressions like, "what did you expect?" or "what else is new?" Or in France, *comme ci, comme ça,* or in Italy, *que sera sera,* together with all sorts of shrugs, sighs, gesticulations, and expectorations: merely picturesque ways of saying everything's black and white or both. So the camouflage of Navy life is a fast-moving kaleidoscope of black and white.

Can my naval career, from Pearl Harbor to Maui and beyond, be described in these terms? Gray, black/white, boring/exciting, and everything in between? In many ways, yes. The Jeep carrier to Pearl, for example, was exciting and every kind of boring. As it happened, Dick Jurgens's popular dance band played on that trip and, on several occasions, I had the fun of playing piano with the band. That part of the trip was not boring.

Pearl Harbor was crowded, dirty, and (while we waited, and waited) boring. Yet Pearl was the heart and soul of the war in the Pacific, so it was also downright exciting. Waikiki, famous beach and a tourist's delight, continued to attract thousands during the war. (I doubt if Yogi Berra had Waikiki in mind when he reportedly said, "Nobody goes there anymore. It's too crowded.")

Service personnel went there precisely *because* it was crowded, because that's where sailors and soldiers went. Waikiki offered the best chance to meet an acquaintance, to find someone from a similar unit, present or past, to meet an old friend, or make a new friend. Pearl was crowded, Waikiki was more crowded. Pearl was dirty, Waikiki dirtier. Pearl was noisy, Waikiki deafening.

I wrote Andrée about going there and said it was "super ugh." Told her I had not been interested in going there, but others in our outfit "dragged me there." "Anyway," I said, "there was little else to do at Pearl. But I enjoyed the scenery and the spectacular views at Waikiki."

A few more days on Oahu and we were whisked away, happy to desert its clamor and bustle but sorry to leave its nightlife and history. I was relieved to be free of daily encounters with its all-too-visible signs of December 7, 1941. As a group, we were ready to leave behind the disheartening signs of poverty amid affluence among the citizenry. Strong feelings, here and there, were elbowed aside by curiosity, wonderment, and excitement.

The short flight, less than an hour, takeoff and landing included, from Oahu to Maui had been pleasantly uneventful. On the ground, the flurry of deplaning activities, the blur of bussing to the base, and registration at the BOQ, gave way to an atmosphere quite familiar . . . gray.

Settling in, however, we discovered almost at once an emerging clarity. While gray areas remained, black was black, white was definitely white.

Contrasts were sharp. Military was tight but casual. The uniform of the day was *work,* and work performance was uniformly precise, uniformly effective. Enlisted personnel and officers treated each other with civility and respect. Mutual friendliness prevailed, but familiarity was avoided; courtesy and support were everywhere, but saluting rare.

Daily operations were carried out with utmost precision with no margin for error. After hours, errors at the bar might be tolerated, but grudgingly, even egregious error. After all, if one made a damn fool of himself off duty, after a hard day in the cockpit, that was usually *his* business. At the bar for enlisted personnel, nights were usually a trifle quieter. "Never a damn fool there," a certifiably sober Marine staff sergeant confidentially informed me one evening.

In sum, Maui was a full-blown Naval Air Station operating in an active war zone, temporarily quiet but technically active and within 15 minutes of Pearl Harbor. Those minutes, it's been said, could look like seconds to combat pilots who were already airborne and at full throttle.

Air Command, Maui, had the triple responsibility of maintaining ever-ready response capabilities against surprise attacks, operating a frontline state-of-the-art training facility, and coordinating planning with advanced staffs in preparation for the invasion of Japan.

Since each of these functions involved sizable contingents of army, air force, and Marines, in addition to our air support control group, the task was huge and all-encompassing. While its tripartite demands were answered effectively, the training part touched me most directly, particularly because of my interest in training and its close association with education.

At ATB Coronado we had gone through the process of simulating countless landings and air strikes against mock targets. On Maui, we repeated those exercises but with much more intensity, more elaborate planning, and a higher percentage of live ammunition. We planned strikes, assembled equipment, and "landed in Japan," all in strict battle mode. Making allowances for the different theater, we found and directed air coverage from "Japanese beaches" on Maui and the other islands in the Hawaiian group.

The NAS Maui program was realistic to a fault. There was more detail, greater thoroughness and, after each exercise, much more debriefing. The term used was always *mock operation,* a phrase that goes beyond *training exercise* or *simulated attack,* a matter of degree, small but significant.

Another difference, more of substance than of degree, was that at Maui we worked more closely with the pilots. We hadn't known them at ATB Coronado and had rarely talked to them other than on radio-phones during simulated runs. At Maui, we saw pilots all the time, whether in debriefing rooms or at the bar or mess area, talking about operation matters, communication problems, weather patterns, news from home.

Some of the differences that existed at Coronado were just built in at Maui: the theater, weather, geographical isolation, and the extended stay in one spot. We lived together, ate together, worked together, drank together, played together, and endlessly gabbed together.

The Command, both air-station brass and air-control officials, encouraged this "togetherness." They arranged cultural forays around the island, brought in celebrities to entertain and dignitaries to lecture, and set up exercise programs.

We had baseball games, tennis matches, and even chess tournaments. This latter I know well, because I actually won the big chess tournament, receiving an emolument worthy of a "king's ransom" ($2.50) and (unofficially) being declared Pacific Fleet Chess Champion.

At Coronado, as at Harvard and Quonset Point (a naval base in Rhode Island the Harvard Command School trainees visited briefly), we had also trained for duty on board the huge communications/command ships that would oversee landings from both the long-range, strategic base and the immediate tactical or operational deployment.

It was evident from the start that such "plush" assignments had already been doled out, mostly to more experienced personnel and at an earlier point in the training cycle. It was ever more difficult to counter the ongoing assumption that an advanced staging base, or Japan itself, was our next assignment.

Faced with the obvious, nobody seemed to be overly concerned about it. We talked a lot, drank more than a lot, worked hard. Morale was good, probably because of hard work and knowing our efforts were aimed at a definite object. There was also a certain bravado, among many, "to get the show on the road. Enough training," they proclaimed, "it's time to put that training to good use."

Their views were also subject to change: optimists became pessimists and vice versa. Passing time brought increases of cynicism, boredom, and drinking, while weeks drifted by without detectable movement toward the next stage.

With war drawing to an end in Europe, the Japanese Empire shrinking, and air strikes against its mainland increasing, one might conjecture that the War in the Pacific was winding down—or, just as easily, conclude that it would drag on indefinitely. As June drifted into July and July to August, morale remained high but uncertainty grew.

Mock operations continued but less frequently. My roommate and I escorted 20 enlisted men on a trip to Mt. Haleakala, an active volcano in Maui's interior. We all found time on weekends to visit beautiful beaches and quaint towns around the island. Jeeps for these excursions seemed always available.

Early on, I had been invited to take on an additional task, a pleasant alternative to the usual nightlife. An official assignment, the project may have been conceived one evening at the bar where officers from various branches intermingled. In pursuit of identical military goals, they followed different routes to attain those goals.

When officers of every rank, every quarter and command, elbowed nightly and politely to the bar, they were not there only to drink. They were interested in learning, exchanging ideas, solving problems, and relaxing in preparation for the next day's challenges.

Conversations were often personal. They could be philosophical and analytical as well (What's wrong? How can we fix it? What's right? How can we improve it?). My idea was that we had officers on board who could teach. Let them use their expertise to offer educational opportunities for enlisted personnel.

A self-fulfilling prophecy? Someone in the command hierarchy may have talked to me or to another officer who knew me. With help from the chaplain, we secured classroom space and set up a course for enlisted personnel with the rather ambitious, and perhaps intimidating, title of Western Civilization.

The class went well enough, with about 25 students attending. On average, they were bright; on average, they were ignorant of history; and, almost without exception, they were eager to learn. How much they learned and how they applied what they learned, I cannot say. Time was too short. I know that *I* learned more than they did.

I learned, indeed, from something I already knew or should have known. Pharmacist's Mate Bill Jones is not called Pharmacist's Mate Jones or Bill Jones in the Navy. He's called Jones. I didn't like that and thought it was demeaning. Wanting to avoid "talking down to students," I called them Mr. Smith, Miss Johnson, or Mr. Roberts.

It didn't work. They were embarrassed. You call an officer Mr. Jones. If an enlisted man, you call him Jones. I'd goofed. But I refused to call Jones Jones. So I quickly learned first names and used those on the students instead. Jones became John. The students all recognized the mistake, noted my correction, and enjoyed the more familiar but less down-putting salutation.

Another mistake had to do with the practical side of teaching. Students were eager to learn but not, I discovered, to listen endlessly. Lectures are for college (they're really not, but that's another story). Anesthesiology not being my thing, I dropped the lectures and, using their first names, started asking questions.

There were always answers, often very good ones. I also lost some of my soporific effect, and a majority of my charges began staying awake (even those who had fortified themselves, before class, at the enlisted men's bar).

The course was reasonably successful because of the chaplain's heroic efforts in getting reading materials to the students in a timely fashion during wartime and also because of the active endorsement of Maui Command. Awareness of my two years' service as an enlisted man as well as the master's degree in history from the University of California may also have encouraged students to accept the class, participate in it, and remain eager to learn.

The idea of someone teaching a class in the humanities on a naval station in a war zone during wartime to enlisted personnel on active duty in, or training for, fleet operations, borders on the surreal. Or, maybe far out. I'm reminded of one of the most innovative and effective civilian programs in history.

On June 22, 1944, President Roosevelt had signed the Servicemen's Readjustment Act of 1944, better known as the GI Bill of Rights. NAS Maui had nothing to do with its legislative development, nor did any of us know much about it. But surely we were all in it together, wondering how to prepare millions of service members for their return to civilian life.

On Maui, I taught the very people who, postwar, would need and seek the educational boost that the GI Bill provided. While it helped veterans buy homes, find jobs, start businesses, and secure medical care, its major emphasis was on education. It subsidized the costs of tuition, fees, books, and living expenses.

By 1951, when the number of postwar veterans had begun to recede, 14 billion dollars had been spent and more than 18 million veterans had received educational benefits (roughly 3.4 million in job training, 3.5 million in secondary schools, and 2.3 million in colleges and universities).

The results were far-reaching and enormous. Government got its money back multifold. Society received ongoing and recurring benefits: doctors, lawyers, engineers, teachers, professors, architects, artists, artisans, musicians, skilled labor, police officers, and any number of highly trained technicians. New institutions and new buildings mushroomed everywhere.

That was postwar. Returning to Maui and my miniature GI Bill, I recall that some benefits accrued to me in a number of small ways. For instance, it confirmed my growing desire to teach. It helped me see my failings and provided an opportunity to correct them. And it quickened my conception of a postwar career, *anything* postwar.

Above all, it was an indicator for students and teacher alike. The very fact that the class existed and that Command had ordered it lent grist to the rumor mill: Is the *skipper* playing games? Or is he off his rocker? Or is the war about to end?

What I couldn't help noticing is that the course started in May, less than a month after our arrival at Maui. I wrote Andrée on May 29th that my class had already met for the second time.

With a bare two weeks' time for me to prepare, the commencement of the class was abrupt. And a course in Western Civilization presented to Navy technicians, gunners, aircraft maintainers, landing-craft sailors? That was strange enough, and definitely a herald of changes ahead. Otherwise, why? "Well," the cynical might allow, "there's nothing else to do but wait and drink. They might as well be learning; meanwhile, what are they fighting for?"

Yes, they might as well be learning. By this time, students in the Western Civilization class were immersed in accounts of Themistocles, Pericles, Alcibiades, and the fall of the Athenian Empire in the fifth century BC.

For some, the history course was a sign of de-escalation. Another sign was the gradual turnover: personnel were shipping out piecemeal rather than by large contingents as replacements after the Iwo Jima and Okinawa campaigns (hostilities on Okinawa dragged on until June 22, 1945).

Within Air Support Control, personnel continued to ship out steadily through the summer. By the end of July, 1945, few of us were left. With weekly departures, it was clear that as a group we were going nowhere, but as individuals it could be *sayonara* tomorrow.

The signs were everywhere. Maui was my Cassandra. Almost from the beginning, she had been telling a story. But I hadn't been listening. Full military procedures and the strict training routine had steadfastly been maintained, mock exercises with live ammunition too. Yet subtly, gradually, the pace and intensity diminished—so slowly that few of us noticed at the time.

Some signs I could not avoid noting, nor inferring their significance. Most remarkable among these was the steady atrophy of the complement of air controllers. This regression came to a head at the end of July. On August 5, 1945, I wrote Andrée, "There are only six of us left here of our original group."

The *bomb* fell on Hiroshima on August 6, 1945.

While Japan wavered, particularly over the meaning of *unconditional surrender,* a second bomb would fall, on Nagasaki.

A third, and last, bomb was ready a few days later, but President Truman issued orders to desist.

On August 14th, Truman announced to the world, "Japan has accepted the Potsdam Declaration," namely, unconditional surrender.

The war had ended at last, and the scramble of reservists, homeward bound, began. To set priorities, a system of points based on length of service was established to determine who would leave first. Mysteriously, the critical number was set at 49. If you had 49 or fewer points, you waited; 50 or greater, you were on your way, subject to transportation availability. No wiggle room there: 50 says *leave*; 49, *grieve*. But what happened to someone with 49½ points? This was an urgent question for me because that's how many points *I* had accumulated.

Days and rumors flew. My colleagues in Air Support insisted that, logically, I was "home free." I agreed with their reasoning, but Command did not, reminding me I was still in Maui and would remain so pending clarification from higher authority.

While that weird chess match approached stalemate, resolution came, quite literally, from higher up. A Navy captain, meeting his flight time requirement, flew in one morning. Still in the dark on the point debacle, the commanding officer of the air station apparently saw the light in the captain's imminent return to Pearl Harbor. "Do you have room for a passenger?"

A phone call and a brief discussion with Air Support Command followed. These two and their respective staff officers, still without information on how to handle 49½ points, now rid themselves of the dilemma: "You can take your case to Headquarters on Oahu, if you and your gear are ready for takeoff in 15 minutes."

Well, they punted. Oahu made a fair catch. Command, never resolving the half-point issue, on the one hand, sent me home on the other hand; actually on a Liberty Ship. Who knows? Perhaps they figured that a voyage on a jeep carrier would take so long that, by landfall, I'd have earned my extra ½ point anyway.

In my haste to catch the captain's flight, I left a few items behind and failed to pay respects to friends and colleagues. I was also sorry I was unable to thank the chaplain for his generous aid in setting up the Western Civilization class. The commanding officers deserved my thanks, too, for their support. I should also have expressed my appreciation for their innovative way of sending me off. It was a resourceful and friendly gesture, even though I might have been killed in the process.

Killed in the process? Maybe that's a bit strong. But I must say that the captain, though friendly and conscientious, had a way of validating his need to complete his flight time. All in all, it was a pleasant day and a smooth flight. Except for one little glitch.

The sky was clear as we made the final turn for the approach and a gentle descent on Oahu. Then, precisely at the proper instant, the captain deftly executed a perfect three-point landing. Smooth! However, for an instant, we still hovered about five feet *above* the tarmac at the moment before landing, which, to say the least, was abrupt. "A little bumpy there at the end," he apologetically joked a few moments later.

Dicey there for the genial captain, and also for me. But I didn't get killed that day, nor later; and thanks to President Truman, under different conditions, neither did thousands of others.

The question of whether my life was saved by Truman's decision to use atomic weapons is not new with me, or for others primed for the invasion of Japan. But it remains important philosophically and pragmatically in reference to wartime use of atomic fission.

The simple facts are these. My training as a naval officer was directed almost from the beginning toward the invasion of Japan. Three months at Harvard, all communications, and, for some of us, an additional month of ground-to-air communications, clearly pointed us toward our next assignment, ATB Coronado.

At Amphibious Training Base, we trained in two areas: landing craft invasion and ground-to-air radio control to facilitate air support of small-boat assaults.

Once at Maui, our training was aimed solely toward assaults on Japanese shores, to provide air support for other units striving to establish beachheads.

Once our troops were on beachheads, casualty rates were estimated to be high, some of the highest in all warfare, 50 percent or more on some beachheads. Such survival rates argue in support of Harry Truman's role in saving my life.

Could the war in the Pacific have been won without using the Bomb? Some claim that the war, in a sense, had *already* been won. The Imperial navy had been destroyed, air force crippled, oil supplies depleted. But Japanese determination, rooted in desperation, remained. Their reliance on *kamikaze* attacks mirrored Emperor worship. As one military authority lamented, "If, like Okinawa, we had to take the islands one at a time, the war could take months, even years, to conclude."

So the answer to that question is yes, but not feasible under the circumstances. "Could the war have been won without an invasion of Japan, island hopping in other words?" No, as per the quotation above, and also no, unless the Potsdam Declaration were interpreted so that "unconditional surrender" meant *only* overcoming the armed forces, not the whole country and not the Emperor.

Even after Hiroshima, Japanese individuals in high places were insisting they would fight on, island by island, naval blockade, siege and starvation, even to the point of invasion of the mainland. Under every condition they'd continue to fight, resisting with such fanatical resolve and guerrilla persistence as either to repel the intruders or succumb gloriously in apocalyptic support of their Emperor.

Such determination prolonged the otherwise waning erosion of military will and would have caused enormous loss of life, mine probably included, in long, drawn-out island-to-island guerrilla warfare. So we give a vote to Harry in avoiding any kind of war of attrition.

The evidence piles up, but before reaching a verdict, we should view some countervailing data. The Japanese, very low in food and oil, also faced both the loss of control of the Sea of Japan and the threat of a Soviet attack from the opposite direction.

Already aware of the atomic bomb and its probable use, Josef Stalin agreed at Potsdam to declare war on Japan. Thus, he gained assurance of Soviet involvement in war-ending negotiations as well as a chance to redress losses of the Russo-Japanese War of 1905. No matter their fanatical resolve, how long could Japan hold out against Soviet armies from the northwest, naval blockade in the east, and all kinds of material shortages at home?

Not long, especially considering the additional impact of a rain of conventional bombs, when control of Okinawa was secured late in June. From then on, Tokyo was well within the range of B-29 Superfortresses. Under the circumstances, the idea of closing in on mainland Japan through costly and time-consuming "isle-hopping" no longer applied when measured against the size and strength of the Allied armada just off the coast.

Even so, direct assault would still have been costly, bloody, and long-drawn-out. Loss of life in such a lengthy campaign surely would have exceeded substantially—on both sides—the devastating losses at Hiroshima and Nagasaki. So Harry's decision certainly may have saved the lives of thousands of American and Allied service men. Whether or not it saved mine remains open, there being another point that must be raised, namely, the hefty Elephant in the Japanese China Closet, *unconditional surrender.*

In his first speech to Congress shortly after President Roosevelt's death, Truman spoke of the war and his determination to follow closely the path of

his predecessor, including prosecution of the war until the day of unconditional surrender. He reiterated this stance at Potsdam. The Potsdam Declaration in time became virtually synonymous with unconditional surrender.

In the six months before the dramatic climax of the war, Japanese and
Allied ministers tried repeatedly to negotiate a cessation of hostilities. The
failure of these talks seemed always to hang on language problems wherein,
according to our people, the Japanese were uncertain as to the meaning of
unconditional surrender and therefore could not come to an agreement.

The truth of the matter is that the Japanese were not one bit uncertain.
They knew full well that the phrase "unconditional surrender" meant *surrender without conditions.*

For the Allies, this phrase was the philosophical basis of the war effort. It
had worked in Germany. Why not in Japan? For the Japanese, *unconditional*
threatened the Emperor and the totality of Japanese ways, customs, mores.
The impasse could not be broken. A *deus ex machina* was needed to provide
a "happy" ending to the tale.

Hiroshima seemed to be that *deus ex machina.* But the "language"
hang-up remained. Emperor Hirohito did nothing. He waited. His negotiators worked hard, though to little avail, for resolution during the three days
that followed. When Nagasaki was hit, August 9th, stubborn behavior on
both sides was at last blown away. The Japanese asked directly, what happens
to the Emperor and "our way of life if we surrender?" The clincher came
for the Japanese with the application of conditions onto the *unconditional,*
in effect a reply of "nothing happens," thereby resolving their worst fears.

The great impediment, the word *unconditional,* lost its significance after
Hiroshima and Nagasaki. Just a word, it didn't kill people. Once Allied
negotiators convinced the Japanese that *unconditional,* as far as the Emperor
was concerned, did not really mean *unconditional,* negotiations could at last
move to closure.

The *Elephant* thus dispatched, war could end, and President Truman
would announce five days later that Japan had accepted the Potsdam
Declaration.

Technically, Japan had not, but that doesn't matter since it was "only" a
language disagreement. Anyway, all ambiguities were resolved September
2, 1945, with the signing of the peace agreement on the battleship *Missouri,*
anchored in Tokyo Bay.

Simply stated, the "language disagreement" prolonged the war. The
Japanese were defeated *before* Hiroshima in every way except determination.

They were determined to fight on indefinitely rather than to surrender *unconditionally*. So my first point is that the life-saving role of the atomic bomb is only a partial one, given the significance of Allied insistence on unconditional surrender. And that's for *all* lives. For *my* life, it's at best a maybe.

A maybe, that is, when you consider that I was still on Maui at the beginning of September and could hardly have reached the battle zone in time to be involved directly. After more than 500 days of training, I seemed no longer to be headed for the Sea of Japan. A colossal invasion force, enormously powerful, seasoned, and ready for action, was already there.

On free nights, the chaplain and others in the chain of command often got together for bull sessions at their respective quarters. The BOQ bar was nice enough, but noisy, so they favored their private digs where the food could be better than the BOQ mess offerings, the atmosphere more convivial, and the liquor choice. I recall Old Forester being one of the chaplain's favorites.

The chaplain occasionally invited me to some of these soirees. As a result, I met a few high ranking officers on the Base, also becoming acquainted with several of lesser rank. One of these delighted in showing me he knew more about Western Civilization than I, while another had fun teasing me about my sore back and sleeping with a plywood board under my mattress.

On the occasion of my surprise departure from Maui with my 49½ points, he happened to be nearby when I learned *officially* of my passenger status. Somehow privy to the news that I had a flight back to Pearl, provided I could be ready in 15 minutes, he saw me outside the BOQ,

"Hey, Webb!" he shouted. Go get your board.

You're out of here."

Acquaintance with members of the command hierarchy could have had some remote influence on where or how I was stationed. But the overwhelming weight of evidence supports the theory that I remained on Maui because I wasn't needed in the active war zone, where the invading force was already in place.

It is my considered opinion, therefore, that Harry Truman did *not* save my life. I am happy to say, however, that his decision saved thousands of lives, both Japanese and American, by avoiding an endless war of attrition. While he had the support of the Allies and the General Staff, Truman alone could make the final decision. Agonizing over it for days, horrified by the thought of innocent lives lost, he decided that the Bomb could shorten the war, resulting in far fewer killed and wounded overall.

Some continue to argue that the Bomb wasn't necessary, that it was not the reason the war ended, that the war was over and only misconstrued words were holding off peace. They have a point since *unconditional surrender* seemed to frighten the Japanese more than American guns and bombs.

But the argument does not fly. The Bomb was a major factor. It set the stage for meaningful negotiations. Importantly, it permitted the Japanese to capitulate, to save face because the Bomb was so definitive, so apocalyptic.

The Bomb may not have ended the war all by itself, but it set new ground rules for negotiations. Moreover, it allowed the Japanese to present to *their* world a convincing reason for stopping the fighting.

Not beaten, just blasted to smithereens, they could aver *metaphorically* that the war had come to an abrupt ending because the Land of the Rising Sun was smitten, in a sense, by monstrous demons from outer space.

President Truman having not saved my life, I don't really mean to suggest that interspatial aliens did, or that a Navy captain failed to take it. Whatever his motives or inclinations, he landed relatively safely at Pearl Harbor, and I lost no time hightailing it to naval headquarters. ◆

Chapter 13

THE GOLDEN GATE, AT LAST

◆ ══════════════════════════════

Riddle of the Points. Pearl Harbor revisited. Jeep carrier home.

𝒫earl Harbor had not changed, yet it was different. The same frenzied efficiency—now more frenzied than efficient—struck one's eyes. The same teeming crowds, festive as always, were there to welcome all comers. Joyous and jubilant, they happily hindered the progress of scores of soldiers, sailors, and Marines, who patiently accepted congratulations from the celebrants milling around them.

Most of these troops, on liberty, leave, or temporary assignment, were on a mission similar to mine, namely, to find a swift and appropriate way out. While they scurried back to "wherever," to *hurry up and wait* for "whatever," I hurried to Pacific Command Headquarters, only to run into one humongous line.

Despite days of scrambling to see key officers and hours of waiting in lengthy lines, I was on a ship for California in four days. Meanwhile, not a single word had been said about *points* or about that exasperating number, 49½.

Once again, it was a Liberty ship, better known as a Jeep carrier or CVE. And once again, the passengers were not "ship's company." Not being ship's company on the trip home meant that passengers—with the possible exception of rescued prisoners of war—were denied most amenities provided for the ship's crew, including decent food. There was actually a separate mess for us, called the passengers' mess. Its food was intolerable, nearly inedible. It was so bad, in fact, I stopped eating there. I didn't stop eating; I just stopped eating in the passengers' mess.

Spam being available, many of us subsisted on Spam sandwiches for the rest of our time on board. We alternated Spam with fasting. In fact, I lost about 15 pounds during the leisurely weeklong homeward jaunt, a loss lamented neither by my parents and siblings nor by Andrée, who immediately dubbed me, "Sir Svelteness." That title, however, was soon abandoned as Spam-generated voraciousness kicked in.

Thoughts of fasting endlessly on that dawdling ship, day after day, often remind me of W. S. Gilbert's lilting words in "The Yarn of the *Nancy Bell*. "That I found alone, on a piece of stone, an elderly naval man." Turns out that the man had "sailed the Indian Sea" on the *Nancy Bell*. "And there on a reef, we come to grief, which has often occurred to me." Abandoned, stranded, and famished, the 10 survivors (from a crew of 77) are desperate:

"For a month we neither wittles nor drinks, till a-hungry we did feel.

So we drawed a lot and accordin' shot the Captain for our meal."

I should add that Spam isn't all that bad. We never once considered dining off the Captain's hide, despite a grievance or two. Besides, compared to the passengers' mess, Spam tasted pretty good . . . at first. Still, in more than half a century since leaving that Jeep Carrier, I've never taken another bite of Spam.

As passengers, we did not participate in any of the crew's social activities nor, obviously, their shipboard duties. With time on our hands, we plodded through the slow-moving hours, Spam and *fast, fast* and Spam. That routine left us endless opportunities to think and dream.

Some made good use of the time by sleeping. Having trouble sleeping, I daydreamed about the future, particularly about being back with Andrée, working out our life together.

"I need to concentrate," I told myself while scrambling around the rolling deck of the carrier in search of a place to squat. Scrounging for a seat—topside, below, inside, or out—was a daily occurrence. *Hurry up and wait* once more, it was *hurry* to beat out fellow-passengers for suitable landing areas and *wait* for the Spam. Constantly immersed in the usual commotion and ship-board clatter, I'd wish for a mind uncluttered and stomach pangs assuaged.

Interruption and turmoil defined my days, my work station, my ocean-going studio. All at sea, so to speak, struggling to keep turbulent thoughts afloat, I reviewed the crests and shoals of an erratic naval career.

Quite naturally, I thought of the questions awaiting my arrival in California. Andrée, already knowing much about what I had experienced, would have far different questions than her parents and various members of my family, with whom I had had little time for correspondence. How might I describe "my war" to them? *Incongruous? Contradictory? Episodic? Miscast? Full of change?*

It was *all* change, I'd have to tell them. Constant change. Change, in fact, was so unchanging, it became ludicrous. Thus it produced the absurd tale of an officer of the line, in good physical shape, with rigorous and prolonged training for one of the bloodiest types of naval action, who—in 52 months and 14 days of war—saw no actual combat, never encountered an enemy, never fired a shot in anger, and experienced no *real* sea duty.

I wondered about the questions my father-in-law might ask, he who fought in World War I; or his wife, directly descended from French naval officers; or my late cousin, Elton McDaniel, who flew army bombers over Germany for most of World War II.

Ruminating on these curious facts led me, in a few days, to the key questions: What did I learn from my extended tour of duty? And what contributions, if any, did I make to the war effort?

First, I learned how to clean petri dishes, test tubes, and latrines. To take blood pressure readings, do "short arm" inspections, and land landing craft on non-Japanese beaches. On Maui, I learned that many high-ranking officers were actually human. Similarly, at NTC, Arizona, I met good people, both enlisted and commissioned. Indeed, one officer there showed me that the worst intentions often produce the best results. Much against his wishes, he helped me find that rarest of rare occurrences, the navy brig masquerading as a convenient and comfortable place for a good night's sleep.

Also at Maui, I learned that Andrée, after a year alone with me, found it difficult spending all her free time with her parents. In turn, her loving and protective, very French, and Old World–oriented mother and father had problems reacting to their grown daughter, now more American than French. She was changing, and so was I.

I was beginning to know myself better. Like Andrée, I had been influenced by changing environments and social interrelations. But I lived in just two worlds, she in at least three, with her parents, in her social world (friends, Cutter Labs, Anna Head School), and in her own head. In my simple worlds, I was learning, or, rather, confirming that education lay somewhere in my future.

Whether I contributed to the war effort or not readily narrows down to two examples: the assignment with US Naval Research Unit #1 and the tour of duty at NAS Maui.

Regarding the former, one may assert that, in wartime, any sailor, soldier, or marine on active duty in a facility working in behalf of the nation's military goals is, ergo, contributing. That's the general statement. Add that at any moment during the war, working on influenza and bubonic plague, I could have been as much at risk as landing on a beach in Japan. Theoretical? Yes. Because risk, no matter how great, does not prove contribution, though it strongly implies it.

Less theoretical, my changing role at Maui made the big difference. From training exercises aimed at the beaches of Japan, a subtle shift began, as Command set me up in the educational program. Ancillary at the outset, it slowly became primary when overwhelming Allied strength in the Pacific heralded a likely cessation of hostilities. Gradually, the course in Western Civilization became more important, certainly to me, and perhaps to a few others who began to realize that the War in the Pacific *was* Western Civilization.

Not officially, not on Maui, but intellectually, symbolically, and self-consciously, I was coming to the conclusion that *my* war, *my* course— even my students' developing minds—were *the* war: Not only were we involved in scuttling the Land of the *Setting* Sun. We were reaffirming, re-creating, and embracing Western Civilization, a political system striving to co-exist with other nations and cultures in a supportive and noncontroversial way.

In holding this view of our society and reflecting it in teaching Western Civilization to a score of sailors, I may have made my only significant but modest contribution during the war and, therefore, to "the war effort" and beyond, postwar.

———— ◆ ————

The eight days—it seemed more like eight weeks—on salt water and Spam fell away in a burst of sunshine with the sudden appearance of the Golden Gate Bridge. The lingering fog of our voyage lifted.

Where we docked and how I got across San Francisco Bay are a blur in my mind, a blur of anticipation, exultation, even anxiety. I probably took a cab. Neither my father nor Andrée could have picked me up, not knowing when or even where I would land. Somehow, I made it to Berkeley, the ever-present Campanile having greeted me, according to its custom, well before I reached the East Bay shore and the Bonno house.

A strange feeling, climbing the long flight of stairs to their door after so long. I was uncertain about the greetings I might receive and apprehensive of how my tongue might act in mixed and non-naval company, including a 29-month-old brother-in-law.

I knew I'd get an exceedingly cordial "Welcome back!" from my in-laws and quite a bit more from their loving daughter who, however, as I had long-since noticed, was always a bit reserved in speaking to me in front of her parents. But Andrée carried it out well and, I am sure, no one noticed we were both anxious to be on our way, alone, in our old Dodge coupe that had been sitting in the Boynton garage most of the time since I'd left.

Once the jubilant hellos and shouts of welcome subsided, and food and drink consumed, Andrée and I politely and thankfully departed. We then made the rounds to friends and relatives. I was pleased to see that all were well and in good spirits. I was overjoyed but not surprised to find that Andrée glowed and sparkled as I had remembered her and that she had lost none of her beauty. Quite, and most emphatically, to the contrary.

Andrée looked very good, but tired. And thin. Her work at Cutter Labs in Berkeley—basic laboratory work—had been interesting but strenuous. And she had been concurrently teaching French during the school year at Anna Head School, which had been strenuous as well. *Un*interesting too, and exasperating, as high school girls of a certain age were young enough to be easily distracted but too old to master pronunciation of foreign words.

Like me, she suffered from our forced separation. I had the advantage of being with men living under similar conditions, while she lived with her parents, who did not always understand her plight. Seldom an easy arrangement, but a recently married, "Americanized" 23-year-old daughter living with her very French parents promised some tense moments ahead.

They were pleased with her teaching French at a prestigious school. They were not pleased to see her exhaust herself at Cutter Labs. They would have been highly displeased had they known her major incentive in continuing to work there was to "get out of the house" (although she, quite correctly, also saw her work at Cutter as aiding the war effort).

Telling me that she did not feel free with her parents, Andrée had about decided to move out when the Bomb ended the reign of tension at Boynton Avenue, averting domestic explosions in that part of the world. Her decision to "wait it out" at home may also have received a boost from a letter of September 20th, my last one to her. Postmarked Pearl Harbor, it included the promising news that I expected to catch a boat within the next few days.

There being no more letters from me, it is evident that we sailed no later than September 23rd and the carrier must have crept through the Golden Gate on September 30th or October 1, 1945. So Andrée had known for almost a week that I'd be home, barring mishaps, before my birthday.

Naturally, we were overjoyed that I was home and the long separation was over. Now, Andrée and I needed to find independent lodging.

I also had to report to ATB Coronado (the first step in getting out of the Navy) and check with various authorities about enrollment, midsemester, in the University of California graduate program.

In the whirlwind of activity those first few days, I have no idea of what happened on my birthday; another party, no doubt. Birthday celebration or no, we cut the Gordian knot by squeezing ourselves into the old Dodge coupe and driving to San Diego.

My release from the Air Support Control Training Command was accomplished in a few hours. A leisurely return to Berkeley gave us a chance to plan our next few steps and to get to know each other again. That was fun. It was serious, too, a long-term project that joyously continued for the rest of our lives together. ♦

PART TWO

Chapter 14

TOO LATE FOR CAL, SETTLED FOR HARVARD

◆ ══════════════════════════════════════

*New friends and unusual living quarters. Three years of
graduate work.*

*B*y the time we set foot again in Berkeley, it was mid-October, 1945, and
late enrollment at the University of California was neither feasible nor prac-
ticable. The Coronado break, at least, had made it tactically and tactfully
possible for us to take up temporary residence at Roble Court while we
searched for an apartment.

On October 22nd, the Commandant of the 12 Naval District, San Francisco, officially released me "to inactive duty-honorable," awarding me credit
for sea duty in the process.

We were fortunate enough, meanwhile, to find a cozy little one-room
apartment, complete with wall-bed, at 1806 Walnut Street, just a few blocks
from the UC campus. From the insularity of this redoubt, we were able to
preserve some measure of objectivity while discussing our next steps with
parents, in-laws, and friends.

In letters to me on Maui, Andrée had written of her interest in finding employment to bolster our finances after my return. She had demonstrated her ability to do so, having worked at Cutter Labs while teaching French at Anna Head School and being promoted at Cutter in the short time she was there. Nevertheless—given the times—family discussions centered around *my* professional future, a perspective with which she was in full accord.

My father, 30 years a successful businessman, saw his son's future in the Berkeley/Oakland automobile business. But he had remained on good terms with Cal athletics since his playing days. So he was not unhappy over the prospect of my reentering the academic program at Cal, much as he desired an additional and immediate hand at the Webb Motor Company. And, optimistically, he saw nothing incompatible with my earning a PhD in Modern European History at the University of California preceding entry into the business world.

Andrée's parents were of similar mind. A PhD? Certainly. At Cal? Certainly. Never a question, although it should be noted that they would have had no objections if I had abandoned the idea of an academic life in favor of a career in a Berkeley business establishment.

My sister, Virginia, busy at work in San Francisco, was neutral: anything's OK, she said, "just so it's not the automobile business." My brother, a natural apple-cart rearranger, was adamant: "Enough of this talk. Get out of town!" He'd been singing that song almost from the day of my return.

Gene may have been influenced by his experience at McGill University, where both he and his wife, Aileen earned MD degrees. Or perhaps he saw Andrée's need to "get out from under." More likely, he saw mine.

Living in Montreal, Gene and Aileen were familiar with Boston, Cambridge, and the rest of New England and traveled there often, always enjoying the local culture and historic landmarks. When it became evident that my entry into graduate studies at Cal would have to be postponed until the spring, Gene encouraged me to apply for admission to Harvard, "just on the off-chance."

When my letter of acceptance miraculously arrived, only a short time later, family discussions heated up. To little avail, though, since Andrée and I had already analyzed the pros and cons at great length. Quickly, therefore, we decided we were going.

Scurry, scurry, scary too. Hurry! Hurry and hope. Little time for parties at Walnut Street. Little time for Andrée to wind up her affairs at Anna Head and for me to do the same at the Webb Motor Company, where I had been employed as a salesman.

Little time for Marcelle and Gabriel Bonno to get accustomed to the thought of a 3000-mile separation from their daughter, so recently a child. Little time too for that same thought to be processed by my father, sister, and other relatives. Oddly, it was a major problem for my brother, despite his role in initiating the move.

Nonetheless, a few days after Christmas, Andrée and I were off, all packed up in a 1946 Nash 600 four-door sedan, one of the first off the postwar assembly lines. A black beauty that my father, who sold it to us, described as "looking like a Cadillac," it was called the 600 because it had a 20-gallon gasoline tank and therefore could go 600 miles on a tankful, provided it delivered 30 miles to the gallon. But at 15¢ per gallon, who cares?

Although I seldom got better than 23 miles per gallon, we liked the 600 anyway. It had three times the interior space of the '33 Dodge coupe and covered twice the distance on a gallon of gasoline. Besides, it cost only $1000, for which we managed to pay cash, an accomplishment we would not duplicate in the next 30 years.

The trip was pleasantly uneventful, in marked contrast to our first cross-country drive, some 18 months earlier. Nash proudly promoted its Weather Eye passenger-heating system. Though not quite so magical as advertised, it proved equal to all but the coldest blasts of January weather. Redundantly, we took the "Southern" route and, naturally, added our own thermal assists.

Somewhere around Bakersfield, I made a great discovery: the gasoline gauge had hardly moved. "Aha!" thought I, "is *Mr. 600* actually going to carry us 600 miles on a single tankful?"

No. I had merely witnessed a phenomenon shared by most fuel indicators. They read high, especially for the first 100 miles.

About five days later, New England welcomed us cheerfully with bright morning sun and light snow flurries. There was little accumulation, affording colorful contrasts—green and white on the ground, and roofs boasting every shade, every texture, every state of repair or disrepair. Driving on, the day still ahead of us, we indulged in some sightseeing, soon finding ourselves in Chestnut Hill, a suburb of Boston, site of the famous Longwood Cricket Club.

Much earlier, in Berkeley, California, a long wire fence once separated the John Muir School playground from a huge estate to the south. Behind that fence, a small boy, half hidden by undergrowth, often peered out longingly at other children at play. Growing up and emerging from his fenced-in cloister, he entered a different social climate. In high school, this lad, Billy Hotchkiss, and I became good friends, quite possibly because he drove, and let me drive, a nifty Plymouth roadster with wonderful appendages such as "free-wheeling," a "hill-holder," and even a built-in radio.

Learning in November, 1945, that I was leaving for Boston, soon, Billy told me that his aunt, Hazel Hotchkiss Wightman, lived there and I "simply had to look her up." Vaguely recalling something about the Wightman Cup, I acknowledged his command and promptly let the information slide into the wastebasket of my mind.

Once in Chestnut Hill, I rummaged in that wastebasket. Finding her name there, and also in the local phonebook, I screwed up my courage and called her. Answering the phone, she warmly greeted me, making me think that Billy had alerted her.

"You and your bride must come right over and say hello," said she, graciously, but in a tone forbidding any contrary-minded response. When I demurred, protesting our disheveled appearances and long time on the road, she insisted in no uncertain terms. My "bride" was horrified when I told her we were on our way—this very instant—to meet Hazel Hotchkiss Wightman. But we went. Mrs. Wightman was charming and charmed. One look at Andrée and she asked us where we were staying and, hearing what she expected to hear, immediately informed us that we were to stay with her until we had found more suitable lodging.

From the vantage point of the Wightman home, I began the process of registering and finding my way to classrooms, offices, and libraries of Harvard University.

I was pleased to learn that the formidable registration fees of a private university had been absorbed by the GI Bill. That aid and a modest monthly stipend helped immensely, though still leaving our finances in marginal territory. Andrée was determined to find employment as soon as possible.

Once my classes began, she was free to do just that as we set up a regular daily routine. At a nominal rent, we now lived in the upstairs quarters of the home, also in Chestnut Hill, of Hazel's friend, Madeline Bryant, and her 14-year-old daughter, Anne. Each morning, Andrée and I drove from Chestnut Hill to Cambridge. There, we parked the car on Mass. Avenue. (Try doing that now!) From there, Andrée had easy access to the subway, and I had a two-minute walk to Harvard Yard.

The very first day, she found a job at Jordan Marsh in Boston. Each evening, either we'd meet at the Cambridge subway station or I'd pick her up at Jordan Marsh. Then, it was dinner in Boston or Cambridge and "home" to Chestnut Hill, sometimes with a show or lecture intervening. We followed that routine for several months until Andrée found a better job—located in Cambridge, too—with General Motors.

In addition to saving her time, the new position paid better, a consideration we could live with. Andrée had a knack for such things, as I observed on a regular basis. Incidentally, in all her life, Andrée never applied for a job without getting it, never "lost" a job, and seldom held a position for a significant length of time without finding ways to improve its efficiency or effectiveness. These characteristics would play a major role in the 30 months or so of our Harvard venture.

We stayed with Madeline Bryant for the better part of a year, remaining on good terms with her and profiting from many household improvements she provided. While still in Chestnut Hill, we also enjoyed seeing Mrs. Wightman from time to time and being amazed by her strong will, forthrightness, and charm. I liked the bonus, moreover, that she had a ping-pong table in her basement.

At Cal, I'd become an accomplished player—not a champion, but one who lost infrequently and was locally infamous because of a wicked serve. Playing with Mrs. Wightman, I might win a point or two here and there, but I don't think I ever won a game. Should have known!

Much later, I discovered that she was one of a select few in the history of tennis to have won a "Golden Match," one in which the loser wins nary a point. Hazel did it in 1910 during the Washington State Championships, demolishing her victim—a certain Miss Huiskamp—6-0, 6-0, by winning 48 consecutive points.

Far from being embarrassed by that thrashing, La Huiskamp could probably be proud of herself for having been on the same court with a woman who was US Women's Champion that year. *And* the year before. *And* the year after. *And* in 1919, after giving birth to her first child.

She was so good. And so modest. Here she was, an amateur champion, fresh out of her glory days at the University of California, instantly breaking into the wider world of professional tennis with a spectacular and concentrated string of victories.

Modest? Hazel Hotchkiss Wightman was the only woman *ever* to win the US national singles, doubles, and mixed doubles championships in one year (1909). A great athlete, universally respected for her sportsmanship and persistence as a winner in one of the longest active careers in sports, she never uttered a word—at least, to us—about any of it.

And *"table* tennis"? "How do you do it?" I'd ask after seeing her smoothly and repeatedly return every smash, every slice, almost every shot. "Oh," she says, "I just try to return everything."

"TRY?" Come on! She returned everything. When she didn't, I *might* win a point. She had a disconcerting way of volleying most of her shots. Devastating in ping-pong. Same in tennis.

Tennis was her game at the beginning of her professional career. As the story goes, growing up in Berkeley, Hazel hit balls against a wall, not letting them bounce since the ground was so uneven that balls invariably bounced erratically. Accordingly, she revolutionized the game with the volley shot. It became a compensating ploy to offset her small stature. For others, it would just become an integral part of their overall game.

We finally moved from Chestnut Hill, finding an apartment in Cambridge closer to everything and with all the amenities, including the all-important kitchen. Andrée enjoyed the work at General Motors, finding new friends there with whom we played tennis and met socially from time to time.

My work at Harvard was interesting and rigorous, at a level similar to what I had known at Cal. But it may have been a bit easier than a full-time Navy assignment simultaneously juggling a master's degree program.

It was stimulating, once again, to be in the company of world-renowned scholars such as Crane Brinton, Sterling Dow, David Owen, Myron Gilmore, William Langer, and Samuel Eliot Morison.

It was exciting and also a little frightening to find myself, along with Alvin Coox, later a colleague at San Diego State, in a class, just the two of us, with the renowned classicist Sterling Dow, analyzing Thucydides and the Peloponnesian War.

And it was exhilarating to see on every side, on every corner, and in every byway, the roots and residuals, the monuments, cemeteries, and assorted artifacts, the symbolic reminders of a nation's birth pangs. It was tantalizing, indeed, to be studying in a library, the books of which evoked the smells and textures of eighteenth-century New England while I was there in pursuit of a degree in *European* History.

I made my choice on the basis of a lifelong interest in European history. How could I do otherwise with a father-in-law who was an active, living example of European history? And with a wife who personified the glory of

France in every way save one? The lone exception was *war*. She definitely was not warlike.

Speaking of war, I'm happy to say our time at Harvard was uniformly peaceful. Struggles with books and curricula were few. Housing and cost-of-living concerns were our major battles. We had temporarily won the housing campaign. But it was a pyrrhic victory, since rent for the apartment increased our monthly outlay.

Both problems, however, were soon to be surmounted by a single, unforeseen stroke. Because of a long-planned trip to California, we had to move from the apartment in the summer of 1947: temporary problem temporarily solved.

On returning in the fall and encountering the same dual dilemmas, we went to the Harvard Housing Office in hopes of securing some sort of lodging. An undergraduate student clerk courteously handed us a sheet of paper with addresses and phone numbers of several rooms and apartments. As we thanked her and headed for the door, she said, "I don't know if you'd be interested in this one." After a meaningful pause, she added, "It's a little different," and gave us a 3x5 card that read:

> Mr. and Mrs. David P. Wheatland
> 11 Gray Gardens West, Cambridge, Massachusetts
> Looking for a live-in couple to help care for children and
> assist in managing the household.

The card included a phone number which, after Andrée and I deliberated at some length, I called. A low-pitched voice, dripping with annoyed authority, answered, "Yes?" I was taken aback by the tone but managed, after a noticeable pause, to recover enough sangfroid to explain the reason for my call.

Later that morning, by appointment, Andrée and I arrived at 11 Gray Gardens West, a huge and stately Colonial sequestered at the far end of a parklike cul de sac. With trepidation—for me at least—and in some awe, we prepared for our assault on this imposing citadel.

Austere and forbidding when we got out of the car, it seemed to have also become impregnable as we saw a handsome couple confidently walking away from the mansion where, presumably, they had just been interviewed. Chattering cheerfully, they hardly noticed us passing near them on our way to the front door.

Expecting to be greeted by a butler or perhaps a keeper of the moat, I was surprised to see Mrs. Wheatland herself opening the door. Looking much like I'd pictured her from the phone call, she was tall, middle aged, elegantly dressed, impeccably coiffed.

But instantly, and seemingly "out of character," she greeted us and—all smiles—ushered us into an immense living room, one whole wall of which was covered with a bookcase filled with ancient tomes that appeared to be original editions.

After a few moments of conversation with Andrée, Mrs. Wheatland turned her attention to me, interrupting my studied and somewhat furtive appraisal of the books with a question.

"Now, young man. Tell me about yourself!"

I told her that I was a graduate student at Harvard and hoped to earn the PhD degree.

"No-no-no-no-no," a sort of one-word-sound-alike burst forth. "We know all that. How are you with a fireplace?"

Not wanting to get slammed with another quintuple *no,* I asked whether she meant cleaning one, lighting a fire, building one, making one, or what?

"I meant building a fire!"

With my reply to the effect that in California we had few fires and when we did, my father usually built them, she nodded equivocally and abruptly ended her grilling of me.

Toasted, I resorted to my role of designated-library-observer, while Betty Wheatland and Andrée Webb conversed quietly: English, 90 percent, French, 10 percent, of which about 1 percent was spoken by our hostess.

Standing up and reverting to English, Mrs. Wheatland said, with a smile, "But you don't have an accent!" and, turning to me said, in a kindly but dismissive manner, "So good of you to come, Mr. Webb. I hope you will have a successful career at Harvard."

Driving away from 11 Gray Gardens West, I remarked that we had done a pretty good job botching that interview. Taking no offense at being gratuitously included in the botching job, Andrée said, "Oh, I don't know. She told me that her husband is the real New Englander, going way back, and that she is a Midwesterner, often out of sync with some of the old-wealth attitudes and therefore a bit overboard at times in trying to assume the reserve and hauteur of a true Bostonian."

Taking that to mean the fireplace questions might only have been a reflection of Mr. Wheatland's point of view, I quieted down, though I didn't believe our chances were very good. I should have known, however, that once Mrs. Wheatland had talked to Andrée, the couple we had seen leaving the house were out of luck.

I still was not believing, when we got a call later in the day inviting us to join the Wheatland household. My disbelief gave way to simple amazement when we were summoned back for details later in the week. We were shown our quarters, a delightful suite on the third floor—a bedroom, a living room, a bath, all colorfully painted and wallpapered, the bedroom in a light green, the rest in beige.

Andrée's duties were endless, the enumeration of which made it obvious why and how *we* got the job. As a full-time student, mine were restricted, essentially, to building the fire every morning *and* making the cocktails in the evening. Andrée was to help with the children, five of them, as it turned out.

Additionally, she was to assist Mrs. Wheatland in managing the kitchen, grocery shopping, room decoration, and flower selection. Each of these duties was enhanced, supported, and—incredibly—not complicated by the participation of another employee, Mrs. Barrett, a sort of super-nanny.

"Barrett," as she was referred to, took care—almost exclusively—of Martha, aged five, the youngest daughter, and David Alan, aged seven. Adept, friendly, and sensitive, Barrett put out fires among the children and sometimes, circumspectly, elsewhere in the household. The children loved her, and she returned the affection. She and Andrée became good friends on the basis of mutual respect and interlocking responsibilities.

We soon learned that these tasks were not the only ones and not, by far, the most important. We became "family" overnight. I didn't always make the cocktails; David Wheatland liked to make them too. But I *always* drank them, a duty I assumed without reluctance when invited to do so. Andrée and I were asked to join the family at dinner right from the start.

Betty Wheatland wanted our company for her own reasons, which may have included the hope of offsetting occasionally awkward moments with her daughters Su, 14, Barbara, 18, and Nancy, 19, and, quite obviously, because she saw Andrée as a role model for the three eldest children.

Our "family membership" status went everywhere: ski trips to North Conway, clothes-shopping sprees, new-automobile hunting, New England Patriots football games, weekends at Pingree Farm, the Wheatland ancestral home in Topsfield, and one fantastic jaunt to New York City.

The latter excursion involved only me and Nancy. I was asked to escort her to a soiree for debutantes at the Waldorf Astoria Hotel, where I would also serve as her dance partner. We had a marvelous time. Nancy was in fine fettle. But *my* fettle faded a little when it came to dancing up-tempo Viennese waltzes; that ability was conspicuously absent from my catalog of terpsichorean skills.

Nancy was a lovely person and, it should be noted, her mother's favorite. She and Andrée jelled nicely. But we didn't see Nancy too much since she was away at Sarah Lawrence College most of the time.

Barbara was different, a little distant. She and her mother didn't always interact smoothly. While we later got along well with her, admiring her independent thinking and startling humor, she seemed to be a little standoffish with us at first. Barbara may have resented her mother's apparent perception of Andrée as someone bringing culture and grace to the dinner table. Only 18 and the second child, Barbara was still finding her way, sometime seeking it in perverse ways, especially at meals.

The dinner table was "something else." The whole household convened most nights, Mrs. Barrett and the two younger children, whom she fed earlier, excepted. David Wheatland presided, but Betty controlled, for a few moments, in an attempt to maintain a formal and civil atmosphere. Formality soon evaporated, everyone talking at once, David jovial, Su animated, Betty fencing, Andrée and I enjoying the show. No problem. Good time all around. But when Barbara was there, civility generally wasn't.

She enjoyed teasing her mother, who usually tried to turn the other cheek as tension mounted. Then, often as not, the civil war would be set aside, pistols holstered, as Mrs. Duran emerged from the kitchen with steaming delights.

With the appearance of the genius of the pantry, addressed only as Cook, the atmosphere changed for the better. Barbara had had her fun. Armageddon had been averted, as *vapeur de la cuisine* mollified our hostess, relieved anxiety, and activated salivary glands. Another show, another happy ending.

After dinner, Andrée and I always had the comfortable feeling that our workday was officially over. We could retire to our quarters or remain in conversation with the family.

Often, Betty and I would put on a concert, a duet on the two grand pianos neatly juxtaposed in adjoining parlor and living room. Su would listen appreciatively. David would dexterously record the session on an array of sophisticated gear nestled amid his huge collection of first editions and *incunabula.* Nancy, if there, would listen politely or help her father's recording. Barbara would discretely disappear.

With mixed emotions, we left them in early spring, 1948, because Andrée was with child. Her pregnancy, Betty would claim—nay, repeatedly insist—resulted from good cuisine, a comment that utterly destroyed my faith in storks.

Life with the Wheatlands—all of them—was a wonderful experience. We enjoyed every bit of it. A marvelous family, and good friends. We would see Betty and Dave again many years later when we lived in Connecticut, visiting them in Topsfield on several occasions and also seeing Barbara there. Barbara was delightful and very friendly.

Andrée and Su kept in touch but, despite phone calls and meeting plans, never managed to get together when she and her new family lived in Lafayette and we were in Santa Rosa, 50 miles away. With Nancy living in Washington, we lost touch. We were long enough at Gray Gardens West for Martha to learn to tolerate us, but she was too young to remember, and though David Alan and I became good friends, he also was too young to retain many memories.

Though short, the Gray Gardens West episode was significant. We were almost penniless, undernourished, tired, and discouraged, about ready to "call it quits." Andrée's natural grace and social charm were critical, and immediately apparent to Betty Wheatland, who definitely knew what she wanted: help with her children and household, but most of all, sophisticated direction for her daughters.

Andrée filled these requirements, and more: the savoir faire Betty cherished. Indeed, she and her family, so pleased with their "adoption," surprisingly included us in their very intimate (and I must say, generous) gift exchange on Christmas morning. I still have several presents (bar items made of sterling silver), reminders to this day of a scarcely credible juncture in our lives that may well have forestalled an early return to California.

Our stay with the Wheatland family coincided with completion of my course work at Harvard. Courses, seminars, and tutorials—from David Owen and Elliott Perkins in English history; Donald MacKay, French history; Sterling Dow, ancient history; Crane Brinton, French history and French revolution; Myron K. Gilmore, renaissance; and Ernest Knapton (visiting professor), French revolution—were all behind me.

They were all scholarly, all thorough. Additionally, Owen was witty and downright funny. Dow was brilliant, precise, and cool. Brinton was brilliant and cerebral, world admired. Gilmore was sharp, well organized, and encyclopedic.

None was more brilliant, more stimulating than Wilbur Kitchener Jordan, president of Radcliffe from 1943 to 1960 and, concurrently, professor of history at Harvard. I was unable to take a course from "K. J." But several of us scrambled over to Radcliffe at every opportunity to hear him. In a packed auditorium, he held my fellow grad students and me spellbound. Owen and Brinton could do that too, as could Sontag and Kerner at Cal. But Jordan was a master at directly involving his students. Sontag was close, with similar techniques but somewhat smaller classes. Professor Jordan's lectures invited questions. His responses effortlessly melded the questions into the main lines of his lecture as, without skipping a beat, he returned to the central theme.

Was Sontag more precise? Yes, not that Jordan lacked precision. Was Jordan more exciting? Yes, not that Sontag lacked excitement. Was Jordan unique? Only in method. He had an intense interest in seeking ways to reach students and in finding effective means for helping them learn. An interested observer of this kind of academic striving, I had seen examples of it at Cal. But the passing of five years had changed education as well as my perception of it.

I would have liked to visit more of Professor Jordan's classes, but already in the research phase of my doctoral dissertation, I had to focus on that process. At the same time, without the formal structure of class attendance, I was free for other things. Eight hours in the library was enough for my eyes, my attention, my willpower.

So Andrée and I had time to see friends, many from California, like Virginia Saam and her husband and Carra Mae and Robert Sproul Jr. (saw a Red Sox game with these four). We also saw J and Billie Ward frequently, and I went to games of the old Boston Braves several times with J. (J Ward was actually his name; it grew into Jay only when he became famous.)

J was studying for the MBA at Harvard. They rented in Melrose, north of Boston, until we told them Hazel Hotchkiss Wightman was adding a rental apartment to her house in Chestnut Hill. The Wards soon became Hazel's first tenants. Billie, a very good cook, had been a home economics major at Cal. She and J invited Andrée and me to Thanksgiving Dinner. It was a wonderful occasion and a great day to be once again in the Wightman home. Everything festive, marvelous fragrances wafting from the kitchen, and a large bowl of eggnog inviting our pleasure. J and I sampled the goods, which I found delicious and J declared anemic.

"Needs ice cream," the ever-flamboyant J announced, whisking me off to the local market to procure the missing ingredient.

J was right. A quart of vanilla ice cream produced a heavenly concoction. The women sampled it. The men demolished it. Then the women brought in the turkey with chestnut dressing, mashed sweet potatoes, stewed onions, and accompanying delicacies. We all sat down. The women partook of the feast. But the men? We just sat. The women ate. The men sat, looking here and there. The women glared.

Disaster. And we didn't even see Hazel. Or play ping-pong. Many years later, I would play ping-pong with J—by then a wealthy impresario—when he rented Marlon Brando's former residence in Hollywood, a bulky, round house. Bulky and round himself, J loved that place and graced its ample basement with a ping-pong table, custom-built to his own peculiar specifications.

He played on one side, *always*. Visitors played on the other side, *always*. The peculiar aspect of the table was that J's side was about one-fourth normal size, his opponents' side about twice normal size. Pre-Brando, J seldom beat me. Never once did I beat J post-Brando. I might just as well have been playing Hazel.

With the exception of his side of that ping-pong table, J did everything *big*. Before the Thanksgiving episode, broke as he was, J managed somehow to get tickets to the All-Star Game, played in Fenway Park in 1947. That was the game with Rip Sewell and his famous "Eephus pitch" with its high arcing loop baffling batters. We saw him strike out Rudy York, and we saw Ted Williams, up next, deposit that Eephus ball in the center field bleachers, some 400 feet away, a great moment. It was the first All-Star Game I saw. Also the last. But I would see much more of the amazing J Ward.

Andrée and I ran into others from California, notably William Chaney, later famous as a professor of history at Lawrence University, whom I'd known when we were both teaching assistants at Cal. And John J. Van Nostrand, professor of ancient history on leave from the University of California, doing research at Harvard.

Like me, after long hours in Widener Library, John and Bill were often weary. Late one afternoon in the stacks, droopily poring over a fat tome, I heard Bill say, "Come on! You need some coffee."

Picking up Professor Van Nostrand on the way, we crossed Mass. Avenue, ensconced ourselves at a friendly table, and started a series of conversations—coffee only incidental—that took place from then on, between 5:00 and about 5:30 on many an afternoon. We gradually became good friends in the process.

On one occasion, we traveled together to Washington, DC, to work at the Library of Congress. Two days of driving in the Nash 600, two days of lodging together, two days of "archiving" together. The trip was successful, a good test of friendship.

The coffee hours were coming to an end, though, as my research was nearly complete and I was beginning the new task of writing the dissertation. Andrée was spending those same hours girding her loins, so to speak, for a promising transcontinental journey. ◆

Chapter 15

SAN DIEGO STATE:
THE ARTHURIAN TRIUMVIRATE

◆ ═══════════════════════════════

First full-time teaching job. A new world. Great faculty colleagues, good students, and the perverse Tale of the Three Arthurs.

Reluctant to terminate the comfortable life at 11 Gray Gardens West but nearing the end of her first trimester, Andrée was anxious to be on her way home to *maman*. A transcontinental trip by automobile, arduous enough under any circumstances, had been ruled out. Deciding to travel by rail, Chicago transfer and all, she was on board early in March.

By the time I was able to clear up last-minute details at Harvard, service and load the 600, and bid farewell to the Wheatland clan, Andrée had already arrived safely in California.

One week later I was there, too, with all my papers, mounds of notes, and a chapter or two of the developing dissertation. The summer lay ahead, and I was determined to finish the manuscript before autumn. So borrowing Gaby's office as well as his portable Royal typewriter, I set to work. Weeks passed slowly, though faster than my fingers.

August came and almost went. As I fitfully labored in the vineyards of a creeping dissertation, my wife labored at Peralta Hospital in Oakland. At last, and in no hurry, an heir appeared. Early in the morning of August 31, 1948, Andrée delivered her baby, Charles Richard Webb III, two weeks late, but healthy.

All joy and jubilation. Relief also. The baby was robust, his mother was well and in high spirits, photographs were taken, and movies were produced, thanks to an 8-millimeter camera I had bought for the occasion.

Andrée was happy to settle at Boynton Avenue, where Marcelle Bonno had prepared a bright and cheerful recovery room for mother and child.

As the joyful furor and excitement calmed down, I was able to return to dissertation writing, and the Bonno household to semi-normal. Six occupants crowded the modest home and made more work for Andrée's mother, who also had to look after her six-year-old son, Charles Henri Bonno.

Charles (pronounced "Shall") was in transports of joy and self-satisfaction over a living, breathing nephew. Charles could hoot and holler that he was now an uncle, while his father, born August 30, 1898, chortled over being "one day older than" his grandson. But neither one was chortling and hollering when we moved to Roble Court in late September, even though the move gave them more breathing room.

The move provided a wide and comfortable space for us, private bed and bath (Tue Gee's old quarters), spacious baby room (dining room), and total access to the huge living room/library with its grand piano that my mother played so recently. My father, staying upstairs most of the time, was delighted with the living arrangement. Roble Court afforded quiet for finishing my dissertation, getting it typed, proofreading it, and sending it off to Harvard in December. The rest of the year was pleasantly uneventful until the holiday season, when tragedy struck.

In a fit of despondency, Virginia's sweet and gentle husband, Richard Geist, committed suicide the day after Christmas. The anguish and sorrow that followed for Virginia and their three young children, Mary, Martha, and Richard, can well be imagined. Virginia was able to pull herself together and to provide a decent living for her children, but the toll was heavy and of long duration.

My dissertation was accepted the following spring. Summoned to Harvard for a final oral examination, I anticipated a detailed defense of the thesis. I considered myself well prepared, since I was probably the world's leading authority on William III and the Spanish Succession.

Instead, I encountered several senior professors who amiably engaged me in a number of general questions on a variety of subjects, more on New England lore than on European history. Not a word was uttered about my dissertation, neither questions, comments, nor criticism.

I was disappointed, yet what could I expect? I had immersed myself in research on an esoteric subject at length and in depth, followed by more than a year of writing. Who among them had the time and inclination to duplicate my research or read my 220-page manuscript dissertation?

Some of them might have read *part* of it, perhaps even approvingly. So it seems I traveled 6000 miles to participate in a pageant that can also be found elsewhere, with similar details, throughout higher education. Curious.

Not that it matters here, since my tome was bound and duly deposited in Widener Library where—presumably approved by a mysterious committee—another generation of scholars could criticize, laud, or condemn it. In any event, I returned to California in the spring as a Harvard doctor of philosophy.

There I ran into old friends, J Ward, of enriched-eggnog infamy, and Lute Nichols, our college pal. On the playground of Emerson Elementary School, we resumed our favorite baseball pastime, North and South. It's a game for three players, a pitcher, a batter (who also caught), and a fielder.

Great game, complicated rules. We played it every weekend. One Sunday, J, who had turned his Harvard MBA into a real estate business, showed up with a new MG, imported from England, no less, right-hand drive and all. I protested,

"J! What's with the MG? You're in the real estate business. You drive clients around."

"Oh," said J, "that's for Brandy."

"Whaddya mean, Brandy?"

"Oh, you, know, Brandywine. My dog."

"J!" (by this time I'm getting a little annoyed). "You don't have a dog!"

J calmly acknowledged this obvious fact and dropped the subject. A few weeks later, he drove up one morning with a puppy beside him in the MG. Did you guess it? The puppy, of course, was Brandywine, a St. Bernard. Brandywine grew up fast and, a month or two later, could be seen all over Berkeley in that MG. No, J couldn't drive customers around in his MG, but Brandywine, sitting up in the passenger seat of a British right-hand-drive car, appeared to anyone—who looked twice—to be driving.

I also happened to run into David Dowd on the Cal campus. A good friend, he had helped me out on a number of historical research problems when we were seminar classmates. Andrée and I had visited him and his Russian wife, Lyla, in Lincoln when he was teaching at the University of Nebraska. They had not been happy there, so David told me he was ecstatic over being "home again" and delighted with a new appointment at San Diego State College.

During this time, I was working at the Webb Motor Company while seeking a position in academe. I was surprised one day to receive a call from my old friend and mentor, Dr. Franklin C. Palm. Could I get away this morning to come to his office on the Cal campus?

There I met Dr. Abraham P. Nasatir, professor of history at San Diego State College. Turned out that David Dowd, after our recent conversation, had been offered and accepted a position at the University of Georgia. After an exchange of pleasantries and respective credentials, Abe offered me the position in European history at San Diego State.

Naturally, my father was disappointed on hearing news of the offer, insisting I'd make much more in the automobile business. He had a point, since my starting salary as an assistant professor amounted only to $4192 *per annum.* We argued, amiably enough, both knowing the pay differential was not critical, long term. I spoke of three years of intensive graduate work to qualify for a teaching position. He countered, "Those studies also prepared you for a career in business." Granted. Nevertheless, I accepted the San Diego offer.

Since I was due in San Diego in a few days, Andrée and I scrambled to pack baby and belongings, muster once again our exciting but sad good-bye routine, and head south. It was a rushed several days, Charles Richard having just celebrated his first birthday party as September rolled in.

The 500-mile trip was uneventful and relatively pleasant. We enjoyed it, exuberant baby most of all. Lodgings were not so easy. We had been offered—and accepted—state housing at the glamorously entitled *Aztec Terrace,* wartime-training temporary buildings whose apartments featured two bedrooms, kitchen, bath, and living room.

On arrival, we were not overjoyed to discover that one bedroom could barely accommodate the crib. The other, only slightly larger, had little space for accessories and none for furniture. Definitely, we were camping, and we were not happy campers, though we were mollified by the correspondingly modest size of the monthly rent at $35.

Life would get better. We made good friends both on campus and at our "new home." We handled the space problem by moving the crib into the living room, where it remained as long as we lived there. The Terrace was a mixed bag, some faculty, young and new to the area, students, non-students, everyone going in all directions, having fun managing on modest, or no, income.

San Diego State was also a mixed bag, a bag of different textures, disciplines, tongues, origins, people. I wasn't sure where I fit in that bag, but I enjoyed meeting the other occupants. Members of the History Department welcomed me cordially.

There were three senior members, Abraham Nasatir (Latin American history), whom I had already met, Charles Leonard (US history), and Lewis Lesley (European history).

Lesley was a capable gentleman but nearing the end of his contract, perhaps a little rusty in his specialty, and always a little on edge with me since I was new and in his field.

Leonard, who would retire a few years after my arrival, was a formidable, powerful faculty member who once, early on, had come very close to becoming president of San Diego State.

Leonard and Nasatir enjoyed a continual shouting match and semi-friendly war in their offices in the Library Tower, much to the amusement and annoyance of those in the same area. John Merrill (Asian history) and I shared a converted closet office on the battlefield, in between Leonard and Nasatir and directly in the line of fire.

All members of the department had PhDs except Merrill and Lionel U. Ridout (California history). Ridout was on leave for the year, completing his degree at the University of Southern California.

There were two other members, Katherine Ragen (US history) and Kramer Rohfleisch (European), an extraordinary pair whom I would come to know under changed but interesting circumstances. (A word about them in a moment.)

Lewis Lesley, nearing retirement at San Diego State, taught the big introductory classes in Western Civilization. Kramer Rohfleisch controlled the upper-division offerings in Modern European History, my field of specialization. I was assigned upper-division classes in English History and, in alternating years, Ancient and Medieval.

In the lower division, Western Civilization being unavailable to me, a way had to be found to fill out my course load. It was decided a bit to my consternation that I should teach two sections of the beginning course in US

History until Lesley's retirement created an opening in Western Civilization.

There is a saying that good teaching usually occurs when the instructor is hard-pressed "to stay a day ahead of the students." With three-fourths of my load concentrated in US History and Medieval, I should have met that condition. I did, in Medieval. But US History presented an unexpected challenge.

There were six sections of the introductory course, History 17A and 17B, first and second semesters, respectively. Katherine Ragen, PhD, University of Wisconsin, US History, was nominally in charge of a team of three; with my addition, she was outnumbered by men and by European historians, the third member being Kramer Rohfleisch, University of California. Katie had no trouble contending with such ratios. Bright, witty, persuasive, she held her own in any company and against all odds. She and Kramer got along well, she the more subject-matter oriented, he a philosopher of education, boating, wine, and all things historical.

Classes in each of the six sections of *American Civilization* (its formal title) were restricted to 35 students, a necessity because of the discussion method of teaching. Guided by provocative and challenging questions, students interchanged thoughts on a variety of subjects. Discussion for each classroom hour was always based on specific reading assignments, specified in a syllabus distributed at the beginning of the course.

The success of the course depended on each of its three major elements: the source materials, students' diligent use of those materials, and the instructors' skill in using the source materials. Source materials were contained in *The People Shall Judge*, a book published by the University of Chicago Press, an excellent collection of documents from the American past recounting the original words of those involved in the great issues of our history. Many books of readings have been published since then, but in my judgment none surpasses *The People Shall Judge*.

Students either applied themselves attentively to their reading assignments or didn't; those who didn't discovered they were unable to engage effectively in classroom discussion. Those who did apply themselves were still dependent on their instructor's skill in clarifying and augmenting the sources.

The instructor's role was paramount. Our job was made easier because we had a good text with original documents, which increased student interest. *Sources* rather than *secondary accounts*, they confronted students with the same problems of understanding and interpretation the authors faced.

Think of the difference for students reading *The Personal Memoirs of US Grant* or Bruce Catton's *Grant Takes Command*. Catton's secondary account might provide more detailed information, especially if you read all 556 pages of it. But you wouldn't need a teacher to clarify or interpret it, whereas you probably would for a dying President Grant's memoirs.

My colleagues strove to interpret, clarify, and explain—but primarily by guiding students to do the job themselves. This concept was their ideal, an ideal they realized more often than not. Informally, we constantly discussed method and practice. Formally, we met regularly.

Every week, we'd meet to discuss reading assignments and various techniques to motivate students. Dr. Ragen was very good in finding parallels connecting the sources with present events and teasing the right answers from her charges. Sometimes she would use her techniques on Kramer and me, Socratic method and all, to coax out of us the best way to spur students so that they'd come up with reasonable solutions on their own.

She might, for example, ask a student whose assignment was an excerpt from the *Federalist Papers*, "Tell me, Bill, if James Madison were alive today, what might he say about immigration policies in Arizona?" Or in a planning session she might ask what was wrong with the question, knowing she'd get an answer from Kramer. Sure enough, he'd say, "Nothing wrong with the question," adding, "but I'd prefer to ask the whole class. If you ask him first, Bill's going to lose his breakfast if he failed to read the assignment. And the rest of the class will relax, or fall asleep, because Bill's stuck with the question."

Kramer might also say, "Beware the discussion stopper! If Bill read the assignment carefully and came up with a good and relatively complete answer, there could be little left to talk about."

Katie and Kramer knew all the ways to manage "discussion stoppers," those students who, unintentionally, play havoc with an instructor's efforts to encourage students to read critically and think independently. "Discussion stoppers" are best ignored early in the hour and reserved for summing-up time at the end.

History 17A and 17B were great courses, effective and popular largely because of the instruction method and the source book. In a semester's time, moreover, students were so absorbed in the method that they became part of it. Question and answer, observation and retort, read and reread, examine and reexamine, and synthesize—who learned more, teacher or student? I certainly learned much from it and thoroughly enjoyed the experience. With the death of Lewis Lesley, I was programmed into Western Civilization, and out of US History. Though sorry to leave 17A,B, I welcomed the shift to History 4A,B, for which my training specifically prepared me. Nevertheless, despite all Professors Ragen and Rohfleisch and *The People Shall Judge* taught me, I wasn't out of school yet. Western Civilization was a large order.

I taught two huge sections (total enrollment, 350), the larger meeting from 11:00 to 11:50, MWF, the smaller from 9:30 to 10:45, TTh. Having been in classes of similar size at Cal and Harvard, I had witnessed a variety of efforts, some spectacularly effective, to teach huge sections.

I did not expect to emulate the brilliance of President Jordan of Radcliffe College or the precision and incision of Raymond J. Sontag at Cal. But I constantly sought ways to turn passive conditions into active learning experiences for the majority of my students.

I encouraged teaching assistants and readers to interact with students at every opportunity, holding office hours after tests and making themselves available at other times, especially right after lectures. I developed a variant on President Jordan's self-interruption techniques and question-answer sequence by using seating charts to facilitate question and response periods.

This was only a limited success, since not all students were receptive to the idea of assigned seating. I also tried creating "volunteer-instructors" after the first-midterm exams, selecting top scorers to lead discussions with their fellow students. This too was a flop. But I persevered as my education progressed.

Then there were the faculty at San Diego State. Very few "flops" there. In the fall of 1949, the History Department, including me, had just seven members. The numbers remained the same the following year with Lionel Ridout's return from leave and Lewis Lesley's departure.

They were all characters and all different. Add the fact that they were friendly, in their separate ways, making it relatively easy for a newcomer to get along. The faculty as a whole were the same way, though naturally more distant, more formal.

That distance narrowed and the formality evaporated once I knew them better. Dead serious in their academic endeavors and fiercely intent on the quality of their teaching, members of the general faculty, easily amused, were appreciative of subtle humor and tolerant of the most outsized guffaws. They'd smile in assent when Frank Johnson of the English Department referred to the college as "the land of the Lotus Eaters" or applaud at a faculty meeting when he complained that literature in a proposed general education program "amounted"—cough, cough—"to what chemists would describe"—cough—"as a trace."

The talented Communications Department had its own share of characters and jokesters. One example of departmental jollity will suffice. Kingsley Povenmire and Paul Pfaff were well known and popular throughout the campus, Povenmire, sharp and jovial, Pfaff, distinguished, scholarly, and a perfect gentleman. Understandably, students had trouble pronouncing Pfaff's name; thus the following episode was widely reported:

"Excuse me, sir, are you Professor Puh-faff?

"No, I'm Professor Puh-fovenmire."

Another wit was Ambrose Nichols, professor of chemistry. He and I were golfing at Singing Hills Country Club in Escondido when, seeing an old dilapidated tree about ready to collapse, I ventured that it "had seen better days." "I dunno," quoth Amby, "this looks like a pretty good day."

Amby and Barbara Nichols constantly hosted parties at their attractive home near the campus. Their social skills would carry over nicely to Amby's presidency, later, at Sonoma State College. Despite usually being the youngest couple at their affairs, Andrée and I always seemed to be invited and became fairly well known in their circle of friends.

It was all part of a developing progression. Andrée met women she liked, usually faculty wives, and they gave parties to which we were invited. People like Ella Harvey and her husband, Ray (mathematics); Dee Benton and Carl (physical education); Evelyn Klapp and Orrin (sociology). In this way, we widened our social circle.

Thus, in this generally relaxed social and professional atmosphere, Andrée and I prospered. My progression through the *cursus honorum* was conventional, not rapid but steady: promotion to associate professor in five years and to professor after another four.

In due course, I served my two-year rotational term as head of the History Department. I did the usual committee work, at one time chairing the College Curriculum Committee and at another, holding the presidency of the local chapter of the California State Employees Association (CSEA).

This latter connection led to my appointment as an affiliate to the newly formed California State Employees Insurance Company, partly because of my previous experience writing insurance coverage on auto sales. I also studied for and secured state licenses in both life insurance and casualty insurance, acquiring a little more professional diversity, I suppose.

*Andrée and I, ensconced between her mother and the cat
and her father and the boy. The boy, Charles Richard, apprehensively
regards the squirming cat, while his uncle, Charles Henri, casually
checks the photographer. December, 1951, San Diego.*

More than an incidental, the appointment gave Andrée and me a modest but welcome addition to the family exchequer, which had become healthier but was hardly robust.

Already fortunate in meeting many faculty members in various departments, I found that insurance activities greatly increased interdisciplinary contacts. Another appointment would further expand the numbers of extradepartmental acquaintances, especially in the Division of Humanities. I was asked to assume the duties of secretary of the division.

This I was happy to do. Like everyone else, I had a high regard for John R.

Adams, who chaired the division. He was the perfect administrator—correct, casual, low key, and hilariously funny in all sorts of surprising ways, salient, dry, witty, and effective. My duties were explicit in only one sense: I was to keep the minutes of the meetings, which occurred monthly throughout the academic year.

It was a simple task. A one-page report of motions introduced, voting results, and actions approved would suffice. Dr. Adams would accept the report with thanks and without comment. Minutes were circulated, but approval in following meetings was not required, since the only things duller than academic meetings are the minutes thereof.

His meetings were not that way, never dull, and they seldom lacked in friendly jousting and good humor. A true reflection of those meetings is not possible. Jack Adams invariably started them with a short summary of recent academic events, spicing declarative sentences with a biting tag or humorous aside, often with a breathless comment on a comment, delivered in his unique, comma-filled voice.

In my minutes, I couldn't reproduce the Adams' repertoire of guttural tics, masterfully exploited, or the resounding cadence of his delivery. So I tried to hit a middle ground, dutifully recording the gist of Dr. Adams's remarks without attempting the asides while imposing fewer restraints on myself in reporting observations from the rest of the faculty.

Sometimes I went overboard, but Jack never cautioned me nor told me what to do or how to do it. Copies of campus minutes were sent to the offices of the various deans, followed by general but sporadic distribution. So I gained some notoriety among the collegewide faculty and, within the confines of the academic dean's office, became borderline infamous.

Andrée and I were enjoying ourselves at San Diego State. Good students, great faculty, superb weather, all ferment and froth, it was both serious and tongue-in-cheek frivolous. The History Department was growing. We had an opening and were interested in a candidate at USC who looked good on paper but whom, otherwise, we did not know, one Arthur T. Smith.

At the time, Donald Watson, dean of instruction, was attending a conference in Los Angeles and planned to interview candidates for positions in several departments. We had asked him to interview Mr. Smith for us.

All proper and customary, Dean Watson interviewed many candidates, taking copious notes on all of them, including one Arthur F. Smith, with whom he was well impressed. Accordingly, he invited Mr. Smith to San Diego to meet members of the History Department.

Meanwhile, Arthur *T.* Smith had sent an apologetic note to Katherine Ragen, who chaired the department at the time, explaining that he'd been detained and missed his appointment with Dr. Watson. He explained, however, that he was free to come to San Diego the following Friday.

There was a little hilarity among local historians upon hearing that the dean had not only interviewed the wrong Arthur Smith but had invited him on campus. Some relief, too, with the news that the real Arthur Smith was still available. But hilarity and relief turned to consternation when we learned that both Arthur Smiths would be on campus the same day.

It was Friday when the Arthurs popped into my orbit, the Friday *after* the Watson/Arthur *F.* interview. It was also the Friday when I had my quarterly naval reserve weekend drill at Los Alamitos Naval Air Station. Since Professor Bonno was then teaching at UCLA, the Bonnos lived in Westwood, a mere 20 miles from Los Alamitos. So Andrée and I usually made the trip together every three months.

I could hardly wait to get home to tell Andrée of the latest development on campus. By the time we reached Los Angeles, we had had fun enough with the Arthurs. In fact, we had exhausted the story, its various ramifications, and ourselves.

Then, of course, I had to relate the developing scenario to Professor Bonno (Gaby—accent on the second syllable—as everyone called him). But I was an innocent bystander. Up to a point.

I don't know where that point was passed, on entering L.A.? or on seeing Gaby's amusement? Or perhaps when we realized the story was incomplete. Keep in mind that Gaby's field was literature. He knew almost immediately that the story needed some sort of authenticator, something to make *bizarre* genuine. Then he lighted on the solution. "That's it!" Gaby cried triumphantly. "You don't have *enough* Arthurs."

With that, Gaby had punctured the tale. Vulcan and a little more *Dubonnet* to the rescue, we patched the puncture and relieved the shortage of history candidates by inventing another Arthurian contender.

Gaby's wife and daughter were bystanders, disconcertingly innocent. Andrée urged caution. She was having fun at San Diego State and had no interest in jeopardizing our status there, no matter *how* good the gag. Reassured by her father's part in the prank and his insistence that one doesn't lose an academic job with a small joke, she let us go to Western Union with the following telegram:

Katherine Ragen, History Dept.
San Diego State College
San Diego, California 92115

Have PhD, Asian History
University of Washington, 1954
In San Diego, Friday Morning, 8/27/62
On campus from 9:00 AM
Hope to see you then.
Yours,
Arthur Q. Smith

Monday morning when I entered the office that four of us shared, Katie was already there. This was the moment I had looked forward to relishing, and suddenly found myself dreading. *She's gonna give me hell!* Instead, as I sat down, semi-nonchalantly, she waved something blue and gray in the air and said,

"You're not going to believe this," motioning me over and adding, "take a look at this."

Walking over to her desk, I managed to keep a straight face as I glanced at the telegram. Muttering, "Guy's gotta lot of guts. What timing!" I quickly turned away, hand over mouth, and thought, "Passed *that* test!"

That self-congratulatory moment was the mistake of the day.

I should have let Katie in on the joke right away, or at least before losing sight of her that morning. I sauntered off to my nine o'clock class, never thinking that hell could be breaking loose within two hours.

After class and a library visit, I headed for the general faculty meeting. As I entered the large lecture hall, the usual buzz sounded loud and animated. Katie, in the midst of a group of historians, was talking excitedly.

Fighting off a sinking feeling, I reasoned, that with three candidates, all with the same name, all on campus the same day, "How could she believe that?" Then, with a U-turn, I asked myself, "How could she *not* believe it? In her mind, how could this possibly be a prank? How could a stranger in Los Angeles know what's going on in the History Department at San Diego State?" Panic time!

And something close to actual panic hit me as several hundred faculty members were taking their seats, President Malcolm A. Love having already entered the hall. I rushed toward Katie, who had not seen me. Finding a seat behind and a little to the left of her, I leaned over, tapped her on the shoulder, and whispered,

"*I* sent the telegram."

She turned full around, staring wide-eyed, and gave me an indescribably fierce look, one that said, somehow, "You rat! You traitor! How could you do that to me? To me!" Then, amazingly, and uproariously, she burst into laughter.

It was the laughter of relief, the hoax discovered—and just like that, "Arthur Q." dissolved. More than that, Katie's laughter was the laughter of forgiveness, the laughter of "Damn, I've been had, but what a good joke. You're a stinker, but my kind of stinker."

Katie knew I had placed her on the fence-mending spot. She could have insisted that since I had done the damage, I should do the mending. But no. She generously assumed that it was *her* job as head of the department to set the record straight. Doing so with other historians would be no problem; they'd enjoy the laughs.

The dean, however, would see nothing funny in the joke, since, in a sense, he had initiated the show. He, and Arthur F. Smith.

I linger over the episode since it has a moral. Actually three, fittingly enough. First, it demonstrates perfectly Katie's grace, humor, and humanity. She was a good and capable individual. A superb teacher, she would become an efficient and well-regarded administrator later on.

Second, behind the scenes, it reveals the character of Donald Watson. The fall guy in the Arthur F. mix-up, he became the goat of my grossing-out on the Arthurs, Smith. Certainly a minor humiliation to him. He took no umbrage. He never spoke to me about the subject nor demanded an apology. Significantly, shortly after the incident, Katie was appointed Dean of Women, an action that certainly had Watson's approval.

Third, I learned a lesson, or should have. I learned to avoid exploiting the incongruous or absurd for their humor, lest unexpected repercussions land me in serious trouble.

In sum, with the dissolution of the Court of the Three Arthurs, things settled down in San Diego. I stayed on a few years, contentedly teaching. Incidentally, I was writing insurance policies, textbooks, and minutes of the Humanities Division, as well as entertaining students and faculty with performances of the Ivory Tower Jazz Quartet.

The Ivory Tower Jazz Quartet in the fifties and sixties at San Diego State. I am on the vibes. Next to me on drums is a student, Ron Withm. Political science professor Vince Padgett on alto sax. Engineering professor Bill Schutts on guitar, and sociology professor Orrin Klapp on bass.

In passing, I should mention that, early on, Dr. Orrin Klapp, professor of sociology, Vince Padgett, political scientist, and I created the Ivory Tower Jazz Society and its creature, the Ivory Tower Jazz Quartet. A rather large quartet, as one of our colleagues quipped, the group had many musicians, comprising over the years Orrin (string bass and guitar) and me (piano and vibraphone), Vince (alto sax and clarinet), business professor Dr. Robert Hungate (trombone and vocals), engineering professor William Schutts (guitar), student Ron Withm (drums), local businessman Ron Turner

Note that the quartet has grown. Drummer Ron Withm has become the bassist. Bassist Orrin Klapp has switched to guitar. All made possible by the addition of local businessman Ron Turner, on drums.

(drums), and others, including student Bob Osborne, a superb tenor saxophonist, who happened to be the son of geographer Dr. Clarence Osborne, chairman of the Social Science Division.

Eventually called away, apparently through no fault of my own, I would fall into situations that made the wretched reign of King Arthur III look like a stroll in the library stacks. ◆

Chapter 16

NUDE DRIVER ON HIGHWAY 99

◆ ══════════════════════════════════════

*First day as Dean of Academic Affairs at Stanislaus State
College. Headline: unclothed professor arrested for driving at
100 miles per hour.*

*W*hile I cannot mention all the good friends at San Diego State, there are
four—in addition to Vince Padgett and Orrin Klapp—who deserve particular attention. They are Ambrose Nichols, professor of chemistry; Allan
Shields, professor of philosophy; and two history professors (in addition
to Katie and Kramer, already mentioned), Richard Reutten and William
Hanchett.

Amby Nichols, in the early sixties, became the first president of Sonoma
State College and, in that position, I suspect, he must have given my name
to the president of Stanislaus State College, Alexander Capurso, who invited
me to apply for the academic deanship there. I was appointed dean of Academic Affairs at Stanislaus State in the summer of 1964.

With a September 1st starting time, there was much to be done. Andrée
and I rushed around making arrangements. Out of the blue, Allan Shields

generously loaned me his old Ford pickup, which had the fetching insignia "DORF" gracing its radiator. One afternoon, Bill Hanchett and Dick Reutten helped me load DORF, books and other junk piled high until it was impossible to load any more.

Next morning early, I set out alone for a hastily procured rental home at 1143 Edwards Drive, Turlock, assuring Andrée and Charles Richard that I'd be back to pick them up in time for his 16th birthday at the end of the month. Without the help of DORF and friends, I could not have maintained schedules or kept promises.

DORF, despite the heavy load, performed handsomely in its stately progression northward. Allan had done such a good job servicing and keeping the engine tuned that it effortlessly surmounted the Grapevine (the mountain range separating Southern California from Bakersfield and Northern California).

Nonetheless, tired and hot by the time we reached the Bakersfield area, DORF and I needed to stop soon. Fresno was less than two hours away on Highway 99. The largest city between Los Angeles and Oakland, it promised decent food and a relatively short drive to our destination. I was also eager to buy a copy of the *Fresno Bee* for information about the area and some news about Stanislaus State College and the town of Turlock, where the college is located. I got my wish. In spades. Splashed on the front page of the *Bee* was the headline:

STANISLAUS STATE COLLEGE PROFESSOR ARRESTED DRIVING NUDE ON HIGHWAY 99

The story went on to say that Keith Crow of the Sociology Department had been stopped for erratic driving and speeding between Modesto and Turlock. It was then discovered that his only apparel was a strong liquor breath.

In smaller print at the end of the article, reference was made to Mr. Crow's statement that he had fallen, or was pushed, into a swimming pool at a party in Modesto and was hurrying home to get dry clothing.

No matter the circumstances, the story circulated and was locally taken as one more sign that the new college was a den of crackpots, weirdos, law-scoffers, and maybe thieves (two years later, an employee of the business office would be indicted for absconding with $10,000 from the college foundation).

For me, it was a big red flag, a sort of preview of coming attractions and general disarray. I would soon lose track of it, however, because of the bustle and excitement of a new job. Besides, the incident was a big joke on campus. The young instructor was new, his appointment temporary, and his chances of retention dim because of his lack of a terminal degree and slow progress toward acquiring one.

President Capurso ordered me to take Crow under my wing, spur him on to earn the doctorate, and tame his social eccentricity.

I would attempt these mandates, with minimal success, remaining silent on the swimming pool incident, convinced it was beside the point and factually weak.

For the moment, I concentrated on unpacking DORF and stowing its contents as well as I could into the ample recesses of the spacious and luxurious home on Edwards Drive. That done, I was off to San Diego to return DORF to Allan, to celebrate C.R. III's 16th, and to help Andrée pack for the return trip to Turlock in time for the September 1st beginning of the fall quarter.

It was all fun and excitement, yet none of us, father, mother, son, had wanted to leave San Diego. I was undecided and, almost at the last minute, was ready to turn down the offer, but Andrée said, "If you don't accept the offer, you'll always wonder whether you should have." Knowing she was right, but also sure she did not want to go, I struggled with the contradictory alternatives and finally accepted.

Professionally, it was probably the right move. For the family, not so much. All of us separated from friends and activities, Andrée the most. Charles Richard took it well but was very disappointed in losing touch with friends, sports, surfing, and contacts within the performing arts.

When Orrin Klapp, Vince Padgett, and I created the Ivory Tower Jazz Society, at San Diego State, we practiced at my house. And that's where, from a tender age onward, one small individual, up past his bedtime, got hooked on live jazz.

The house on Edwards Drive had a large, finished basement, a perfect place for a budding musician to hone his skills, first on drums, accompanying recorded jazz. Later, as a guitarist, he would play with rock bands. A shared love of music and performing had become a significant connection between son and father.

Thus, the decision to move was showing signs of not being too bad. Andrée was just as pleased as I with the musical progress of our son, and, as always, she easily made friends and adjusted to the new surroundings.

I learned a lot at Stanislaus State, made lasting friendships among faculty and staff, and was amazed by the techniques of fellow administrators, both skillful and the unbelievably inept.

There were many capable faculty members, including Larry Berkoben and John Gill (English), David Stenzel and Jack Rasmussen (history), Lloyd Ahlem (education and psychology), Steve Grillos (biology), Fred Kottke (economics), Dean Galloway and Miriam Malloy (library), and Zaki Habashi (physical education), to name but a few. Several were borderline, and one or two older instructors coasted comfortably along.

All in all, a good faculty, but they were fiercely divided on several fronts. The president, a brilliant but insecure individual, exploited the divisions when he could and invariably backed down when confronted by the contrary-minded. Two examples should define the manipulative and vacillating sides of his personality:

The college had an opening in philosophy. Allan Shields, he of DORF fame, applied for the position. A superb teacher with an excellent publication record, he was interviewed by numerous faculty members and recommended to the president, who arranged to meet him in Los Angeles.

The president, well impressed, offered Shields the job on the spot. When a few members of the Humanities Division, jealous of the candidate's formidable attainments, protested vaguely but forcefully in the president's office, he withdrew the offer.

Embarrassed, I apologized to Dr. Shields, who replied graciously, though naturally angered, that he felt forewarned by the experience, concluding, "I consider myself lucky not to be working for such a pusillanimous president."

The other example is quaint, a clever ruse. In cabinet meetings or with smaller groups, even of one or two attendees, the president liked to tell stories. When doing so, he invariably dramatized the presentation, his voice rising. Almost shouting at the crescendo, he'd abruptly dismiss the group. There'd usually be a person sitting in the anteroom waiting to see him. Witnessing both ends of this charade several times, I deduced that the act was deliberate, a technique calculated to intimidate the supplicant at the door.

Faculty/administrative tensions eased somewhat in 1965 in anticipation of a pending move from the old campus (temporary buildings at the fairgrounds) to a beautiful new campus. The move itself was also a distraction, as was the prospect of inaugurating a four-year program, called the

Freshmen Core Curriculum, to accommodate freshmen and sophomores for the first time.

The new campus was expansive, over 200 acres, well laid out, a long and attractive pond running midway between parallel entrance and exit roads, and much field space, including a complete baseball diamond. My office was ample and convenient to other offices, the classrooms, and a spectacular theater-in-the-round.

Happy times, excellent quarters, assistant deans close by, secretarial staff highly qualified, efficient, and personable. The secretary to the dean, Olivia Stalter, was simply a gem, capable, correct, and well liked by her cohorts, whom she directed and assisted but never scolded.

Outwardly, everything was going well, but I still had the growing pains of adjusting to a new campus and lower-division courses. The core freshman program, hammered out at the fairgrounds with the assistance of many faculty members and the frantic opposition of a few, still rankled, though students absorbed it without complaint. Yet I could tell that any creative academic work I might have contributed had probably been done already.

Every day brought new evidence that the college would not grow academically and educationally so long as professors fought turf wars and an embattled president hid from the faculty and seemed constantly on the road. The scintillating and acerbic Jack Rasmussen called him the Vanishing American.

The president did say yes, however, when I asked permission to take on another task. One day in autumn several students dropped by my office. Telling me that Zaki Habashi, our only physical education instructor, had declared himself unqualified for coaching baseball, they wondered if I could take on the job in the spring. I said yes, provided approval could be secured.

We had a fairly good team and season, despite only 11 or 12 players regularly showing up. Off to a slow beginning, we ended up losing more games than we won, but we steadily improved throughout the season. We had fun, laughs, and, amazingly, some good baseball. I'll share two anecdotes.

The first: We were playing Sonoma State. I had spent the morning on the golf course, as usual, on Saturday morning with Frank Balbo, business manager, a capable administrator and a good friend. After, rushing to the diamond in time for warm-up drills, I was greeted by Dave Gomes, our student manager. "Hey coach!" he hollered excitedly, "We got only eight men."

I pondered this tragic intelligence for a moment, rejected the notion

Baseball on three campuses (clockwise, from top): At bat for the "Grand-padres" at San Diego State (faculty vs. students), 1951 ("Grand-padres" won!). In early spring 1972, throwing in a ballgame's "first pitch" while presiding at Eastern Connecticut State. With team captain Ron Harrelson while coaching at Stanislaus State, 1967.

of playing another 18 holes of golf, and said tentatively that I might ask Sonoma State's coach if *I* could fill in. My team agreed.

I talked to the other coach. He doubled over in spontaneous and needlessly extended laughter before saying OK. I put myself in right field. Conveniently, no flies come my way. Strike out twice. Scratch a single third time up.

Last inning: We're way behind. With five guys in front of me in the batting order, there's *no way* I bat again, so the game will end, and I'll still be one for three (.333, not too shabby for a substitute). Then, against the odds, we get two runners on base, 2nd and 3rd, no less, and I have to bat after all.

Team captain comes to me as I'm on my way to home plate, "Coach. Why don't you lay down a bunt?"

"Squeeze play?" I reply, "When we're already down 9-0?"

"Yeah, but you've been drilling us all week on bunts."

"OK." I'm resignedly thinking, "Oh well, *sacrifice*, leaves me at .333, better than .250, and, anyway, with the surprise element (9-0! might work, avoid a shutout)."

I bunt. And, of course, it's perfect. After all, *I'm* the coach. It's right between the pitcher and third baseman who, playing back, doesn't have a chance. Pitcher makes a great play, one handed, and a perfect throw home, but too late. Run scores, and by the time the startled receiver catches the ball and relays it to first base, I'm way past the bag.

Base hit and, as a bonus, a run batted in, not to mention that I am officially 2 for 4 for the day—possessor, as it turns out, of an official lifetime batting average of .500 at Stanislaus State.

The second tale is merely revelatory. No times at bat. But it does give me a sort of game winner, enclosing, like bookends, my two years at Stanislaus State. Our catcher and team captain, Ron Harrelson, and I, were driving back to Turlock from Tracy, where we had played a doubleheader against the prisoners' team at the Deuel Vocational Institute. The rest of the ballplayers were on the team bus.

Ron and I got to talking about Keith Crow's immersion in the Modesto swimming pool. I was of the opinion that he had simply *fallen* in. Ron insisted that Keith had been pushed. Attempting to resolve the shoving match among witnesses to the event, I asked. "Why are you so sure about how he fell into the pool?"

"Because," Ron calmly replied, "I pushed him in."

A doubleheader sweep of the prison team marked the turnaround point of our team's season. From then on, we lost only one more than we won. Similarly, "I pushed him in" turned Keith Crow's image around and, in so doing, summed up my "season" at Turlock. It was a good season in several ways, many wins, a few losses.

While I was absorbed in college work, the family was settling in at Turlock. Andrée took advantage of our elegant abode on Edwards Drive by throwing a grand lunch for faculty and staff wives. She was roundly criticized for serving wine—"never done here"—and roundly applauded, "well, it's about time!" Richard (he'd dropped the Charles by then) enjoyed and did well at Turlock High, acquiring friends and playing in rock bands. His world was also expanding with growing access to family cars, and soon his own.

I found some compatible tennis partners, all wins regardless of which side prevailed. Weekend golf with Frank Balbo and Lloyd Ahlem, and, occasionally, with students was rewarding as much for the laughs as for the golf. No jazz, but I did make it, one weekend, to participate in an Ivory Tower Jazz gig in Poway, north of San Diego.

Andrée and I were invited to a number of faculty parties, guardedly at first. But invitations increased when people discovered we were relatively harmless and that one of us added grace, charm, and elegance to any shindig.

Then there were friendly jousts with faculty and students, as I regularly attended *T.G.I.F.* sessions on Friday afternoons. Formal speeches too. One of them, apparently, prompted a librarian to dub me "Dean of Puns." May have been the speech wherein I warned emotional faculty not to "get the heart before the course."

There were other wins and losses, one of which was win/loss combined. That was the Freshmen Core Curriculum, already mentioned. Academically and intellectually, it was a modest triumph. Tactically, it was a loss. The speed with which it was created and implemented offended the punctilious. Its simplicity offended the pretentious. And its insistence on factual detail and avoidance of sweeping generalizations offended some educational philosophers.

Its particular, pragmatic emphasis on courses within disciplines where appropriate faculty were already available on campus, offended members of the entrenched Education Department who, as they liked to say, "teach students, not subjects."

In sum, where breadth and depth applied, the Freshmen Core Curriculum invariably preferred depth. And that is the heart of the matter. Faculty, secure in mastery of key elements of their discipline, stood for depth. The insecure preferred breadth, mostly because it was safe.

I recently ran across a copy of the plan, entitled *Proposed Freshman Program*. There are compromises in it, and there would be more coming, especially since the document calls for ongoing experience-based adjustments. It is 17 pages long, every word advocating *rigor* and depth.

It still looks good to me, after half a century. It should; I wrote much of it, conceived all of it. In the process, I studied innovative, highly successful, and similar programs at Sarah Lawrence College, Reed College, Evergreen College, Stanford University, and others, including both the University of California and Harvard University, where I had firsthand experience.

The plan was described as "an effort to concentrate faculty talent and administrative resources on a standardized curriculum designed to give all freshmen a thorough and intensified grasp of our cultural heritage, the basic principles of science, the development of systems of knowledge, and the refinement of intellectual processes."

With this general introduction, the statement goes on to reproduce the course outlines of each part, stressing both the interrelatedness of the various segments and the interdisciplinary theme that runs between and among them, and among the faculty teaching them.

Those who supported the program worked hard and enthusiastically to make it work. Some who opposed it buried their misgivings and worked hard, if not enthusiastically, to support it. A strident and unrelenting small minority, however, resented it and resented its perpetrators. They opposed it, inveighed against it, and seized every opportunity to sabotage it.

"The operation was a success," as my father used to say, "but the patient died." The core curriculum sustained a lingering illness. My successor, Maurice Townshend, a good politician, killed it rather than contend with a few recalcitrant faculty members. I cannot blame him. I can only sorrow for him and the students.

Looking at the *Core* from another viewpoint, I also sorrow for a man who was "his own worst enemy."

The president of Stanislaus State destroyed himself gradually, by very slow degrees. He had all the talents. While not a particularly handsome man, he projected a striking presence, a ready wit, and a powerful demeanor. Well educated, with a PhD in psychology, and an accomplished violinist, he had an easy command in most conversational situations. His voice was strong and well modulated. He used it effectively and deliberately, together with a great—though rare—smile.

These positive attributes were nullified progressively by a general dis-trust of other people and their motives, which probably reflected a deep insecurity. He had a disdainful way of dismissing the problems of, or those caused by, associates: "I'll have to wipe their noses again." "First, we'll have to give him a spanking." "Don't bother me with the birdseed." "Now I have to play nursemaid again."

At the same time, he could be expansive and outgoing, "Yes! Let me concretize that." Or the manic, "Good point! I'll be covering that very thing in my inaugural address, 'The Education of a Prince'" (a phrase oft-repeated in cabinet meetings).

He had a fear of faculty, especially in groups. But he could handle them one at a time. Manipulative, and adept at playing one against another, he genuflected at the church of divide and rule.

The faculty, who cordially disliked him, did a tolerable job of dissect-ing his personality. Unfortunately, they learned in the process how to counter-manipulate. Dissident minorities among them could confront him and frequently get their way, thus subverting the general will of the faculty at large.

There was much resentment of his frequent and lengthy junkets, which were usually justified as recruitment or money-raising trips. Seldom pro-ductive, they were viewed as wasteful expenses against a tight budget and as more evidence of his perceived incompetence.

An odd example of the fallout from these excursions was that in the summer of 1966, at the very edge of our return to San Diego, an extended presidential jaunt resulted in my official appointment as acting president of Stanislaus State from early June until mid-July.

A nice honor. But meaningless, except for the fact that it was an expres-sion of faculty insistence, through the agency of the Academic Senate, that an *academic* dean generally holds precedence over an *executive* dean in appointments of this kind and that I was better qualified than the previous temporary chief, or, at least, so perceived.

There wasn't much on the burner; I had only to preside over five or six cabinet meetings and such like. Andrée and I were packing and otherwise getting ready for the return to San Diego that we'd been planning for weeks and discussing for months. Andrée was delighted with the prospect but concerned about *my* concerns. Richard was simply delighted.

I had mixed feelings about leaving, as Andrée knew but carefully refrained from mixing further. I was troubled about deserting what many faculty members thought was a sinking ship. I was convinced that some of the college's problems were temporary. For instance, I was aware that the president was actively job-hunting. I had real misgivings about leaving the baseball program and also knew that the History Department at San Diego State had greatly changed in my absence. There were many new members, several departures, and one or two habitually absenting themselves.

My concerns were allayed in early September, 1966, at the first departmental meeting, a cordial, welcoming affair despite a lingering anxiety over the fact that the Stanislaus State leave had officially broken tenure at San Diego State. At one point in the meeting, however, I happened to be making a comment when Bill Hanchett suddenly interrupted, loudly exclaiming, "Shut up, Webb, you don't have tenure!"

That did it. The ice was broken, solemnity dispelled, and my anxiety relieved as the crowd laughed, chortled, and applauded, everyone knowing that Bill and I were the best of friends.

Recovering its purpose and dignity, the department returned to the chief item on the agenda, *recruitment*. Before long, I found myself dragooned into joining Al Coox in a recruitment committee of two, Coox chairing it.

Morale had been low in the History Department because of marked understaffing and, consequently, a very heavy teaching load for faculty. Al and I managed to secure a promise from President Love permitting us to recruit 12 new faculty members, an unheard-of allocation, more than for the entire Humanities Division. This development caused some grumbling elsewhere within the college despite the fact that History, the fastest-growing department, had been understaffed for years.

In a recent campus reorganization, the History Department had been moved from Social Sciences to Humanities, a move that was greeted sardonically by campus jokers: "History! From 'Queen of the Social Sciences' to 'Whore of the Humanities.'" The canard, quite naturally, resurfaced with a vengeance when news of our windfall circulated.

So Al and I got to work with what amounted to carte blanche from fellow historians, there being only a reasonable proviso that we make no commitments without departmental approval.

Actually, *all* appointments, upon recommendations from the department, the division, and the academic vice president, had to be approved by the president and ultimately, as it turned out, by the governor.

We compiled a formidable list of prospective candidates, got in touch with all of them, arranging for some to come on campus for interviews and others to meet us at the annual convention of the American Historical Association in New York City the week after Christmas.

We had already been able to hire two and make provisional offers to other candidates before we left for New York. At this juncture, Governor-elect Ronald Reagan persuaded Edmund Brown to place a freeze on *all* new hires.

We lost two of our best prospects as a result of the freeze, one because he received another offer and, despairing of a timely thaw, accepted it. The other, not waiting for thaws or "feelers" from *any* California institutions, curtly directed us to withdraw his name from consideration as he had no interest in "teaching in a state where Ronald Reagan was governor."

Nonetheless, we pushed on. President Love generously and wisely permitted us to go through with the recruitment trip on the assumption that a thaw would come soon enough for a few more appointments that year and, even without a thaw, future hiring opportunities should result from the trip. So we went, and we interviewed scores of worthy candidates.

Making no promises, we told the best qualified to keep in touch and when the ice melted, we would so inform them. With the eventual thaw, we reestablished communications with the candidates who were still available, still interested, and still fit our changing needs. Final count: 11 hired by late spring, 1967.

No sooner had our task been done—*it seemed*—than I received a phone call. Actually, it was exactly one year after the New York trip, but intervening summer and fall terms had gone quickly, quietly, and uneventfully. The call was from Gerhard Friedrich, dean of academic planning for the 19 California state colleges, soon to be universities.

Having met him on several occasions at Stanislaus State, I was highly impressed by his understanding, intelligence, and sensitivity, as well as by his acute awareness, ready wit, and dry sense of humor. Since he had reviewed the Freshmen Core Curriculum and approved it, he was familiar with my work. He invited me to join his staff in the chancellor's office, Los Angeles, as associate dean of academic planning, at the start of the spring semester, 1968.

Having just forsaken administration to return to teaching and curious to see new faculty members in action, as well as enjoying old friends at San Diego State, I was reluctant to leave, especially on such short notice. At the same time, I admired Gerry Friedrich. The idea of working with him in the

Office of the Chancellor of the California State Universities and Colleges had appeal.

There were interesting people in Los Angeles as well as some prestigious and high-powered relationships. Some intrigue too, which was definitely *not* an attraction. A pay raise was also involved, a major consideration as we continued to dig out from under the financial doldrums that clouded the early years.

The increased salary had been one of the reasons why we went to Turlock. And at "The Learning Tower of Wilshire Boulevard," I'd earn much more than in Turlock and be working with a man whom I knew to be the exact opposite of the president of Stanislaus State.

Besides, we would be in Los Angeles with its many attractions, a city I had known and enjoyed as a child visiting relatives there. Moreover, Andrée's parents lived in Westwood, where they'd moved when Gaby transferred from Cal to UCLA. Hot weather, traffic, and smog might have deterred us. But they didn't. Considering them mere incidentals, we decided once again to make the leap.

We had no argument from Richard against the move, since he was enrolled at San Diego State, living in a dormitory, and reasonably independent. We found an apartment to our liking in Hollywood, where we lived for two years, seldom bothered by smog, oblivious to traffic, and enraptured by the countless wonders of the city and its environs.

Andrée discovered a French restaurant on Sunset Boulevard, just 1¼ blocks from our apartment. Its proprietor had been the head chef on the liner *Ile de France.* He was delighted to find a customer, new and steady, who knew French cuisine like a native and expressed her culinary wishes in his native tongue, spoken, of course, in *her* native tongue. The proximity and high quality of his establishment guaranteed the frequency of our visits, so much so that we began referring to the restaurant as *the neighbors.*

We invited J and Billie Ward to dinner at our small apartment. Andrée informed them and our four other guests of a (prearranged) kitchen mishap. Dinner spoiled!

"No problem!" said I with a straight face. "Let's take up our constantly entertaining neighbors, across the street, who always insist that we drop in on them anytime."

Nobody, even after a drink or two, was going to buy that whopper. But suspecting—and willing to go along with—some sort of gag, they allowed us to walk them out the door, across the street, around the corner, and through the *backdoor* of our cozy "neighbors." There, we wined and feasted on a preplanned, fixed menu, totally delicious, "family-style" dinner. No ordering, no checks or gratuities visible. Served by the proprietor and his family.

Complete success. The women loved the "impromptu" style (a well-rehearsed ad-lib?). The men enjoyed the food. J was wowed by the gag. A little chagrined that it was *my* gag and not his, he'd figure ways to turn the "one-upmanship" tables on me. That goal line would be crossed more than once.

The neighbors' party was a metaphor for my years in the chancellor's office, where the work was demanding and hours long, but only five days a week. Staffing was hierarchical; people at different levels seldom socialized with one another. Without the extracurricular obligations of a college campus, moreover, nights and weekends were free for excursions, exploring, dining out, and frequent visits with Andrée's parents.

There were some exceptions to the nose-to-the-grindstone life, mostly to be found in *Academic Planning*. The dean, Dr. Friedrich, captained a taut ship, everything trim, tightly controlled, but lightly administered. *Play* was seldom condoned. *Playfulness* was, provided it was quiet, unobtrusive, and reasonably work related.

Application of the rules, however, were subtle and highly subjective. Few of us would test the limits. But if one inadvertently slipped the bounds of propriety, the dean had his ways, usually with a quip or gesture, of gently redirecting the offender onto less hazardous byways.

Academic Planning meant just that for the System, and more, including approval of new programs. Approving, disapproving, or guiding the development of new programs was a tricky business, requiring long hours of negotiation and explanation on various campuses. Explaining the need to avoid duplication among the colleges, especially duplication of expensive or low-enrollment programs, was often a topic of negotiation and always a delicate one. Gerry and I spent many hours on airplanes, busy while flying with bulging briefcases, voluminous notes, question-and-answer periods, and endless repartee, of which Gerry Friedrich was the invincible master.

In the process, Gerry and I became good friends. He relished opportunities to engage his colleagues in intellectual discussions, to analyze the pros and cons of various program proposals, and to explore the motives of those who proposed.

His sense of humor was all-encompassing, from the intellectually arcane to modest puns. He loved plays on words and thrived on obscure puns and double-meanings. Our correspondence was full of them and continued five years beyond my departure from Los Angeles.

Indeed, my last letter from him was dated June 24, 1974. He spoke of a trip planned for later in the summer to Alsace, Germany, Austria, and England, mentioning in passing that he had been seriously ill from "an insect bite transmitting a tiny wolf [a pun on the Latin derivation of lupus] in sheep's clothing known as 'systemic lupus.'"

He was dead from that "wolf in sheep's clothing" less than three months later. As I sorrowfully closed the book on the long and very rewarding friendship with Gerhard Friedrich, PhD, the illustrious "dean of epidemic punning," I reflected on his many warm gifts to those of us who knew him well, the wit he shared, the probing insights he rendered, the sly "put-downs" he sometimes felt obliged to utter, such as: "interdisciplinary programs are OK, but first you have to have disciplines to be inter." Regarding a problematical proposal from Chico State College: "Are they talking tongue-in-Chico?" "Extrafunicular?"

I remember his undisguised laughter, admonishing me for making a paper airplane out of the last page of a calendar on a month-ending Friday and sailing it at Helen Fluher, the office Latin scholar, with words on its wings and fuselage proclaiming *Tempus Fugit!* Helen was not amused. But Gerry was.

I learned much from him. About education, teaching, people, and the application of humor to unpleasant situations (pleasant too). I learned where the best onion soup in Los Angeles could be found. Not too far from the "Learning Tower," at Maison Girard, on Rodeo Avenue. On relatively quiet days, Gerry and I would often go to lunch there and puntificate.

Perhaps best of all, I found a man who was able both to put up with my puns and to joyfully top me in appreciative reciprocation. Wondrously, he could do so along with serious talk. If I had to summarize in two words my years in the Chancellor's Office, they would be *Gerhard Friedrich.*

Among the other good people in Academic Planning, I should mention Bill Mason, a business administration professor from San Jose State, my counterpart in the economics side of Academic Planning and a good, straight-shooting man. There also were Julian Roth and Jack Baird, capable and congenial academicians, and Michael Harada, everyone's favorite.

Michael, an English teacher at Eagle Rock High School, was dubbed "Sweet Drawers" by the adoring members of the secretarial staff who profited from his habit of regularly slaking their candy cravings with boxes of chocolates. Unfortunates who somehow missed the handouts he appeased with a ready wit, cheerful efficiency, and unfailing good humor.

Years later, visiting us in Connecticut, Michael took Andrée and me to dinner in Hartford. Oddly enough, being Japanese, he chose a Chinese restaurant. During the meal, needing a waiter, Michael wondered if "this one" was our waiter. When Andrée suggested ours might be "that one," Michael graciously withdrew and motioned to "that one." After "that one" brought the needed item, Michael slyly leaned over toward us, smiling, and quietly confided, "You know, I can't tell *them* apart."

Toward the end of 1968, I received an invitation to visit Eastern Connecticut State College, where there was a vacancy at the academic dean level. With Gerry's approval, I drove from a meeting in Philadelphia to Connecticut one morning, lunching en route with Eastern's president, Searle Charles. That afternoon, I met with the faculty and staff of the college.

Though favorably impressed by the faculty, I withdrew my candidacy after some thought, largely because it would have been a parallel move economically (from Turlock, at least). And why leave the wonders of the Miracle Mile for less money in a distant clime? Anyway, I had been contemplating for some time the pros and cons of departing the Chancellor's Office.

I had a great "boss." Relations with, and visits to, the 19 campuses were a fascinating part of my job. Being a backdoor witness to all sorts of in-house machinations added an intriguing aspect, but a troublesome one as well.

Too often Gerry Friedrich and his office were the object of the intrigue. He was goal-oriented amid a tribe of career-driven individuals who sometimes saw him as an obstacle. More than that, he often *was* an obstacle.

Often *the* obstacle in an obstacle course, he deliberately stood in the way whenever he saw ambitious individuals pursuing self-serving goals he considered unworthy. He made good use of a certain word, *reputable*. Subtly suggesting antonym connotations, he delighted in stressing the need for developing "reputable programs" (or courses, or centers).

But usually—rather than implying something might be *dis*reputable— he was straight to the point. "This won't work," "Duplicative," "Contrary to the Master Plan," "Needs more work, for the following reasons."

He could be very supportive, but when conditions were negative, he too had to be negative. Often excoriated for being obstructionist, he was under enormous pressure coming from many directions.

Much of the pressure rubbed off on Bill Mason and me during the spring of 1969. We felt it indirectly, living in a rumor mill. We also felt it directly, because Gerry took us into his confidence regularly. We'd talk endlessly after hours, both of us inclined to resigning. Usually I'd leave first. Bill would stay on. He was even more set on leaving than I.

Gerry did all he could to keep us both. He got our titles changed to Deputy Deans of Academic Planning from Associate Deans and applied for salary increases for us, which were denied. Gerry put me in charge of the newly established systemwide publications program and Chancellor Dumke asked me to prepare a paper and deliver it, in his stead, to the Chula Vista Historical Society. Bill and I fed on other carrots from the small storehouse.

But meanwhile, there would be tragic news. ◆

Chapter 17

THREAD CITY

◆ ════════════

*Back to San Diego State for a year, followed by two years at
"The Learning Tower of Wilshire Boulevard," and then into the
Connecticut frying pan.*

Early in June, 1969, only a week after having officially confirmed my determination to return to San Diego State, I received a phone call from Andrée. She had been visiting her mother, who had suddenly lost consciousness, presumably from a stroke.

Although Andrée was able to take her quickly to a nearby hospital in Westwood, her mother never regained consciousness. All efforts to resuscitate her failing, she died a few days later.

In addition to the grief that struck us all, Andrée's father fell into a deep depression from which he recovered only partially during the following year, before he would also die. Mimi's death poignantly affected our lives directly. It also affected us indirectly through its powerful impact on Gaby.

People quite reasonably assumed that our plans to return to San Diego would be cancelled and that we would move into that big, beautiful house in Westwood to take care of the lonely, bewildered widower.

Gerry Friedrich, for one, figured I would stay in the Chancellor's Office. He extended sincere condolences and thoughtfully arranged time off for me. But he believed that we had little reason not to stay, an opinion that he candidly and confidently expressed. Perfectly logical, yet the reality was a bit more complicated.

The complications, though varied, need not be discussed since one of them overrode the rest. Ironically, that one complication was the condition of Andrée's father. He was so distraught that he simply could not function. Numb and disoriented, he seemed either to have lost interest in his surroundings or, worse, to have become unaware of them.

Lengthy discussions among Gaby, his son, Andrée, and me followed. Andrée thought it would not be safe to leave him unattended for as much as five minutes in the multi-storied, Spanish-style home on Wellworth Avenue. Gaby said nothing, and I had little to say.

Charles said the situation was "impossible," adding that he was out of it, away at UC Hastings College of the Law, and asking us to take care of matters. Which we did, finding a large, one-story rental in San Diego with separate quarters for Gaby just off the dining room, complete with kitchen and bath. The attractive home provided privacy and safety and made it easier for us to take care of Gaby. Further, we expected that my more flexible schedule on campus would be more convenient for all of us than the regular, nine-to-five of the Chancellor's Office and its many trips, often overnight.

There was another factor in our return to San Diego. Unlike the transfer to Stanislaus State (cutting ties with San Diego State and breaking tenure), the period in the Chancellor's Office was classified as simple leave time. I could rejoin the faculty as a tenured professor of history at *my* convenience when and if I wanted.

Unlike the Turlock transfer, my return would require approval neither from the History Department, the Division of Humanities, nor from the vice president for academic affairs. But there was a corollary, the decision being unilateral, mine and Andrée's alone, and well before her mother's death, we felt honor bound to abide by it.

And *abide* we did. Not easy to do, however, since other factors, mainly Gaby's unpredictable health, played a heavy part in our decision. But he didn't balk over the move, and it went well enough. He liked his apartment and was happy to discover that most of his large library had survived the trip in good condition.

But he didn't like his new refrigerator which, he complained, kept him awake at night. He was pleased to give up its convenience in exchange for the reward of not hearing its recycling. We simply moved it inside, where he had access to it as well as to the large kitchen version.

That arrangement solved the problem nicely, it seemed. But within a few days, other problems emerged. Then others. He soon followed his refrigerator into the main house. All was contentment from then on. He and I took nightly walks through the Hillcrest section of San Diego. Andrée found books and magazines for him and drove him to medical and other appointments.

His limited existence was comfortable and tranquil yet anything but idyllic since he was consumed by his loss. Efforts to console or distract him had little effect. We offered to take him to Los Angeles and to local events at colleges, libraries, and museums, all to no avail. He would thank us politely and appreciatively but invariably in the negative and with few, scarcely audible, words.

Sad it was, especially for Andrée, to see this man who could enrapture audiences with his brilliant oratory sitting listlessly and unresponsively before us. Sad, too, to reflect on his wild sense of humor, now totally absent. For example, as recently as our residency at Norton Street in Hollywood, we were playing canasta in Westwood after one of Mimi's fabulous dinners. Gaby controlled the game, both in its formal arrangement and in the general atmosphere, always jocular, always wild. And always "bitterly" contested, two sides in mock war, men against women, tightly ordered by the official scorekeeper, Gaby. We weren't great players, nor very serious, except for Mimi, who correctly understood that the object of the game was to win. Actually, not simply to win, but to win *big*. She and Andrée had won the first game of a best-of-three match by a small margin.

The second game was decidedly different. Andrée and her mother had all the cards. I mean *all* the cards. They were simply clobbering Gaby and me. The winning tricks stretched out in front of Mimi so far that they were falling off the card table.

The game was obviously over, our chances beyond redemption. But the massacre continued. Mimi had no mind to stop the slaughter. But Gaby did. He deftly removed the first letter of *slaughter*, by turning to me in a confidential pose, "Don't worry, Deeck," he fairly shouted, black eyes glistening, "SHE'S BLUFFING!" Mimi graciously submitted at that point, accepting victory as we all broke up in laughing recognition of the delicious absurdity of the moment and appreciation of the shrewd two-word exploitation of its incongruity.

Now in San Diego, the keen, incisive intelligence that proclaimed *two words from Gabriel Bonno are worth a thousand pictures* was submerged in gloom. We did what we could to provide comfort and to ease the uneaseable pain of the sudden end of a half-century marriage. We waited for improvements that did not come and, we feared, never would. We made do, gradually resuming our own lives but with restrictions, especially at night.

Restaurants were out. Gaby quietly refused to go, and we were unwilling to leave him alone. Andrée could attend social events as could I, but not together. We all could sit outside, enjoying the fall weather and the pleasant garden. The first semester moved along quickly, and our lives assumed a regular, generally predictable pattern. Predictability vanished a few days before Thanksgiving.

I received another phone call. In fact, there were two calls. One was from Vice Chancellor Ray Rydell in Los Angeles. No. He wasn't asking me to return. It was an interesting call, but let's take the other one first so as to avoid breaking the narrative. It was from Searle Charles, president of Eastern Connecticut State College, whom I had met during the vice-presidential search there.

Said he: "I have been appointed president of the Connecticut Community College System, and we've started the search for my successor at Eastern. Some faculty members here have asked me to call you to see if you would be interested in becoming a candidate for the presidency of Eastern Connecticut State College."

"Here we go again," I thought, "the revolving door revolveth," as Gerry Friedrich described the turnover rate in the Chancellor's Office. In no mood to revolve, I told Searle I'd think it over and "get back" to him. Not knowing whether to laugh or curse, Andrée and I began once again trying to decide whether to leave, stay, or "go blind," as the saying goes.

Our first thoughts centered on how any new course of action would affect her father. Attempts to get his reaction to the question were fruitless. He either did not understand the situation or, quite logically, decided discussion was premature at that time since the offer was only an invitation to candidacy. At this juncture, another voice was heard.

My brother, Gene, called from San Francisco to ask, as he regularly did, how and what we were doing, inquire about our health, and to hear

Eugene Webb, my brother,
at about age 48.

the latest on Gaby, whom he knew well. Regarding the letter from Searle Charles, he said, instantly and predictably, "Go for it!"

The news on Gaby prompted Gene to reaffirm his belief that psychiatric intervention was needed. He recommended the prestigious Langley Porter Psychiatric Hospital and Clinics at the University of California, San Francisco. As a clinical associate professor of medicine at UCSF, Gene was well aware of Langley Porter's worldwide reputation and also was in a position to get Gaby in. He urged us to persuade him to go.

Andrée and I were convinced. But her father was not. Nothing we said would change his mind. In fact, he was so adamant that it seemed to both of us that he was fearful of a cure; that, weirdly, any release from the depth of his mourning would somehow be an affront to his dead wife's soul.

Whatever the cause, we simply could not get him to consider Langley Porter or, for that matter, any kind of intervention other than that of his general practitioners in San Diego and Los Angeles whose sole intercessions in his behalf were pills.

Andrée was disappointed because we'd missed the most promising avenue of return to good health for her father. I was disappointed for the same reason. Besides, his unwillingness to follow Gene's suggestion meant that Andrée could not accompany me to the presidential search interviews in Connecticut, an important part of decision-making involving a major relocation.

So, after prolonged discussion, I went alone on December 19, 1969. Put up luxuriously at the Sonesta Hotel in Hartford, I walked to the headquarters, nearby, of the Connecticut State Colleges, where I met and had breakfast with J. Eugene Smith, the executive secretary of the system and, incidentally, the former president of Eastern (immediately before Searle Charles).

Dr. Smith was a delight—unpretentious, thoughtful, and aware. He would become a friend, and a good one, for more than 20 years. Leaving him after breakfast, I spent the rest of the day at the college with faculty, staff and, students.

A good dinner followed, in Hartford, with members of the board of trustees, a pleasant group, well informed, well mannered, and well oiled, a fact that may have prevented their noting that the candidate had become sleepy by closing time.

Flying home, I reflected on the day. "Now, what am I getting in for?" The head "revolveth." I had been impressed all over again by the campus, the setting, the quintessentially New England town, Willimantic, site of the historic American Thread Company.

More than on the vice-presidential search visit, I was impressed by the faculty. I was especially impressed by the wild, witty, and profound historian Francis Willey. He amazed me with his encyclopedic knowledge almost as much as he terrified me by the wildly inventive character of his automotive improvisations while we traversed the back roads of Eastern Connecticut.

Everything and almost everybody I'd seen were attractive to me. But my thoughts were on Andrée and San Diego. "Beware of foreign entanglements" and similar cautions helped calm me down. As the churning mind relinquished its hold, my thoughts returned to Ray Rydell and his call from Los Angeles. He had asked me if I had any information that he should hear concerning the president of Stanislaus State. When I answered *yes* but said that I did not want to talk about it over the phone, he asked me to come see him.

Arriving in the Chancellor's Office while thinking about my former boss in Turlock, I assumed he was applying for another presidential post, confirming news from the rumor mill. I was surprised, therefore, with Rydell's first words after we exchanged greetings,

"Do you know anything about *The Education of a Prince*?"

"Yes. It was his inaugural address."

"Did he actually deliver it? And were you there?"

"Yes. I introduced him."

"And what was it about?"

Strange question, I thought, as I answered that the *prince* was a metaphor for students being educated to assume eventual leadership of their country.

No more questions. Ray then relayed the shocking news that the head librarian at Stanislaus, R. Dean Galloway, had discovered in a collection of published speeches a copy of the original speech, once delivered by

Chancellor Tolley of Syracuse University. My meeting with Ray Rydell must have served as confirmation of Galloway's discovery, that it was indeed the same speech and that it was actually delivered.

Chancellor Dumke would give the presumed plagiarist his choice of resigning or facing a public inquiry. The president's resignation soon followed. I left Rydell's office feeling both disgusted and sad. As Longfellow and others have said, "Whom the Gods would destroy they first make mad."

Why did this intelligent, resourceful, and very private man commit such an absolutely crazy act?

Why did he consistently pit one faculty group against another, one person against another, skillfully playing games to unsettle perceived opponents? And why, invariably, did he undermine subordinates, such as the four capable and frustrated assistants to the president whom he "ran through" in less than two years? Why?

Did he fear his intellectual raiment might appear shoddy in the eyes of his scholarly, elegantly costumed subordinates? Was *The Education of a Prince* his set of new clothing? And did Mr. Galloway discover that this enigmatic emperor was proudly sporting new and completely transparent threads?

Driving back from Los Angeles, reflecting on the parable of invisible garments, I concluded the man was simply an enigma. He had all the talents, all tainted. Brilliant/clumsy; intelligent/stupid; insightful/clueless; mentally wealthy/intellectually impoverished—if he wasn't the befuddled emperor duped by mendacious garment makers then, who was he?

Surely he was James I and VI, King of England and Scotland, whom seventeenth-century scholars cannily lampooned as the "Wisest Fool in Christendom."

———— ◆ ————

Shortly after returning from Connecticut, I received a phone call from J. Eugene Smith with an offer. The presidency of Eastern, said he, was mine, effective immediately, starting no later than February 1, 1970.

I called him back the next day, telling him that I could not be available until the end of the spring semester at San Diego State. Saying he'd try to get an extension, he called later to inform me that members of the board were reluctant to leave the position vacant that long and had decided to reopen the search.

I had been surprised by the offer but was disappointed at its being rescinded over a four-month differential. Board members must surely have known I was morally bound to complete the academic year in San Diego, especially having so recently returned from leave.

Deducing the board or faculty must have been split—more likely the board—I swallowed my disappointment, let loose a sigh of relief, and contentedly resumed preparations for the spring semester.

That was the end of it. Or so I thought. Andrée was not so sure. Her intuitive reaction to my analysis was that a *second act* was not out of the question. We had talked much about the situation, the place, the various interviews, the attitudes of my hosts. While accepting my view of a split, she also assigned equal weight to concerns of the local establishment over a long vacancy in the presidential office.

Andrée also believed, regardless of what I'd say to the contrary, that the reopened search could bring a second offer. Since she did not argue the point, I don't know exactly what she thought. But I do know what she did. She charmed another woman.

Halfway through the spring semester, I received a message from Laura Johnson, a board member of the Connecticut State Colleges. She'd be in San Diego on such and such a day, would it be convenient for her to meet me? The day fit Andrée's schedule, so I invited Laura to join us for tea.

Laura Johnson was a bright and friendly person. We got along well as we chattered away in the spacious living room of the house on Arcadia Drive. We had been sitting through the proper amount of small talk, partaking of tea from a silver pot—a wedding present seldom used—and Andrée's freshly baked cookies, when the time for business abruptly arrived. Glancing at me, Laura exclaimed, "What do you think of *parietals?*"

Almost before the words were uttered, Andrée had arisen, offering tea and casually admitting her unfamiliarity with the arcane word. "Oh, sorry! It's our word for dormitory rules," Laura apologized. "I guess, we're a bit provincial at Eastern." Andrée must have sensed my consternation and, suspecting I didn't know *parietals* from a pajama party, instinctively intervened.

Laura's brief definition provided the clue I needed to say a few words along the lines that dormitory students need some flexibility within a system of reasonable rules rigorously enforced. Apparently, there had been no malice behind the question. My answer was graciously accepted, and Laura cheerfully went on to other less thorny subjects.

I doubt that she noted Andrée's gentle intrusion. But *I* noticed the smooth and effective intercession. I saw it as critical, giving me breathing space to respond to the most difficult question of the session.

Her timely intervention was not contrived. It was natural, easy, instantaneous, and intuitive. And thinking back to my anthropology studies at Cal, I might add that it was essentially female (quintessentially, Andrée).

Seeing a tight situation, Andrée had bailed me out. Did it in a way that was neither obtrusive nor obvious; in a way that was part of a piece: the friendly and proper hostess who charms while at the same time enjoying the charm of her guest.

However Laura Johnson may have perceived the candidate or the candidate's wife, her verdict must not have been too bad. Scarcely a week after her departure, I received another phone call from J. Eugene Smith.

I accepted the offer he forwarded, but not before Andrée and I spent days agonizing over what to do. Gene, of course, urged me to take it. Richard was noncommittal but reckoned it was "sort of cool" that his dad had been offered a presidential position.

Gaby surprised us by saying it was "a great honor" and by taking a position neither for nor against. The prospect of moving with us to Connecticut did not seem to bother him, nor was he overly concerned about leaving good friends in Berkeley and Los Angeles or his son at Hastings.

But *we* were concerned, and worried about his overall health, not just the emotional side. He suffered from digestive disorders vaguely attributed to diverticulitis and other intestinal complaints. Doctors in Los Angeles and San Diego gave him painkillers and sleeping pills, and more pills to offset side effects. No pills were prescribed for bereavement, which had moderated somewhat but not enough to permit nonchemical sleep.

We knew—and he knew—that there were many good friends, especially in Berkeley, who would have been happy—and said so—to have him stay with them. He would have none of that, even for a short time during our initial move. He knew also that Charles Henri was able and willing, despite law school–imposed inconveniences, to take care of him during a transition period.

We had several weeks to put it all together. We stretched our time a bit with extra flights back and forth, one of us at a time, to handle critical tasks simultaneously at opposite ends of the continent. With two houses and their contents to dispose of, our hours were tightly measured. Reassured by Gaby's willingness to take on a 3000-mile transplant, we easily persuaded ourselves that the change would be good for him and that the new environment might help him shake himself out of the doldrums.

To finesse the requirement for being at San Diego State at roughly the same time as my reporting date at Eastern, I flew to Willimantic at the end of May, officially assumed office there on June 1, 1970, and flew back to California in time for commencement exercises. A few days later, Gaby and I set off together to Connecticut.

I had been apprehensive about how he might react to the flight, but all went well and he showed no signs of distress. The flight was relatively smooth, landing on time at Bradley Field, where the academic dean, Bob Wickware, met us. Affable and entertaining, Bob kept us informed and amused as we drove to his house to drop him off so I could take possession of the car, a Ford sedan assigned to me.

Once behind the wheel, I began to relax. It was good to be on the ground safely and with a companion who, much to my relief, apparently suffered no ill-effects from the trip. I'd had enough air travel lately, rushing back-and-forth between Lindbergh Field and Bradley International. How could I know I'd be flying again very soon?

We drove to the Willimantic Motor Inn, temporary lodgings I had secured with the idea of hunting for more suitable quarters the day after our arrival. After registering, Gaby and I went out for dinner at Friendly's, a local favorite.

We toured the town for a while, driving by some of the historic homes on High Street and then circling back to the river and the American Thread Company. This diversion provided an opportunity to tell Gaby about the glory days of Willimantic when the American Thread Company was a potent force in American industry.

"Thread City" became a thriving *entrepôt* until the Great Storm of 1938 destroyed vital bridges that had connected Willimantic to areas it had once dominated. I'd have told Gaby more but was wary of making him sleepy too far before bedtime.

Late next morning, as I was getting ready to leave my office and the college and take Gaby to lunch and to house-hunting, I received a phone call from the Motor Inn: Gaby had fallen. Shaken and confused but otherwise all right, he was transferred, "as a precaution," to a small hospital up the road a few hundred yards away.

I rushed to the hospital. Apparently comfortable, he recognized me but said very little for the half hour I was there. When I returned later that afternoon, he had lapsed into a coma. The doctor had been there earlier but was unable to awaken him.

The hospital staff looked after Gaby, moved him around to avoid bed sores, rubbed his back and neck, and did what they could to comfort him. One nurse seemed to have adopted him. She massaged his neck, hugged him, and told me that he was a wonderful patient. Well aware of his charisma, I knew that even in the throes of despondency and, as now, in mortal illness, he could entrance young women. A sad moment, yet, even under the circumstances, it was a revealing moment that this was no ordinary man.

The doctor did not return until much later, after I had left, weary, distraught, and profoundly disturbed. The news came early the next morning. Gaby had died during the night.

The shock and surprise were overpowering, with a contextual enormity that is hard to describe. Here we were in Connecticut, my huge and pending confrontation dwarfed by his, also pending. His preparation was better than mine, far better. I was not prepared for his sudden departure, and I was completely unprepared for the pain—mine and hers—of telling Andrée.

Her response to my call, after her first anguished cry, was quietly controlled. I could tell she was numb, her dismay submerged under a distressed semi-acceptance and a struggle to reach out in support of me. Each of us knew, or tried to understand, how the other suffered. We also knew that "arrangements" had to be made, and at both ends of the country.

The mortuary took care of details in Connecticut, including shipping Gaby's remains to California. I flew home shortly thereafter and drove with Andrée from San Diego to Los Angeles, where funeral services were held at that same church in Westwood in which—almost exactly one year before—they had been performed for Andrée's mother.

It was a solemn day but still a wonderfully memorable occasion as a crowd of Cal friends drove down from Berkeley, joining us and many UCLA professors, to reminisce. Faculty friends reminded us after the ceremony of the many contributions that Andrée's father had made to the University of California and its students. They also helped us laugh again at the many past episodes that displayed the transcendent wit and scholarly humor of the inimitable Gabriel Dominic Bonno.

Driving back to San Diego after the funeral, Andrée and I were alone together for almost the first time since her mother's death. We were well out of Los Angeles when, at last, Andrée broke the silence, "I really don't understand it. True, I know only too well that I've lost both parents in less than a year. But . . . they're still here."

Quickly acknowledging the contradiction, she said that the service in Los Angeles and the exchanges with old family friends afterward had helped her gain perspective. That perspective was similar to mine. At age 69, her father was just two months and a few days short of his 70th birthday when his Mimi died. He was in comparatively good physical shape. But his emotional health was so bad that it unrelentingly and fatally wore down his physical condition. Though terribly shocked and saddened by the news, Andrée was not caught entirely by surprise.

Nor was I. In retrospect, observing the gradual deterioration daily, we knew that we had witnessed an inexorable march back to Westwood. ◆

Chapter 18

REVERSE DISCRIMINATION

◆ ══════════════════════════════

A bizarre incident in "The Land of Steady Habits," engineered by a student at Eastern Connecticut State.

$\mathscr{W}$e also knew that time was short and had gotten shorter. Andrée had made good use of the hours when her father and I were in Connecticut. Most details had been efficiently dispatched.

Some still beckoned. One curious one was ancillary transportation for small stuff. We bought for $400 an Oldsmobile station wagon from my good friend, Ralph Grawunder, professor of physical education at San Diego State.

Old but serviceable and in excellent shape, it was a great car. I mention this story only because of its revelation on *character*. We drove the Olds to Los Angeles (not the funeral trip). On the way we had a flat tire. Big deal! I liked the car so much that I let Ralph know my pleasure with it and its top-notch condition. In the course of our conversation, I made the mistake of mentioning the tire episode. He instantly insisted on reducing the Olds's price by $20. My protests to the contrary were annihilated. He said, "I told you that the car was in perfect shape. It had a bad tire. That's my fault. I have to pay to make it right."

"Brow-beaten" and embarrassed, Andrée and I reluctantly surrendered to his uncompromising honesty. The car performed beautifully for several years, carried huge loads cross-country, and earned the name RALPH, an honest car bought *used* from an honest man.

We filled that beauty with all our precious possessions, including some not precious but deemed necessary, and traversed the country in five days. Smooth and uneventful, the trip was free of stress and full of anticipation.

Those five days also went quickly, for there was much to talk about: new job and associates; new environment, physical and social; poignant comparisons of friends and habits; and a certain amount of "second-guessing." San Diego was still much in our minds; we didn't feel regretful, just wistful about all the good times we had had there.

There had been changes in San Diego, too, good and bad. For instance, a significant change lay ahead for the San Diego Chargers professional football team, who played at the old Balboa Stadium in downtown San Diego. The stadium situation was similar to games played at the University of California, when I was a child. In those days, my father's trick was to park a car near the stadium early Saturday mornings in preparation for a quick getaway after the game.

Our trick was a trifle better. On football mornings, Andrée, Richard, and I would "plant" our car near Balboa Stadium and walk to the El Cortez Hotel, half a mile away. Feasting on the hotel's brunch, we'd walk back in time for the kickoff, smugly fleeing the premises in our waiting automobile when the game ended.

As Andrée and I sailed through Nebraska on our cross-country trip, we had no regrets about losing that particular delight since the Chargers had already moved their home games to a new stadium in Mission Valley, and Richard, a student at San Diego State, would be attending college games only, during the tenure of the great coach Don Coryell.

Incidentally, parking a car on streets of downtown San Diego (or of Berkeley) for three or four hours is inconceivable now. And Balboa Stadium is probably long since gone. But the El Cortez, with its glassed-in outdoor elevator, remains. I wonder if it still serves brunch.

While Balboa Stadium became a "lost" friend regardless of where we lived, our move caused the most disruption, with some exceptions. For example, Andrée's very close friend Ella Harvey had recently moved to Whitby, Ontario (just outside of Toronto), a one-day drive from Connecticut. So with our cross-country move, we regained a "lost" friend. As Andrée and I drove, we talked about other changes in San Diego, but travel time passed quickly, and the more it passed the more our conversation turned toward the life awaiting us in Connecticut.

On arriving in Connecticut in midsummer, Andrée and I proceeded to Glastonbury, a small and picturesque town on the Connecticut River. I had been lucky enough to rent a lovely, nicely furnished old house there within walking distance of the river and an ancient riverboat ferry, still in daily operation. The home belonged to the parents of my secretary. Unfortunately, it was temporary. At the time, however, it suited our needs perfectly.

Soon I regained use of the state car, and Andrée took possession of RALPH, using the next few weeks to find a house. But first, I had to reappear at Shafer Hall, 83 Windham Street, Willimantic—also known as my office—so as to make a "grand *reentrance*."

Once again trying to hit the ground running, I discovered this time that the ground had been so thoroughly recontoured that a cautious jog was about the most to be expected.

Although it wasn't a professor driving nude on a busy thoroughfare, the situation was just as bizarre. The subject of my pending confrontation, at least, was fully clothed.

The first alert of what awaited me came from my secretary when I called en route, but I think the news had hit the newspapers as well. Had I stopped in Manhattan, I might have encountered a back-page headline in the *New York Times* reading something like this: STUDENT CALLS PRESS CONFERENCE IN PRESIDENT'S OFFICE.

I arrived on campus thinking, "Oh, no! From the frying pan I'm jumping into?"

I was informed that security had been alerted and would be on hand for the "press conference." I had no information about the student, why he had taken this unique route to the president's office, nor why permission had been granted.

When a decently dressed, clean-shaven young man was ushered into my office at the appointed hour, with no signs of bombs, daggers, or handguns about him, I relaxed a little. Just a little, because this was the seventies, a time of constant bomb threats—bombs, too—on campuses.

Rising from my desk, I escorted him to the conference table toward the back of the room, took a seat next to him, and—mustering as much cordiality as the circumstances and my nerves would permit—asked him, "Why are you here?"

There was no need to enquire about the press. Its representatives did not show. I wondered if there had been an actual invitation. Or was it simply the imaginative ploy of a mind overtaxed with visions of storming the presidential barricades?

In the course of his reply, I soon discovered he was *not* a student and, indeed, that his *not* being a student was the apparent source of his disgruntlement. While his reply was long and involved, his complaint was short and simple:

"What I'm saying is your admissions office won't let me back in . . . 'cause."

"Because?"

"I'm white."

"You're saying you have been denied readmission because of skin color?"

"Yes, sir."

When a records check undermined his discrimination claim, his demeanor changed. In the conversation that followed, he assumed a different tack. He eventually reversed himself so abruptly that I simply looked at him in astonishment when he confided in me that he was actually of African descent.

This surprising comment, either a gratuitous revelation or a bald contention, closed his case. One way or another, *reverse* or otherwise, only his grades discriminated against him. He was smart enough to accept that fact and to leave quietly with a handshake and an implied promise that he would find a better way to regain admission in the future.

In the 18 years in office that followed, I never had another confrontation with a student, with one notable exception. Students often came to see me but invariably in groups. I held weekly drop-in office hours in the library, but the few visitors were usually faculty. Afternoon-tea sessions for various student and faculty groups fared a little better.

My efforts, as president, to make myself available were the exact opposite of my experiences at Stanislaus State where, as dean of Academic Affairs, I had constant student visitors. Differences in perceptions of deans and presidents? Or between East and West?

Oh yes. What about that exception mentioned above? It refers to a determined young woman, weighed down by a heavy chip on her shoulder. The reason she gave my secretary for our appointment was simply "academic matters." Once in my office, she clarified that explanation by wandering around the general theme that her professors were a bunch of clods. She did not stop talking when the secretary called to say time was up.

Ignoring my reminder that we had run out of time, she went on, and on, eventually turning to her religion, already revealed as fundamentalist Christianity, more fundamentalist than Christian. A sophomore, she knew everything, including the fact that I was just as ignorant as her professors.

The futile exercise consumed almost an hour, nothing accepted by the student, nothing achieved by her exasperated victim. Running out of breath or concluding there was no point explaining the truth to the intellectually disadvantaged, she vanished.

I ruefully reflected on the plight of this poor soul. She had squandered a beautiful morning laboriously confirming the fact that there was nothing she would be able to learn at Eastern Connecticut State College—she still had two years to go—or any other college, given her mentality.

We attend college to learn, to learn how to learn, to make ourselves educable. In the process, we need to become wary of our preconceived ideas, especially when they are unsupported—or worse, unsupportable—by scientific study and research.

The world is full of individuals who cannot learn because education is not available. How discouraging, then, to deny oneself learning because of a conviction that *truth* has already been attained. The woman in my office was an extreme case.

But there are many out there, plagued by bucketloads of preconceived notions, who *can* learn. All they need is a little humility and a lot of good teaching.

Returning to Katie Ragen (see chapter 15) and the US history course she and several others developed at San Diego State College, I'm reminded of an example of good teaching there. The basic US history course was so effective that it might even have reached the "unreachable one" of the previous story.

Visualize the following: Dr. Ragen has asked the class as a whole about a reading assignment on the writings of Thomas Jefferson and Alexander Hamilton. Having received some answers from various students, she turns toward *Ms. Truth*, and cheerfully asks, "From your reading in today's assignment, whose opinion do you prefer?"

The question is deliberately phrased so that the student can answer coherently even if she had not read the assignment. Her answer will serve as a guide. If it's faulty, and early in the term, Katie will gracefully release the student from further questioning without embarrassing her. If it's later in the term when Katie knows her students better, she'll ask more detailed questions.

"Well in that case, what would Jefferson say about the National Bank?" "And do you agree with Hamilton's response?" "Why?" Then to the class, "Anyone think of something going on in Washington right now that reminds you of what these two were writing about?"

Even a supreme know-it-all learns something, or flunks. She learns from the readings, which present two or more points of view (troublesome for a fundamentalist). She learns from other students, both from their answers to questions and from the fact that in a discussion class, students generally have few inhibitions about criticizing one another.

And finally, she had better learn from the guidance of the instructor. She learns, that is, or fails the course.

I may have flogged this horse too exuberantly, but we can ride it in several directions, uppermost among which are teaching and learning. First, back to a myth: "There is no such thing as effective teaching; there is only learning." The aphorism is interesting and compelling, but it simplifies and overstates.

The evidence that there *is* good and effective teaching is overwhelming. I saw it at Cal, at Harvard, at Radcliffe, at San Diego State, at Stanislaus State, and—again and again—at Eastern. If an instructor merely provides the atmosphere for learning or consciously avoids getting in the way, it still is effective teaching ("First, do no harm" as Hippocrates had it).

Good teaching can inspire, awaken, stimulate, confirm, broaden, balance, equip, startle, and calm. It can arouse curiosity, open doors, provoke creativity, encourage innovation, provide incentive, and instill confidence.

I recall a great innovation, both in teaching and in educational conception, at Eastern. Professor Bruce Clements, with my support, combined his course in freshman literature with a classroom of 4th graders at the F. R. Noble Campus Laboratory School. He taught the course that way for the whole semester. It was a success, I know, because I attended several of the classes.

I mention it here because it was more than great teaching. It was a spectacularly innovative example of creative education on several levels—sociological, psychological, and pedagogical. Beyond that, it took the current vogue of interdisciplinary education to a different level, call it interchronological.

But one might ask, was it good teaching? It was, but only because Bruce

R. Buckminster Fuller outside Hurley Hall in November, 1973, with Andrée and me after consulting with us on the contemplated arboretum and outdoor theater at Eastern.

could get away with it. He was a marvelous teacher and, besides, he was an accomplished storyteller. He could enthrall those 4th graders just as easily as engaging college freshmen in textual analysis.

But he gave up on the experiment after the first term. It was demanding, strenuous, wearing. And anyway, as he remarked, "The college students were intimidated by the 4th graders." The 4th graders were free, fresh, uninhibited, and creative. He had thought to combine the grades because he feared his freshmen were becoming deficient in creativity because they were college students—older, established, set in their ways, well informed.

So there *is* good teaching. It's everywhere and takes many forms. But it doesn't exist in a vacuum. It needs a supportive learning environment. Bruce deliberately tampered with the environment, mixing 4th and 13th graders. As instructors are key elements of the learning environment, so are students. Good teaching flourishes in an atmosphere where instructor and student are in sync, a condition that can exist only when minds are open.

I found the learning atmosphere at Eastern much to my liking. The faculty were capable and hardworking. School traditions were strong. There had been a succession of able administrators who encouraged good teaching and maintained high academic standards.

School spirit was robust, existing everywhere among students, faculty, and staff. All these characteristics were evident to me from the outset, occasional bomb scares or disgruntled press-conference-callers notwithstanding.

Generally, things at Eastern went smoothly. Faculty-administrative squabbles, common on many college campuses, were rare. It helped that I had 20 years' experience as a member of a teaching faculty. I had been "on the other side," *their* side. In most ways, I was in basic agreement with the faculty. What they wanted, I wanted. I even had the effrontery one time—after retiring, of course—to remark that I had had a 20-year honeymoon with the faculty at Eastern Connecticut State University. Faculty members vehemently disagreed with me. Heatedly, they insisted that my assertion was way off since I had served for only *18* years at Eastern. ◆

Chapter 19

ANDRÉE HYPNOTIZES THE LOBSTER

♦ ══════════════════════════════

She actually did, but the chapter is primarily about Dr. Warren Hill, a remarkable man and one-time Commissioner of Higher Education in Connecticut.

𝓑ut it was not all that simple. There were ups and downs and periods of economic duress in Connecticut. Political reactions to austerity usually alternated between demands to reform the antiquated tax system and proposals to reorganize public higher education.

While there were several changes in the way higher education was organized during my time, proposals were far more numerous than actual change. The major thrust of most of these proposals was toward centralization. Those who proposed generally did so in the hope of saving money, or of using money-saving claims to justify alternative projects.

Sending greetings from the State of Connecticut on the news of my appointment, Warren Hill, commissioner of higher education, was surely just apprising me of a common nickname for the state, when he said, "Welcome to the Land of Steady Habits."

Or was his tongue tucked lightly in his cheek, as he reflected on the *steady* stream of proposals from legislators, private colleges, and various public organizations all vociferously advocating either the *strengthening* or *abolition* of the Commission on Higher Education (CHE) and the Office of the Chancellor?

The CHE was originally a coordinating council with little authority and considerable influence. Under Warren Hill and his capable staff, it played a significant part in administrating the sprawling system of higher education in Connecticut. Customarily, Dr. Hill employed persuasion, suggestion, and argument from his offices. Other times, he worked his magic more informally at the campground and barbecue pit, where he excelled.

He combined rare verbal skills with the ability to motivate action. A great *raconteur*, a good cook, and a bit of a showman while barbecuing or mixing drinks, he enjoyed entertaining in his woodsy garden. One summer evening, the theme—and also the delicacy—happened to be lobsters. Before the pièce de resistance could be prepared and served, Warren delivered a little lecture.

He told us that he was troubled by the practice of immersing a live lobster in boiling water. Moreover, he considered it less effective, and almost as cruel, to put lobsters in warming water, expecting them to relax in the rising heat and be happily unconscious before reaching 212°.

"Bunk!" he said. "Contented lobsters? There's only one way to avoid cruelty in boiling lobsters: you have to hypnotize them first."

He then picked up a squirming, very-much-alive lobster and, to the amazement of his now-enraptured audience, "hypnotized" it. Andrée— whose mother was a *chef de cuisine, par excellence*—must have said to herself, "And I thought I'd seen *everything.*"

She innocently asked, "How did you do that?" to which the good Dr. Hill responded, "I'll show you."

Andrée was instantly there by his side, watching him gently stroke the back of the lobster's neck, or what I figured was its neck. As the lobster cooperatively fell asleep, while we all applauded, Warren deposited the entranced creature in the boiling water and asked Andrée if she'd "like to try one."

Even today, as I write this, I find it hard to believe that she took the lobster and, with a little guidance from her host, put it to sleep. This was my wife? Married to her 25 years and still she surprises me?

Following this act of sangfroid, she nonchalantly proceeded to deliver the coup de grâce and *hypnotize another.*

Unbelievable. Yet the way this act developed, had Andrée's "solo run" not consigned the very last contented crustacean to the cauldron, she and Warren could have been mercifully tranquilizing candidates-for-the-boiling-pot the rest of the evening.

The other part of the "lobster tale" should be a question: how many *guests* did Warren Hill hypnotize that night and other nights? And of those, how many were politicians, college presidents, entrepreneurs, benefactors, or foreign dignitaries? The question is rhetorical now. In a few years, Warren was out, victim of the first of many CHE reorganizations that contributed little or nothing. Yes, Dr. Hill, "Welcome to the Land of Steady Habits."

The many changes and threatened changes faced by Warren Hill and the Commission on Higher Education had no counterpart in the board of trustees for the Connecticut State Colleges, except for the threats, which were legion.

The main difference from the CHE was lack of ambiguity in the role of the board of trustees. The CHE was vaguely assigned the coordination of all of higher education in the state: private colleges, the University of Connecticut, four state colleges, twelve community colleges, and seven technical colleges. Changes for the CHE came from outside and emanated from every quarter. The board of trustees, on the other hand, was unambiguously charged with developing policy for the state colleges. Changes came from within.

At the time of my appointment in 1970, the board of trustees had been in operation only five years, its executive secretary, J. Eugene Smith, barely three years. Quietly competent, keenly perceptive, and politically aware, Dr. Smith unobtrusively counseled the board and its able chairman, Bernice Niejadlik.

As a trained historian and a broadly experienced educational administrator, including 19 years as my predecessor at Eastern, Eugene Smith knew that the trustees—well-informed laymen—served to develop policy and regulative structure, leaving administrative details to professional experts operating within the policies established by their respective boards.

On my arrival in Connecticut, I encountered a system where each president was expected to administer his institution locally; in addition, he was to inform, consult with, and report to the board in a cooperative and mutually supportive manner. In fact, I first met another college president, Don James, the president of Central Connecticut State College, in one of the final interviews before my appointment. Don was serving as a representative of the presidents and assisting the board of trustees in the interviewing process.

It was joint governance. The presidents administered, and the board set policy. For example, one item of policy setting occurred over housing for college presidents. The board reasoned that college presidents—in keeping with their academic status and educational experience—should be publicly housed in quarters commensurate with their rank and the prestige of the colleges they headed. The state general assembly and the ever-generous governor, John Dempsey, were *generally* in favor; even the CHE was not adamantly opposed.

Andrée. Truly remarkable in that it
was actually a passport portrait.

On-campus housing for state college presidents had many advocates, but opposition to the idea *steadily* grew. Elements within the private colleges, the University of Connecticut, and elsewhere, uncomfortable with a perceived aggrandizement of one segment of higher education to the exclusion of others, protested the cost to taxpayers.

With economic concerns, dwindling legislative support, and the CHE wavering, the idea was no longer afloat when Andrée and I arrived in Connecticut.

Disappointed by this bad news regarding our housing, we were unable to foresee that it was actually good news for us in the long run. Andrée, already busy with closing the house on Arcadia Drive, organizing its contents for transcontinental transfer, and winding up her father's estate, now found herself flying to Connecticut in search of housing, and then *back* to California to wind up last-minute details there. The routine, which continued for most of the summer, exhausted her. But she found just the right house in the pleasant village of Storrs, site of the University of Connecticut.

We closed the deal on our new home in early September. Andrée flew to San Diego—a one-way ticket this time—and I joined her a few days later. We piled all the small and valuable items not taken by the movers or RALPH into her 1968 Cougar coupe and, once more, set off cross-country.

It had been a difficult but exhilarating summer. The temporary home in Glastonbury was a godsend. A delightful place in a most interesting setting, it gave us a head-start glimpse of the Connecticut past, so much of it in Hartford, just across the river from us. The daily trip from Glastonbury to Willimantic along the well-kept highways gave me an extra awareness of the state and its byways.

Everything in a rush, we were conscious of each moment.

We were even reluctant to spend time for meal preparation and cleanup. So we took advantage of the long summer evenings and Glastonbury's central location to dine out whenever we could, exploring the countryside in the process.

I took particular delight in introducing Andrée to Parma, a famous restaurant in Hartford where Gene Smith had already taken me, explaining its history as *the* place for members of the General Assembly's Democratic contingent. As we entered the dining room for lunch one day, a large, round-faced man, with reading glasses resting lens-up on his forehead, casually greeted us (greeted Andrée, more likely).

We casually survey our home from the deck. But a better view is gained from the vantage point of our pond where— probably not at the same time—Andrée contentedly navigates her inflatable boat, some 200 feet away.

As we sat down, I whispered, "That's John Bailey, the Democratic 'boss' and 'king-maker.'" Andrée was surprised at my knowledge until I told her that one ran into him here constantly, spectacles and all, and that was how I recognized him.

John Bailey became chairman of the Democratic Party of Connecticut in 1946, at a time when it had wallowed in the political doldrums for about a decade. With great energy and political insight, he managed to turn the party around and secure the election of a string of Democratic governors.

John Dempsey, third on that string, was governor when we arrived. Any interest he might have had in resurrecting the idea of state-financed presidential homes—pretty much "down the drain" by then—became moot when he decided to contribute the $250,000,000 deficit to his successor, announcing in 1970 that he did not intend to run for reelection.

So, the $250,000,000 deficit was left for Governor Thomas E. Meskill to deal with and for Eastern to suffer the consequences of *how* he dealt with it.

As for state-financed presidential housing, its demise guaranteed Andrée the joy of a summer of house hunting. She found a lovely home for us. And 18 years of owning that home, together with inflation during those years, enhanced our equity enough to produce a substantial profit. Without that profit we would have found it difficult to finance a post-retirement home.

A small footnote: Glenn Ferguson was one of three presidents at the University of Connecticut during my time at Eastern, the others being Homer Babbidge, before him, and John DiBiaggio, after. Facing the reverse of our housing situation (UConn's campus had a presidential home) and properly worried about postretirement housing, Ferguson and his wife, Patty, bought a beautiful house in Rhode Island, though during his tenure they lived in the on-campus president's house.

Babbidge was friendly, correct, and distant, DiBiaggio was simply distant. Glenn Ferguson, however, was not only correct, but a close friend. Patty and Andrée were good friends and did things together. We were constantly invited to their homes in Rhode Island and on the UConn campus and they, in turn, to our home.

John Dempsey's last-minute decision not to run for reelection in 1970 left John Bailey and the Democrats in an awkward position, unprepared and poorly organized for the election. The large deficit didn't help either. In the election that followed, the Republican candidate, Thomas J. Meskill, handily defeated Emilio Daddario.

Thus, including Dempsey's post-announcement "lame duck" period, Meskill would be "my" governor for all of his days in office, a time so neatly paralleling the governorship of Ronald Reagan as to make it seem like old home week to me. Like Reagan in California, Meskill immediately clamped down on state expenditures, especially in education.

As far as the fortunes of Eastern were concerned, the Meskill years are easily summarized by the following episode. I had invited him on campus to show him the college and incidentally to let him see that we had more students than dormitory space. In the process, I hoped to plant a seed for future building and, above all, to urge him to end the freeze on the Student Center, already authorized and currently at the point of construction.

At a critical moment in our conversation, we entered the new field house, which combined physical education facilities, classrooms, and a gymnasium. "Beautiful building," he said. "What is it?" Halfway through my answer, he interrupted with a gubernatorial "harrumph," fixed me with a cold stare that seemed to say, *OK, that's your piece of the pie,* and then, said out loud, "Another one of those crazy Dempsey extravagances."

That was in the spring of '71/'72. The following year, a modest budget thaw began. The Student Center that I was trying to pry off fiscal dead center that day would finally be completed in 1975, by which time Ella Grasso was governor and that horrendous "Dempsey Deficit" had shrunk from $250,000,000 to $200,000,000 under the austerity of the Meskill regime.

No money, no new faculty nor faculty travel, no buildings: stifling, yet there was some flexibility among the four colleges. The presidents met regularly with the board's executive secretary, Eugene Smith, who tactfully and effectively moderated our deliberations. (The five of us, comprising the Council of Presidents, were mutually supportive in most everything each of us introduced.) We hammered out problems and developed solutions, programs, and joint suggestions to present to the board of trustees.

Board members would discuss these and other matters. The board reached conclusions through open discussion with the Council of Presidents, and lingering issues were referred to committee. In short, it was an effective, problem-solving system.

In this process, Dr. Smith played a key role by being available, giving advice when asked, offering opinions when asked, and seldom initiating, except when asked. His experience as a president and three years as executive secretary gave him a foundation to support his natural acumen and a firm basis for guiding the board and the presidents.

He guided me, for example, in dealing with the legislature, our board, and the CHE as I urged them to accept an idea that had never been tried in public education in the state. We proposed a high-rise dormitory financed on a lease-buy basis with a wealthy contractor from New Canaan, Gene de Matteo. With Gene Smith's help and guidance, and his close relations with the General Assembly, we were able to secure the necessary approvals.

The dormitory, all eight stories of it, went up in a matter of months and was completed in 1972. A building of that size and height, under normal Department of Public Works procedures, would *probably* have taken five years to plan, secure approvals, and construct. Eastern sorely needed it, and needed it "right now."

The building brought an instant jump in enrollment. The novel idea that helped produce it attracted considerable interest from the other presidents and soon led the way to similar projects on their campuses. (Another idea implemented at Eastern, which was quickly replicated at the other campuses, was the creation of a foundation, critical for fund-raising and promoting college interests with the legislature and the CHE.)

After completion of the high-rise dormitory—the logjam in dorm space now broken—student enrollment doubled. It would nearly double again in the following decade, quadrupling from 1970 to 1988. Despite hard times in Connecticut, construction on campus increased. There were four buildings on the North Campus in 1970. Twenty by 1988.

While adding classroom buildings and dormitories brought more students, more students required additional faculty. Connecticut's biennial budget for 1971–72 recognized this fact and provided 34 new positions at Eastern; however, a bad economy (and Governor Meskill) meant that the 34 positions would not be filled for some time.

Still, through the financially bleak seventies, an occasional new building appeared. How explain? Two reasons, primarily: first, the Physical Master Plan for Eastern, approved by the board of trustees and the CHE in 1970, provided a formal justification.

Second, buildings are generally financed through bond sales, effectively postponing major expenditures, whereas personnel costs are absorbed by current budgets. Our arguments for buildings, therefore, might be heeded. But new hires? "Not needed."

Consider: New buildings = good vibes, dedication ceremonies, publicity, public celebrations, and public appearances from the Public Works Department staff all the way to the governor's office. New faculty appointments = new charges to the budget, never popular and very hard to justify in penny-pinching times.

Another difference between capital budgets and operational budgets involved dormitory furniture. My staff and I, as well as Dr. Smith and his staff, struggled with Governor Meskill's office through most of 1971 for a release of funds, already authorized, to buy furniture for the high-rise dormitory.

In desperation to get the funds released, with classes starting in 10 days, I wrote letters to Adolph Carlson, commissioner of finance, and to the governor, and then drove to Hartford and hand-delivered them to Stuart Smith, the governor's assistant, and to Gerry McCann, deputy commissioner of finance. We got the release. The furniture was installed in time only because the crew worked all night to finish the job.

I recount this hassle and time-consuming adventure as another example of how tight in tight times operational budgets can get.

The election of the Democrat Ella Grasso in 1974 might have made a difference, as many expected. But she was confronted with that still-clinging $200,000,000 deficit and by an antiquated and regressive tax collection system.

The General Assembly had passed an income tax in 1971, but, with the steady uproar that followed, the act was rescinded, and Connecticut's taxes remained near the highest level in the United States.

At Eastern, in the following few years, buildings continued to be built, new students continued to appear, and faculty kept on not-coming. (The faculty freeze was still in place.) We were delighted to see a new science building go up, even though student enrollment also increased.

The only thing growing faster than enrollment was the anxiety among faculty and administration alike over a difficult situation that bordered on the impossible.

By 1975, the times had become so desperate as to call for desperate measures. Eastern remained 30-shy of the 34 vacant faculty positions, and we had a much higher student–faculty ratio than the other four campuses.

We were trapped. I saw only one escape route, one that I was exceedingly reluctant to take. ◆

Chapter 20

HAMP!

◆ ══════

*Lionel Hampton, superb musician, famed worldwide on
drums, vibraphone, and piano, who performed in unique
circumstances, marked by strange coincidences.*

$\mathscr{M}y$ reluctance to make the necessary move stemmed from its involving a central part of the learning process, the elementary school. So in 1975, I cut the Gordian knot, closing the Campus Laboratory School housed in F. R. Noble Hall.

Despite prior consultation with faculty, the uproar was deafening. I was excoriated from one end of Willimantic to the other and from Windham to Hartford. Laboratory School faculty let me have it in no uncertain terms, pummeling me in language, colorful and lofty, and decibels loftier still.

I thought I had all the answers, but even so, no one was listening. A lawsuit erupted, landing me repeatedly on the witness stand. Eventually, I won in court, but nowhere else. Though we found positions for faculty and classrooms for students in the Windham schools, few were mollified.

Several Laboratory School faculty members, moreover, were qualified to teach at the college level. We were happy to transfer them to the Eastern faculty and overjoyed to see some 15 new vacancies, the budgeted funds for which were now available to finance positions, long since authorized but never filled. Those new positions made all the difference. We were able to make gradual corrections in the dismal student–faculty ratio and, very important, we could now create new programs and strengthen old.

New programs included an economics major, concentrations in business administration and data processing, and minors in law enforcement and in several areas within the Arts and Sciences division.

Despite the anguish suffered by some and protested by many, discontinuing the Laboratory School conferred significant and long-lasting benefits. Other than increases in college faculty, Noble Hall represented a huge accretion of real estate, a solid building occupying a city block.

I decided the building should be reinvented as a dormitory. Then, for more than a decade, we lobbied the board of trustees and the CHE in its various iterations (Commission on Higher Education, Board of Governors, Board of Higher Education, Department of Higher Education) until at last the legislature appropriated design funds in 1987.

As for the protests over the closure of the Laboratory School, they soon abated. Court proceedings confirmed that we had negotiated with the Windham Schools, the local elementary school district in Willimantic, beforehand to find employment for Laboratory School teachers. Also, five transferred to the college faculty (two in Education, one in Physical Education, one in Psychology, one in Communications) and were warmly accepted by their new colleagues.

The year 1975 also saw completion of the Student Center. Now it stood handsomely there, ready for occupancy, and needing only an assistant to the dean of student affairs. That position had been authorized and funds appropriated and released. We began a search, and several attractive candidates emerged. One of them, pleasant, mature, and well spoken, impressed me with his quiet self-assurance and calm demeanor. His name was Warren Kimbro.

Robert Meshanic, dean of student affairs, had recommended Mr. Kimbro for the position because of his sterling character and outstanding capability—and despite the fact that Warren had been convicted of murder.

On May 21, 1969, as a new member of the Black Panthers, Kimbro had been forced to pull the trigger, sending a bullet into the head of Alex Rackley, a Black Panther suspected of being a police informant.

Dinner on the Bateaux Mouche *on the River Seine in the heart
of Paris, June, 1982. Andrée and I supped with my sister-in-law, Aileen
Webb, MD, and her son, Eugene McDaniel Webb Jr.*

Bobby Seale, the Panther's National Chairman, was charged with ordering the execution but was freed in 1971 because of a hung jury. Kimbro, not
so lucky, was sentenced to life imprisonment, with a 20-year minimum.

Repentant, as he has said, from the moment he pulled the trigger,

Warren became a model prisoner, counseling fellow inmates, directing—on work-release—a youth drug-counseling program, and editing the prison newspaper.

By such earnest efforts, he secured a huge reduction in his sentence from 20 years to 4½. Later, on parole, he became director of Perception House, in Willimantic, and then managed to gain admission into Harvard, where he earned a master's degree. The man was capable, likeable, and deserving. His past was *his* past.

Dean Meshanic and I, however, were dealing with the present. And we were also dealing with the board of trustees. They came from all walks of life and from every corner of Connecticut, with fish to fry, families to protect, and associates to consider. When we apprised them of Kimbro's merits, as well as the risks involved, board members resolutely supported the appointment.

My niece Carolyn Wagner, Gene and Aileen's eldest child, in the 1960s.

As anticipated, when the Associate Press and other news agencies published the story, it provoked a nationwide uproar. Protests, recriminations, and denunciations came from everywhere, including one particularly vituperative blast at me, emanating from Oregon. But the protests could not stop us from hiring Warren.

The naysayers—at least, those who paid any attention once "the tumult and the shouting" passed—were treated to a banquet of well-prepared crow, courtesy of Warren Kimbro, whose performance at Eastern was exemplary. Students adored him, his colleagues admired him, and we all appreciated his tactful, cheerful, and effective discharge of duties in the Student Center and throughout the college.

When Hampshire College managed to spirit Warren away, after four years of admirable service, Eastern's students threw an enormous, tear-filled going-away party in his honor, lamenting his departure but wishing him well in his new endeavors.

In 2009, full of years and honors, Warren Aloysius Kimbro, aged 74, died in New Haven, Connecticut, a credit to humanity, a life vindicated.

The forced contribution of the Campus Laboratory School to Eastern's faculty-student ratio provided an important measure of flexibility. One significant outcome was the reorganization of departments and divisions into three schools in 1977: the schools of Arts and Sciences, Professional Studies, and Continuing Education, each with a dean.

We created deans for the first two schools out of "whole cloth," or, to be exact, with departmental adjustments and promotion of well-qualified faculty, an impossible feat without the flexibility of the extra faculty positions.

For the dean of Continuing Education, we first had to establish the position—with the approval of the board of trustees and the support of the other presidents—and then start a nationwide search.

The search ended in Delaware, where we were lucky to find a real winner, Owen Peagler, and to coax him away from his administrative position with Governor Pete du Pont. Dean Peagler had great references, all the technical qualifications, and a solid set of human assets: highly intelligent and capable, personable, creative, goal-oriented, imaginative, pragmatic, and conscientious.

He immediately took hold of the position and its challenges and opportunities, working closely with the deans of the two other schools and the vice president for academic affairs. Administratively, our picture was complete: the three schools, under the vice president for academic affairs, directly, and the vice president for administrative affairs, indirectly.

So we had a "chart," structurally clean, one that made sense for a school of our size and development. One, indeed, that anticipated the structure that would be required, some five years later, for the college to be renamed Eastern Connecticut State University.

While the deans and vice presidents were capable and multi-supportive, it was Dean Peagler who took over, sensing the unique role of the School of Continuing Education. He had not risen to the deanship from a departmental structure. In fact, he *had* no department. Therefore, he reasoned, he had *all* the departments. Accordingly, he introduced a series of innovations, drawing academic support from various departments and from wherever else he could.

Continuing education programs, common throughout the country, derive a substantial amount of their operating revenue from course fees. Anyone desiring access to college-level instruction but short of admission standards can find a reasonable alternative available. If they can pay the fees, they're admitted. Administrations use continuing education tuition for operational support and, with few restraints, to facilitate programs in a variety of ways. Faculty welcome the system for flexibility and extra income.

Understanding all these advantages very well, Dean Peagler appreciated the operational flexibility the system provided him in helping the college as a whole. The more courses offered, and enrollment-gains achieved, the more opportunities for academic innovation.

I'm sure he also recognized that he had been presented a challenge: truly making continuing education into a *School* of Continuing Education.

Under his guidance, new course followed new course and new programs followed new programs. One spectacular achievement, after months of planning and negotiation, was the creation in 1979 of "Eastern Under the Sea," a joint program to educate submariners, developed in cooperation with the Atlantic Submarine Fleet of the United States Navy.

Another winner, which took longer but was just as significant, was a consortium. For years I had worked on projects with the presidents of surrounding community colleges, Hartford, Mohegan, and Quinebaug Valley. Dr. Robert Miller, president of Quinebaug, and I tried to develop some joint programs that only partially got off the ground.

I asked Owen Peagler to take over. He did. There followed more negotiation, more hard work, and more accomplishment: the consortium with Quinebaug Valley. But not just a consortium, it was a complete package, including a program and, importantly, a home: the former Motor Vehicle Department Office, in Willimantic.

Peagler could accomplish projects like these because he had *vision*, follow-through, and perspicacity; because he was likeable, logical, pragmatic, and resourceful. Resourceful? Consider this: suffering initially from a staffing shortage, funds already authorized for an assistant but having not yet been released, Owen conjured up a *genie*: Andrée.

Andrée fit well within the budget since she would not accept pay. Conscious of faculty and staff reactions, she asked my opinion (I hesitate to say she asked my permission, though Dean Peagler certainly had to). I was happy to consent and pleased that Owen trusted me enough to chance interpersonal risks. More likely, knowing Andrée, he was sure there'd be no problems.

There certainly were no problems. Andrée had been well accepted by the faculty and staff, who found her available when approached but never intruding. They liked the "French flair" that imparted a subtle flavor to the ambience while remaining totally free of display.

Her parties, elegant but understated, were always popular. She had many friends among faculty wives and—cautiously, to avoid charges of favoritism—among faculty and staff. With faculty members, she established the Day for Women in 1978, an event still thriving.

Also, from the beginning she had worked with students, faculty, and staff on improving the college grounds, becoming an originating member of the Campus Beautification Committee in 1973.

Generally, people were pleased to see her volunteering in Continuing Education and delighted to discover that Owen had found a small office for her. I, too, was delighted, having had nothing to do with it.

It was in *his* assigned area and was *his* decision. It is possible from then on, however, that I may have found a few more reasons to visit Dean Peagler in his quarters.

Certainly, I stopped by on occasion to take the dean and his volunteer to lunch, combining business and pleasure. I don't recall Owen's ever being reluctant to join me, though at times his assistant may have been too busy.

The arrangement worked well, continuing until the funds were released, permitting the appointment of Carol Williams as assistant to the dean of Continuing Education.

Later, on October 29, 1998, writing to me on the occasion of his retirement, Owen reminisced about our "ten great years that we worked together" and referred to "the help of Andrée to jump start the new office of Continuing Education until the arrival of Carol Williams. (Not to forget the supply of Andrée Roca!)"

Dean Peagler, as we soon discovered, had a sweet tooth, and he thoroughly enjoyed a dessert Andrée made on occasion, a variation of the commercial delicacy Almond Roca. Andrée and I had become good friends with Owen Peagler, and we went out to dinner together often. We even went together to a formal state dinner that Pete du Pont threw at the governor's mansion. A great adventure, the trip was a learning experience for the three of us, as was a breakfast alone with Owen the morning after the banquet.

It may not have been on the trip to Wilmington, but somewhere along the way we discovered that Owen knew the great drummer and vibraphone player Lionel Hampton. Eastern students were enthusiastic patrons of the arts. With their financial help, we were able to bring Stevie Wonder, Dave Brubeck, and other famous musicians on campus.

Once I learned of Owen's connection to Hampton, I wishfully said, "It would be great if we could get Lionel to bring his band to Eastern." To my surprise, Owen answered, "Sure. No problem."

I asked, "What makes you so certain?"

"He owes me one."

"Oh? How's that?"

"He loves my chili."

So we invited him and he accepted. On the afternoon of November 13, 1984, Owen and I picked Hampton up at Bradley Field. The band would arrive later, in the early evening. On the way to the airport, I told Owen I was excited about the day ahead.

"I have a special reason for excitement."

"Oh, I see . . ." Owen began, and then, "No, no. I *don't* see. What do you mean?"

"I played a duet with Hamp, once upon a time."

All ears now, Owen pressed me for details. So I told him about a day, years ago that the Benny Goodman Quartet appeared on campus at the University of California.

Tom Haven, my friend since childhood and a member of the Welcoming Committee, grabbed me, early that day, on the sidewalk outside Stephens Union and told me to go upstairs to the building's main hall.

"Get on the piano around 10:30 this morning. Don't let anyone get you off it."

When I protested, he said, "I don't care about the hoots and hollers and complaints of other musicians awaiting their turns; just get on that piano and stay there." Then Tom was off, leaving me agitated and bewildered.

By this time, Owen was hooked: "So, what happened?" he asked. "Did you obey?" I told him I did. And I finished the story:

After about an hour, Tom appeared at the door with none other than Lionel Hampton by his side. "Hamp" joined me at the piano for a rollicking 20 minutes of "China Boy," a tune I selected, having heard his recording of it.

After relaying these details, I said to Owen that Hamp probably would not recall the incident after all these years, to which Owen replied, "Tell it to him. We'll see if he does, and even if he doesn't, he'll enjoy the story."

So, on the way back to the university after picking up Hamp at the airport, I recounted the tale. Hamp readily acknowledged that it could have happened, since he was there at the time and always liked to play "China Boy."

After I changed the subject to give him some details about the convocation planned for the afternoon, he returned to the performance at Stephens Union, asking, "How are your chops? Could you do it again"?

Whatever I said, we agreed "to do it again," Hamp clinching it by saying, "We can do it just like we did before."

He asked for the location of a barbershop in Willimantic for a shave. We found one, left him there, and arranged to pick him up and drive him to the newly completed dormitory, Occam Hall, where he would be spending the night and could also take a nap before the convocation later in the day.

Residents of Occam were delighted over having so distinguished a visitor share their home, though I doubt that he got much of a nap. No matter, he told me he thoroughly enjoyed talking with the students and that he liked his room.

While Hamp was at the barbershop and then, presumably, napping, I hastened to round up Ed Drew and Ken Parzych of the music and business departments, respectively, to see if they would like to join a session of "The World's Largest Trio." Ed laughed, and asked, "Who's the fourth member?" Ken merely inquired as to where and when.

I then asked members of the maintenance department to complete the setting by placing Ken's drums and Ed's bass on stage but behind a curtain, with a Steinway grand piano and my Musser Golden Vibes in plain view in front of the curtain.

At the appointed hour, recordings of Hampton's music playing continuously, students and faculty members in academic regalia marched into Shafer Auditorium. Roy Merolli, vice president for Administrative Affairs, opened the program with introductions and general welcoming remarks.

Dr. Merolli then introduced Carole Lee, a talented pianist who chaired the Music Department at that time. She enlivened the program with some choice words and turned the podium over to the dean of Continuing Education. Owen responded by amusing the audience with a few anecdotes about his friend, Lionel Hampton, and then deferred to me for the formal presentation.

After brief greetings, I bestowed upon Hamp the official title of Honorary Professor of Music at Eastern Connecticut State University, adding the formal salutation:

> You have played before royalty as well as before more humble folk throughout the world. You have entertained at least five presidents of the United States.

For our part, in appointing you Honorary Professor of Music today, we register recognition of your extraordinary contributions both to music and to the quality of life around this earth. But in addition, in accepting this tribute, you do honor to this institution, to its student body, to its music faculty, and to all who are associated with Eastern Connecticut State University.

Lionel Hampton, citizen of the world, humanitarian, musicologist, peerless percussionist, master of harmonic invention, and performer *par excellence*, we salute you and we thank you.

So ended the formal program. Then, for a moment, we returned to the Stephens Union episode so many years before. I repeated parts of the tale, telling the audience I obeyed my friend Tom Haven's command: I stayed on that piano until my fingers hurt and my ears were sore from all the shouting from other students, including, "Come on, Webb, you've been on the piano for an hour." And "Get the hell off and let some real musicians play." Suddenly the complaints died down, interrupted by a disturbance at the door. It's the Marines, to the rescue.

No, it's Hamp and Tom to the rescue. *Allons, mes enfants. To the barricades!* Well, something like that: *to the piano!* Hamp sat down, and we commenced playing. As Hamp and I ended "China Boy," I remember looking up at the major part of our audience. There they were, congregated in the shape of an upended tunnel, one on the shoulders of another, and another, reaching up about 10 feet, an astonishing acrobatic feat, albeit short of the ceiling, which is very high at Stephens Union.

At the podium, as I finished revisiting the Stephens Union memory, I looked around to see if any Eastern students were reacting to the "upended tunnel" image. But at that exact moment, Hamp called out, "Hey, Doc! How're your chops now?"

"OK, I guess."

"All right! So what do you want to play?" as if he didn't know.

Looking directly at Carole Lee, of Chinese descent, I replied with little political correctness in mind, "Let's try 'China Boy.'"

So the two of us, in our academic robes, sat down at the keyboard of that big Steinway grand, with Hamp, treble, on my right. What was I thinking as I contemplated the bass notes before me, rapt with the moment, wrapped in a microsecond? Something like OMG, my hands are frozen.

Without a word, Hamp lay down a rapid arpeggio with such clarity and

At a student/faculty convocation on November 13, 1984, in Shafer Hall, Eastern Connecticut State University, honoring Lionel Hampton, "Hamp" and I repeated a duet we had performed 40 years before at the University of California.

In an impromptu session following Hamp's and my duet, we are joined by Ed Drew (bass) and Ken Parzych (drums, not shown).

Owen Peagler, Hamp, and I.

musical authority that it seemed to declare in no uncertain terms, "Take this as an introduction, man. Thaw right now, and come in at the end of the second bar. We own this audience."

I heeded his unspoken words and, for the next few minutes while we ripped and sliced and cut and coddled "China Boy," two thoughts entered my mind. "How does he do it? Such invention, variety, inversion, diversion, revision, precision, harmony: all up-tempo yet with a steady, unhurried cadence, every bit as well done as nearly half a century earlier?"

My other thought? "Don't mess up!"

We put "China Boy" out of his misery in three or four minutes, considerably fewer than at Stephens Union, when we both were younger. As the applause and hoots and whistles subsided, I took the podium once more to announce that there was still another act. On these words, the curtain parted, revealing drums, bass, Ken Parzych and Ed Drew. More applause. Then I asked our guest if he would join me and my colleagues, Parzych and Drew, in an impromptu presentation by The World's Largest Trio.

He said, "Sure. What are we playing?"

"With Mallets Toward None," I replied.

I stayed at the piano, Hamp walked over to the vibes, and the four of us swung out on "With Mallets Toward None." We all improvised since I was the only one who knew ahead of time what we would play, alerting the others in a stage whisper, "blues in B-flat."

After our exercise in joint-creation—a work never performed before or again, rendered by musicians who never played together as a group before or again, in a unique setting, unlikely to recur unaltered—Hamp was back at the podium. Making complimentary remarks about the students, faculty, and staff of the university, he graciously accepted the honorary professorship.

He then launched into a general statement on music and life peppered with a string of anecdotes that had everyone laughing and applauding. One of them involved Louis Armstrong. He and Hamp, while appearing in a series of European concerts, were invited to meet the Pope and tour the papal palace. Louis was in a state of awe over the pomp and glitter. But when they visited the Pantheon, awe turned to unease. Nervously, he turned to Hamp:

"Hey, Gate! This is spooky. What'll we do?"

"Calm down, Pops. Just say something in Italian."

So, according to Hamp, the jittery Armstrong cooked up, "'Spaghetti and meatballs.'"

On that hilarious note, Lionel Hampton sat down. The house erupted in applause. Dr. Merolli, at the podium again, signaled the recessional and formally declared the convocation closed.

The indefatigable Hampton then appeared at a reception for him put on by residents of Burr Hall, next door to Shafer, talked endlessly with the students there, and finally returned to Occum Hall for a short rest, a change of clothing, and an escorted dash to the Francis C. Geissler Gymnasium, just barely in time for his full-band evening concert.

The students of Eastern and the Committee for Arts and Lectures that sponsored the concert got their money's worth. Hamp and his band put on a show for more than three continuous hours, with only one intermission, otherwise broken only by constant applause of the cheering, appreciative audience.

One member of that audience happened to be a visiting professor at Central Connecticut State University from China. He was there with Don James, president of Central, and his wife, G'erti, whom we had invited to the concert.

During the concert, Hamp and his band had "traded fours." (Jazz musicians often expand their improvisations by exchanging "the fours"—short solos within a song, usually of four measures each—with one another.) Don told me the next day that his Chinese colleague was enchanted with hearing this device. He particularly enjoyed two saxophonists who repeatedly traded breaks during several of these exchanges, which he referred to as "debates," an apt expression with an accurate oriental twist.

After the concert, Owen Peagler invited Andrée and me, Carole Lee, and a few others to join him and Hamp and to partake of the famous chili that, I am sure, had been promised much earlier to the now-famished star. The chili was every bit as good as we had been led to expect. Everyone had a good time.

Hamp was enjoying himself immensely, handing out autographed vinyl copies of concerts in Japan only recently recorded. He was apparently unconcerned about details such as how he would get back into Occum Hall at two in the morning.

Off to New York early the next morning, he promised to be back the following week for an interview on my *History of Jazz* show on WECS, Eastern's radio station. But Ronald Reagan cut me off at the pass by inviting Hamp to perform at the White House.

Carole Lee was also off the next day, in a different direction: to California, over the Thanksgiving weekend, to visit her father. Before leaving, she had asked about obtaining a copy of the convocation tape to play for her father, but it wasn't ready yet. When Carole mentioned this, I asked for her father's address, "I'll try to get a copy to you."

I called Tom Haven to tell him about Hamp's visit and the almost exact repeat of the Stephens Union duet Tom had "arranged" when we were Cal students. Since Tom lived in Atherton and Mr. Lee lived in Menlo Park, nearby, I asked if he would be willing to take a tape I'd sent him over to Menlo Park and play it for Carole's father. Tom was happy to do so, his tape having arrived before the end of Carole's visit.

Upon returning to Eastern, Carole told me that Tom had brought the tape and her father had listened to it silently. "But he had a strange look on his face, so I asked, 'What's the matter, Dad? Didn't you like it?'"

"Yes."

"Something seems to be bothering you."

"Well, . . . you see . . . I mean, actually, I've heard it before. In the student union at Cal. I was there. In that same room." More than 40 years ago. ◆

Chapter 21

MARK HOPKINS AND THE LOG

◆ ═══════════════════════════════════

Quote from President James A. Garfield. An extended discussion on the art of teaching.

I would see and talk with Hamp only once more, seven years later, at the Buena Vista Winery, in Sonoma, California on August 18, 1991.

But with his friend, Dean Owen Peagler, I have had a long-standing friendship and, even after retirement, a fairly constant written correspondence. Owen played the key role in bringing Hamp to Eastern. I doubt the musical genius and performance whirlwind that was Lionel Hampton would have brought his superb act to Eastern Connecticut State University without Owen Peagler's intercession, or, at least, without his chili.

Andrée would phase herself out of the Continuing Education Office when the very capable Carol Williams was appointed assistant to the dean in 1978. Carol and Andrée worked well together. But Andrée limited herself henceforth to projects begun prior to Owen's arrival on campus. In 1973, for example, she had encouraged various faculty members to set up a campus beautification committee and instigated the "Green Leaf Review," a series

*The Grooves of Academe. Left to right: "Doc" Mirliani,
Ed Drew, me, Ken Parzych, and Tom Pavone.*

of live performances and shows to finance beautification efforts in general
and the "Arboretum" in particular.

The Arboretum was Andrée's idea of developing a 17-acre wilderness
area bordering the North Campus. Too deep and rugged for conventional
buildings, it was wild and naturally attractive. Its shape—steeply walled on
three sides but fronted by a gradual incline—suggested an open-air theater.
The name, *Arboretum*, stuck; the concept, *Theater*, enticed; the two together
motivated.

With small grants—$4000 being the largest—and enthusiastic student
involvement, the plan quickly got off the ground. The Green Leaf Review
caught on, raising enough to provide ongoing support for the project as well
as for general activities of the Beautification Committee.

The "Grooves of Academe," my faculty jazz band, played for the Green
Leaf shows, aiding fund-raising, as did the faculty and faculty-wives chorus
line. Ever popular among the student body, they danced the traditional
cancan. Andrée taught them the steps and routines. She also directed
rehearsals and, much to the amazement of the audience, led the performance onstage.

Progress on the Arboretum was slow at first, as general interest was
greater than financial support. But gradually, students, faculty, and nearby
townsfolk became involved. With Evergreen Review receipts, more

*When Dave Brubeck brought his quartet to Eastern in 1985,
we had much to discuss because Andrée's father taught summer
sessions at Mills College, in Oakland, when both Darius Milhaud
and Brubeck were in residence there! Also, I knew Dave's older
brother, Howard Brubeck, when we both taught at San Diego State.*

*Andrée with Madeleine Milhaud, widow of the great French
composer Darius Milhaud, in the Milhaud home, Paris, France.
Incidentally, Dave Brubeck named his eldest son Darius.*

donations, and student labor, we were able to plant 200 evergreen trees around the perimeter.

Ideas began to take on substance when the rough outlines of an outdoor theater were hewed from the rocky soil, thanks to members of the Connecticut National Guard and their bulldozers.

Months of modest progress climaxed in the mid-seventies when we inveigled R. Buckminster Fuller to visit the campus and particularly the Arboretum. Well impressed with the potential of a "theater in the woods," he brought his grandson and his architectural associate, Shoji Sadao, to the site.

Buckminster Fuller liked the idea of a natural amphitheater completely open to the elements, but cautioned that it might be impractical, given Connecticut's weather. He sketched out for us a structure of intertwining vines to cover the stage area and spoke of ways by which geodesic domes could provide shelter.

He and Mr. Sadao sent us several samples of geodesic domes applicable to the theater and promised to help in any way they could. I appointed R. Buckminster Fuller Adjunct Professor of Conceptual Mechanics. He liked the title, writing not only of his gratitude for the appointment, but also of the precise designation. "Conceptual Mechanics—that is the nearest anyone, including myself, has come to identifying my preoccupation," he said.

That letter of July 21, 1976, together with his regard for the Arboretum project, left us with great excitement. But in time, with the completion of the Student Center, campus pathways changed, and ecological passions found other outlets. The dream of the Arboretum gradually faded. Its soaring concept was postponed as campus expansion partially bypassed the Arboretum and excluded neighbors, their access blocked by new buildings and parking lots. Given the circumstances, no one was particularly dismayed by this development. We simply came to a major turning point.

Or, as Yogi Berra reportedly declared, "When you come to a fork in the road, take it!"

We actually followed Yogi's zany instruction. We took it. Well, in a sense, we took the fork, since the tines pointed in the same general direction. Significantly, the fiscal health of Connecticut changed in the second half of Governor Ella Grasso's administration. Coffers opened. Buildings rose.

Good times continued during Governor William O'Neill's term in office. Eastern's north campus took shape, dramatically expanding. The Student Center was completed, which led to more construction. Dormitories, new and old, filled instantly. It became obvious to most of Connecticut's official-dom that fully occupied dorms required dining halls.

Connecticut governor Ella Grasso and I, at commencement, 1975.

Margaret C. Hurley Hall, completed in 1978, answered that need. A beautiful building, it provided high-class dining facilities for students, faculty, and staff; space for all sorts of student and faculty activities; and a large set of rooms for the Admission and Records Office.

Hurley Hall, which completed the first phase of North Campus development, provided a well-rounded and environmentally attractive experience for present and future generations. There would be much more to come, but most of the fiscal frustrations were behind us, and basic needs had been met. As for that other tine of Yogi's fork, the route was indeed different, but the results were more or less the same, and where they differed there was little that could be done about them at any of the institutions of higher education in Connecticut.

So our next turn happened to be toward a resurfacing of the old trait in the Land of Steady Habits: correcting one troublesome aspect of Connecticut politics, life, or infrastructure by changing another.

Higher education did not come cheap in the Nutmeg State.

Not really expensive so much as viewed so by those who saw the four state colleges, the ten community colleges, the seven technical colleges, and the University of Connecticut as a ruddy redundancy and a waste of "taxpayers' money."

"Consolidate or eliminate them!" "Tear them down and start over!" How often did I hear suggestions to combine UConn and Eastern, or to absorb the four state colleges into the University of Connecticut, or the technical colleges into the community college system? As for the Commission on Higher Education, the number of pleas to strengthen it were exceeded only by those that called for its closure.

Actual changes were few. Those implemented had little or no effect on duplication and administrative costs. The Commission on Higher Education survived the nomenclature onslaught with a minimum number of substantive alterations. It is interesting to note, however, that in all these changes and near changes, the predominate direction was always toward more centralization.

That trend predicted the latest incarnation, the Board of Regents for Higher Education, enacted in 2011 (twenty-three years after my retirement). The legislation also consolidated the community and technical colleges and placed all public higher education, excepting the University of Connecticut, under a single board.

Changes in governance and organization were variously motivated, but a major driving force was the quest for economies in higher education. Initial savings may have been achieved through reduced duplication. But such savings will surely be offset by increases in personnel to support the regent's staff requirements.

When Dr. Gregory Gray, the erstwhile president of the system, was interviewed a couple of years ago at Eastern Connecticut State University, he apparently made no mention of central staff augmentation required by the board of regents to attain its goals.

Centralization of authority can win some victories, but financial economies are not one of them. A look at the development of the state college system, where my interest and expertise lie, should throw some light on the subject.

J. Eugene Smith, who retired in 1972 as executive secretary of the Connecticut State Colleges Board of Trustees, was a wise and highly capable administrator. He firmly believed the proper role of a board of trustees was to set policy, leaving local administration to local administrators, individuals who had the training and academic experience to run a college effectively and within the policies set by the board of trustees. The role of the executive secretary, he insisted, was to advise board members and to serve as a go-between, from board to presidents and vice versa.

Smith's successor, James A. Frost, a capable administrator out of the New York system, brought to Connecticut an entirely different view of educational politics.

Dr. Frost may have agreed with Smith's views in rough outline, but he intentionally adopted a different plan of action. He assumed that the state colleges were vulnerable because of the many threats to consolidate with the University of Connecticut or otherwise reorganize them. He insisted, therefore, that a strong defense must be mounted, and the best way to achieve that was to strengthen the board of trustees.

The steps he took to that end were so uncompromising—*necessary*, to him; *devious*, to others—that he later admitted they would not have been accepted nor he respected if he had divulged them at the outset of his regime, as he states in his book, *The Establishment of Connecticut State University.*

The Frost plan was simple. To strengthen the board, the title of its secretary needed to be changed. So the "secretary" became "executive director" and would eventually become "president of the Connecticut State University." Frost insisted that a strong board must have a strong staff and that the presidents should report to *him* rather than to the board or its committees.

The central staff had to be augmented to facilitate this control by having college deans and vice presidents report to their newly appointed counterparts in the central office. The end result of this centralization was twofold: first, a rapidly developing and costly augmentation of central office personnel. Second, in the process, the situation would become so complicated that the trustees would gradually become dependent upon the know-how of their staff. In the extreme, the staff—not the trustees, not the presidents—could end up running the institutions. On the winding road to Mark Hopkins's log, I must pause to insist that as a general rule, systems that operate on a centralized, top-down basis get complicated, often leading to bureaucracy. Dr. Frost deliberately placed himself in that kind of position to gain ends he considered imperative. He achieved those ends, but at the price, before and after, of complications.

The reaction of the four state college presidents was unanimous. With Frost's aims, they disagreed on principle; with his methods, in disgust, contempt, and anger. They vented their displeasure at meetings of the Council of Presidents and, achieving little, withdrew in frustration.

Dr. Haas, a marvelously warm and successful individual, was everyone's favorite, well spoken, charming, and gentle but firm. If Gene Smith was the heart of the group, his very long-term friend, Ruth Haas, was the soul. Like Hilton Buley, she was of retirement age. There were no other similarities.

Dr. James was the youngest, by far, of the foregoing group. A natural leader, he was attractive in every way, with a beautiful voice and a quick, incisive mind. Like Haas, he was steady, seldom wrong, and clear in his sense of propriety, as well as capable of indignation with those who possessed a dim regard for it.

Ruth Haas, Western's president, lashed out at Frost regularly. Winning the battles and most of the arguments, she decided to retire in 1975, after 29 years of service, when it became evident that none of us could win the war. Her successor, Robert Bersi, left after only five years, taking a position in the Nevada higher educational system.

Hilton Buley, president of Southern, retired in 1971 and was replaced by Manson Van B. Jennings, a capable and scholarly gentleman with impeccable credentials. In 1981, after a difficult decade in office, he chose to retire, hounded out of the presidency by weird events and troublesome people.

When Jennings arrived at Southern, he "inherited" from Hilton Buley a fractious faculty, some fiscal problems, and a collection of "old school" middle administrators against whom some faculty held long-standing grievances. Trouble boiled for several years, bubbling over in the late seventies with hints of mismanagement in the Extension Division.

The board of trustees intervened, sending Frost to Southern, where he negotiated with faculty and eventually counseled Dr. Jennings to take a medical retirement because of a heart condition.

Presidents and faculty alike at the other three colleges bristled over what they considered interference from the board by its vicegerent. But Frost felt that he had to intervene because, in his view, matters were out of hand, and he was obliged to move whenever integrity or effectiveness were threatened on any campus.

I cannot be so charitable in assessing Frost's treatment of Dr. Jennings's successor, Frank Harrison, 1981–1984. With Dr. Harrison, it was war almost from the beginning. The two were at odds on function, demeanor, and anything having to do with internal affairs at Southern Connecticut State University.

Frost didn't like Harrison's style of governance. Harrison didn't like Frost's viewpoint. The latter was irrelevant; Frost held all the cards.

Some of the faculty at Southern, moreover, did not accept Harrison's style. They cared little for his way of addressing problems that persisted there, and many of the old-timers considered his manner reminiscent of Hilton Buley's authoritarian style.

Buley, a product of his era, simply took the unflinching stance that there was a job to be done and *he* was the one to do it. Harrison, at times, appeared to be like that. Witty, resourceful, decisive, he could also be impatient and dismissive, characteristics sometimes shared by his adversary.

Reacting to sporadic faculty discontent and rumors of nepotism, Frost decided to step in once again. After extended investigation on-site, he convinced the board of trustees that Frank Harrison had to go.

Dr. Harrison was forced to resign—railroaded, according to his colleagues among the other state universities; his own fault, according to Frost and members of the board. While I do not have all the evidence to judge, the very fact that I don't, because of the hush-hush nature of the proceedings, casts some clouds over the issue.

The action taken against Frank Harrison had its justification in Jim Frost's premise: To survive, the Connecticut State University required a strong board of trustees and a strong executive, with centralized authority vested in the board and administered by the executive. If you accept his premise, you've bought the rest.

I do not accept his premise. I cannot accept it as it played out under Frost's aegis. Beyond that, I reject it in principle. As Lord Acton said, "Power corrupts. Absolute power corrupts absolutely."

Frank Harrison got a raw deal. He and Mrs. Harrison lost a large amount of money in the house they were forced to sell. He was humiliated to boot, through action—right or wrong—that was arbitrary. Frost upheld the integrity of the system, avoiding, in his view, a situation at Southern that threatened to become messy. He did what he had to do, according to his premise, and that is exactly why the premise is flawed.

For years, Frost lobbied the legislature and various commissions on higher education in behalf of the state universities and their educational role. His concept was that state universities played a necessary midlevel role between the research-oriented University of Connecticut and the technical and community colleges. The state universities, he said, were high-quality institutions stressing *teaching* rather than *research*.

I am at odds with Frost's bifurcation of *teaching and research*. I consider that a false dichotomy.

It is misleading to separate teaching and research. In higher education they represent two legs of the same animal, the animal being the learning process. High-quality teaching should ultimately be based on research.

If a dichotomy were to be drawn, it would apply more accurately to state colleges and community colleges, an observation that Dr. Frost might accept. Practically and politically, however, he saw no threat from the community colleges. The *whale in the room* was the University of Connecticut. His whale, not mine; the only swallowing possible was that of nearby Eastern, an act of ingestion UConn deemed improbable, and I have that *straight from the whale's mouth.*

What's all this have to do with Mark Hopkins and the log? Well, I'm working on it. But the best way to get to it is by way of boards of trustees, commissions, boards of governors, and regents *on, of,* and *for* higher education, and staffs to serve and educate these august bodies. At the outset, let us recall that Executive Secretary J. Eugene Smith conducted system-wide activities with just a staff of two colleagues: a finance expert and a multi-responsible secretarial assistant.

His successor, James A. Frost, persuaded board members to assume hands-on direct control of the colleges. He wanted a strong board, and a strong board needs a strong executive officer with a correspondingly strong staff. That's what he lobbied for. We have a universal problem here, a course of events that have played out again and again throughout the nation, along with its concomitant phenomenon, centralization.

Some states have centralized education only to reverse course and abandon such systems as ponderous, inefficient, and expensive. That trend is ironic in that one of the main reasons legislators have been attracted to centralization is that they have heeded the siren song of economizing.

Economies are often realized at first, but soon give way to costly and time-consuming struggles to keep up with ever-growing personnel needs.

Another major problem of educational centralization is decision making. There has to be someone at the top. Decisions taken at top levels of centralized educational administrations are, by definition, large. They affect and involve thousands of people, students, faculty, staff, alumni, parents, families, legislators, and the general public.

Because the system is large, and its problems numerous and complex, central offices require all sorts of administrators from all sorts of disciplines, to respond to all sorts of questions, too complex and varied to be functionally accessible to lay boards.

Decisions, therefore, are necessarily made—or avoided—at the top.

There will have been some discussion and consultation at lower levels, but because of the monolithic administrative structure and its monolithic authority, choice is exercised at the top and by the chief executive with the advice of appropriately informed staff.

The system can work, and sometimes does. But it has its flaws. One is that if a wrong decision is taken, there is very little recourse in the system to alter it or modify it in a reasonable time.

And, when governing institutions grow still larger, they tend to become unwieldy, ponderous, and inefficient. Thus, they find it increasingly difficult to adapt, or change course. When they finally do, it can be too late, a hasty decision or, at best, result in an overreaction.

These flaws are not unique to education. They have brought down businesses, governments, and social institutions. Organized education is unique, however, in that its prime purpose is to provide an effective learning process for its students. Every step taken away from this mission reduces its effectiveness, and every reduction of its effectiveness takes organized education closer to its downfall.

And that observation brings us to the title of this chapter, James A. Garfield's memorable portrayal of the ideal university:

> Give me a log hut, with only a simple bench, Mark Hopkins on one end and I on the other, and you may have all the buildings, apparatus and libraries without him.

President Garfield (Hopkins's student at Williams College in the nineteenth century) may not have realized how perceptive his remark really was; nor how contrary to current conditions was this quaint conceit extolling the rhetorical powers of a famous orator.

Mark Hopkins was professor of Moral Philosophy and Rhetoric at Williams College from 1830 until his death in 1887. Significantly, he became president of Williams College in 1836, serving until 1872. Thirty-six years! How could he do that?

Well, first, because he was a good and capable man. But mainly, despite time spent on countless speeches, he ran the college all by himself, perhaps with the aid of a secretary. He did not share duties with faculty committees. He did not have to answer to a board of trustees or a commission on higher education. He knew nothing of collective bargaining nor academic councils and academic senates.

Alumni associations did not exist. Parents were friends and associates for the most part who may have spoken to him individually but never as a group, never on college governance, and seldom in protest. Neither the federal government nor the state of Massachusetts gave him money and directions on how to use it. Nor did he need a collection of deans and vice presidents to help him deal with the foregoing or interact with students or parents.

But he *did* need something more than that fabled log. He needed a teaching faculty. And they would teach or get fired.

From Mark Hopkins's day until the twentieth century, colleges and universities would change gradually as enrollments grew and faculty became more numerous. A revolutionary change, however, came with the end of World War II.

Passage of the GI Bill enabled more than four million returning veterans to attend college. It was wonderful legislation, comprehensive and far-reaching and with vast educational benefits for a generation that might otherwise have drifted aimlessly.

On balance, it was money very well spent, even though it had some unforeseen consequences. Administration became more complicated and more costly, as it simply became *more.* The GI Bill brought the federal government into education in a big way. Funds passed to colleges and students in such quantities that all sorts of rules and regulations ensued.

Wherever there are rules and regulations there must be reporting and compliance. Reporting and compliance require staff to report to and "regs" to comply with. Despite the generous underwriting of books, supplies, and living expenses, students often ran short. Government loan programs, scarce in the past, were augmented appreciably, anticipating to a degree the student loan problems that confront college students today.

Unprecedented and far-sighted, the GI Bill clearly marked an educational watershed. The good results it produced were enormous. The unforeseen consequences, less dramatic, were also enormous.

A critical factor was the huge building, and overbuilding, of American colleges. A mixed blessing, they were all needed in 1945, but many, unneeded, eventually became a burden. Vacant or underused buildings on campuses contributed to the burgeoning financial costs as the program receded. But reductions in enrollment were not accompanied by a reduction in administrative personnel, due in part to increasing federal government involvement, general growth, expanding loan programs, and collective bargaining.

In total, it is apparent that American higher education is at a crossroads, fighting a two-front war against the implacable army of financial exigencies while contending with the forces of alternative education, the ever-present computer, and online innovation. Business concerns setting up their own schools has not helped, either.

It's hard to separate the problems of excessive costs from those of over-administration. They feed on one another. I doubt if the computer is the answer to each, although there are many who consider it the solution to both.

Perhaps President Garfield would say that there are just too many people between Mark Hopkins and the other end of the log.

If we use Mark Hopkins as a symbol of the modern professor in the classroom, can there be a scintilla of a doubt that in American higher education, too many and too much have gotten in between?

How to define "in between"? Anything that stands in the way of professors being able to do their jobs in the most effective way, including cuts in the financial pie that affect the quality of classroom instruction. (I exclude online instruction, because the pros and cons change too fast.)

There are all sorts of "in betweeners": state, local, and federal governments, government loans, grants, aid to for-profit colleges, unfunded laws mandating state expenditures, collective bargaining, affirmative action, and so on. I have nothing against the last two. They have done a lot of good, but the financial and administrative costs run high.

The bottom line, as always, is the dollar, both to students and to the institutions they attend. Escalating costs since World War II have caused colleges to explore any and all correctives to their growing financial woes. One obvious revenue source has been tuition and student fees.

Therefore, a college education, either public or private, is costing more each year, opening up a Pandora's box of alternative choices, mostly bad, for students, like dropping out or enrolling in for-profit institutions such as the University of Phoenix or the Great Courses.

No bargain, these institutions generally offer much and deliver little. Their revenues come preponderantly from the federal government via student aid, which is not cost effective considering that few degrees are granted and the dropout rate is high, as is the rate of student loan defaults.

The for-profit colleges' marketing is good. They advertise hassle-free matriculation, a dubious incentive considering their few restraints from accrediting agency's standards.

It's easy to denounce these educational carpetbaggers. But the majority of them are legitimate businesses, roughly half of which were started by publicly traded companies intent on developing a system that was more responsive to the educational needs of their own employees.

In fact, I was asked to serve on the educational committee of Aetna Insurance Company in Hartford in their efforts to develop an instruction program. They were knowledgeable and resourceful, sincerely looking for something legitimate and effective. But clearly, Aetna was dissatisfied with some aspects of public higher education, just as some "fly-by-nighters" were eager to exploit that dissatisfaction.

Many for-profit colleges took advantage of the financial straits of public colleges; these businesses were quick to note that tuition increases were pricing thousands of students out of an education while loan debts were condemning others to repayment servitude.

For-profit colleges sought to entice students to enroll by cannily exploiting governmental mechanisms for offsetting students' costs. The "for-profit" people knew full well that federal largesse was everywhere.

Or as my former colleague Gerry Friedrich used to say, "There's a lot of money in poverty." ◆

Chapter 22

"AH, YES! LET US INVOKE THE DEITY."

♦ ══

*Dr. Jack Rasmussen, at Stanislaus State College, slyly and
presciently uttered these words half a century ago. The
computer in education, a modest appraisal of its ever-changing
use in teaching.*

"*A* lot of money in poverty"? What did Dr. Friedrich mean here, aside
from indulging himself in his lust for witty observations? Well, of course,
he was referring to federal money. And poverty? Where else? In public
higher education.

Specifically, his concern was that grants to public colleges could have
"strings attached," altering local educational programs to conform to federal
dictates. Or, just as bad, that they might reflect interests of grant seekers
whose parochial motives conflicted with the mission of the institution they
represented.

While *external* money can change or derange and *internal* self-interest
can aid and abet, it should be noted that Friedrich's wry jest was uttered half
a century ago. Federal "aid" to education was in its infancy. Growth since

then has accelerated. It has been costly at Washington's end and sometimes threatening to academic integrity at the receiving end.

Much good has come from this precious largesse but, as Dr. Friedrich might have said, "Beware! Free lunches can be expensive."

Just as the GI Bill greatly increased enrollments, leading to construction of new buildings and new colleges, so its gradual dismantling dug deep holes in college budgets. Ever since, the wolf has been howling at college doors, some doors more than others. Public and private, large and small, independent or state controlled, they have all faced hardship, austerity, and—occasionally—bankruptcy.

The big private colleges, with their large endowments, suffered least in good times. Likewise, public higher education had little difficulty if the economy flourished; when it stumbled, *bleak* was the name of the game. Small independents, especially the new ones, became fiscally creative or crashed.

In good times or bad, all types resorted to strenuous fund-raising. Even great land-grant institutions, such as the University of California, have been forced to mount comprehensive public campaigns to help sustain their educational and athletic programs. As an alumnus, I ask in proud wonderment, "How many times have I been reminded that two-thirds of the University of California's daily operations are financed by private donations?"

Similar figures illustrate the economic plight of other public universities and underline the fact that states and municipalities share the wealth-flight. When states, with their own woes, are unable to respond effectively, college administrators desperately seek other income sources, and intensify the monitoring of waste.

The computer has long been the object of such searches. Everyone has jumped in to a certain extent. Some have jumped for the money, others for the educational promise, many for both. The "both-ists," so far, are out-of-luck. The consensus among experts on the subject, as was mentioned earlier, is that there have been no financial advantages in *online* education.

Generally, startup costs outweigh returns. Experts in the field have had some limited success dealing with the problem. But the verdict is still out, critics maintaining that you can't teach philosophy by a machine, the anti-critics replying, "Who's talking about philosophy?"

They're both right. But the anti-critics have much more and better answers than the snide one above. There are many promising signs. For one, we have to consider that the idea of computerized education is not new.

I well remember talking about it in graduate school with William Burkhardt, whose specialty, more than half a century ago, was computers.

Later, in the mid-sixties, at Stanislaus State College, several colleagues were involved in an amiable but reasonably serious discussion. One person in our group was a bright young history professor, Jack Rasmussen, a witty and perceptive observer of the current scene. We had stalled on a practical issue, when someone solemnly suggested we resort to *The Computer* to get ourselves untangled. Jack raised a hand in mock obeisance and quipped, "Ah, yes! Let us invoke the Deity."

It was the perfect moment for noting this technological *newcomer* and, at the same time, making *fun* of it, as did Gerry Friedrich, who loved to "invoke" the computer's blood brother, "*The weird processor.*"

On a bit more serious side, I recall the Media Center at Eastern Connecticut State University, completed in 1974. Along with all the activities its name implies, the building has a lecture hall, sophisticated for its day, with all sorts of devices that bring student and instructor closer together, including "state of the art" blackboards (called *whiteboards* these days). Actually, they're green.

At each seat (or *student station)* there is an array of devices—all the bells and whistles—that permit students to communicate with the instructor, to interrupt (God forbid!), ask questions, get answers, and take tests (corrected answers showing instantly on short quizzes). All computerized and great for students, not bad for professors too.

Primitive, especially as compared to the new and highly computerized Charles R. Webb Classroom Building, dedicated October 15, 1999. But the idea was there at the Media Center. In 1988, moreover, the entire campus, north and south, was electronically integrated. Most modern colleges are similarly equipped, but few excel Eastern in use of the computer and to exploring its future potential.

Outside the halls of conventional education, much has transpired and much money made by "nonprofit" entities. But their financial success, so far, has not been accompanied by significant educational accomplishment.

"Enroll 'em and forget 'em," critics protest, citing figures on the abysmally low graduation and high dropout rates of these institutions. More moderate objectors have cautioned, "Clean up your act" or get lost, an admonition that could apply to elements within the "pure" academic world as well.

The irony here is that the computer, itself, can be the "act-cleaner" in many ways. It can identify quantitative problems quickly. Counting and

Andrée at the Charles R. Webb Hall naming ceremony, in 1999.

The Charles R. Webb Classroom Hall on the campus of Eastern.

numerical errors can be dispatched with lightning speed. Record keeping, storage and retrieval, and other details of post-matriculation administration are processed *pronto*. These are small strokes on a broader canvas of which "profiteers" are well aware.

They see the picture. And so do the major universities around the world, most of which are involved in ongoing, online research. In this country, MIT, Duke, Princeton, Harvard, Johns Hopkins, Stanford, the University of California, and many others have joined the digital scramble, offering nonprofit courses, available worldwide.

As the spread broadens, depth deepens, pace quickens, the naysayer retreats to the last redoubt, in expressions such as *there is no substitute for face-to-face interaction with professors and other students.* In classes offered so far the attrition rate has been sharp, and critics say, "Told you so," smugly asking whether anyone will stay very long, staring at a screen, listening to a professor's canned lecture day after day.

When academic Neanderthals *and* Luddites cry, "It's too *boring*, can't happen here," they may also be crying wolf too often. It *can* happen, probably *will* happen, is already happening here and there, and one day soon will be happening practically everywhere.

The experts, professors, scientists, artists, universities, dreamers, and entrepreneurs working on this mini-deity are aware of its critics, acknowledge their concerns, and are determined to find answers. It's taking time. Lots of time . . . and money.

In contemplating the impact of this benign monster on teaching and learning, it is critical to distinguish those online peculiarities that can aid teaching from those that cannot. Good teaching can be found wherever the teacher contrives an effective learning situation. And that can be achieved in numerous ways, including not getting in the way—live or digital—of a student's learning.

A relevant example was Myron P. Gilmore, one of my professors at Harvard. A good teacher and speaker, he was not an orator. He excelled in communication, and he excited his students by his intensity, his thorough preparation, and an indefinable way of identifying himself and his class with the personalities discussed, and their times.

I still recall Dr. Gilmore's colorful depiction of the great scholars of the fifteenth and sixteenth centuries, Erasmus and Reuchlin and Lefèvre d'Étaples. And, certainly, the brilliant torch Pico della Mirandola, who flamed out

At the Charles R. Webb Hall naming ceremony on October 15, 1999. University of Connecticut professors Bruce Bellingham and Dan Patrylak surround me at the piano in solid harmony. Below: Also at the Webb Hall naming ceremony. Dan Patrylak (trumpet), Ed Drew (clarinet), me (vibes), and Nat Picarelli (guitar).

at age 32 but not before condensing all human knowledge into 900 theses and challenging scholars to come to Rome to hear and dispute them.

Incidentally, for those who suffered the inconvenience of living far away, Pico offered to pay travel expenses to Rome. Such magnanimity. Such flamboyance. And, one might say, such arrogance; but then, he was only 20 at the time, an age when it is quite proper to know everything, and to proclaim everywhere.

Look at it this way: six centuries later and not being able to do a *Pico* and bring the educated or educable to our podium, we digitalize *our* 900 theses to *their* world.

Dr. Gilmore's classes were fascinating, his subject exciting, and his teaching excellent. But might they be brilliant in a Harvard lecture hall and dull online? Not necessarily. From location in Italy? Outdoors? Costumes? Help from Hollywood? Dull online? Why?

Which takes us back to *my* podium: teaching, learning, and the methods thereto. In Gilmore's fifteenth and sixteenth centuries, great scholars offered public lectures, usually in outstanding educational centers like the University of Paris or the University of Bologna. Scholars from all over the European world attended those lectures, by the hundreds and sometimes the thousands. No microphones, probably no megaphones; benches, usually; but few interruptions and damn few hecklers. People went, and stayed, that being the main form of teaching (outside the monasteries, church schools, and royal courts); few books before the "invention" of moveable type around 1453, other than the *incunabula*.

These early public lectures were effective. Effective because those in attendance wanted to be there, wanted to learn, saw few other opportunities, and were confronted by a body of knowledge that, while vast, was nothing compared to the immense amount of knowledge, and still greater amount of information, facing today's students.

Five centuries of development brought little change to the system. Students came to classes, sat at the feet of the great ones, and listened to them expound. The last century has seen a slight acceleration of efforts to improve the lecture system and massive striving to create workable alternatives.

The marvelous irony in all our thrashing around to invent new wheels is that one of our most promising means to that end, truly revolutionary, is none other than that ungodly deity, the computer.

The simple, relatively unsophisticated computer has become an instrument enabling one professor to lecture to hundreds, thousands, even tens of thousands. It's a neat circle. Pico! Are you envious? Mark! Better than a log? Jack! Called your shot, didn't you?

A neat circle, indeed. But not really, not anymore. The teaching computer is a multi-generational creature. Remarkably, the first, and longest, generation began sometime in the 19th century and closed out the millennium. The second generation saw the creation of actual courses online, primitive and largely ineffectual.

The third brought increased sophistication and an accelerated involvement of major universities. New programs were everywhere, some good, some better. Internationally, both independent and consortial exchange of ideas increased dramatically.

The advent of the fourth generation, just a few years ago, brought change so rapid that the word *generation* no longer suffices. There are generations within generations, it seems, and a proliferation of companies and consortia such as Udacity, founded in 2012 by Professor Sebastian Thrum of Stanford University; Coursera, a large consortium of major universities; and edX, made up of Harvard, MIT, the University of Texas, and the University of California.

These and others have had marked success in their efforts to solve or resolve all the digital riddles. Vexing concerns persist, however, including the central one, as Dr. Thrum and associates have been asking, "Since we're rid of all the bugs, all the technical problems, why aren't the students learning?"

He's working on that one, along with colleagues nationwide. Solutions are coming.

The answers are out there, but we must ask the right questions, such as: How do we improve student interaction? How improve student/professor exchange? How overcome obstacles to effective testing and grading? How confer degrees? Achieve accreditation?

There are many more, including the big ones like how improve student learning? How solve the problem of information overload? And how to help students separate noise from fact, and the disconnected from pertinent information?

There remain all sorts of present and future questions related to face-to-face contact, endless efforts to provide a better education at a lower cost, and the all-consuming question, when "the day" finally comes: what do we do with all those beautiful campuses?

Where will the students riot?

Will the computer help solve its own problems? Is it doing it now? Will the pantheon of 'puter pundits produce the right questions? Will *Artificial Intelligence* produce the right questions?

Can information scientists solve the central problem of *Information Science,* that information feeds on itself? The more it grows, the faster it grows. Can experts cure the ancillary problem of *IS,* its apparent need to "acronym"? MOOCs (massive open online courses), another attempt to squeeze elephants into mouse-like clothing, identify without curing the acronym disease.

If not incurable, the disease is certainly MOOC (massively open to operation or cauterization), as is the larger problem of IA (information avalanche). It is not a new problem, its rate of growth, now exponential, began accelerating half a century ago. I was an eyewitness to its apparent effect upon students way back in the San Diego days.

At the beginning of my teaching career, students did their work routinely, with a predictable course of movement toward a conclusion. Years later, I noticed a distinct difference: on average, the students were articulate and well informed, *very well* informed, but not always coherent. While they were well supplied with information, they had a tendency to misapply it or get swallowed up by it, often having difficulty in winnowing out the salient facts from the mass of information.

This was years ago. The contrast was palpable, even then. Now, the information overload has become a significant factor in education and elsewhere.

The challenge is enormous and growing every day. The computer is largely responsible for the *Information Avalanche* and, perhaps, will be part of the solution.

If the computer is going to help solve the problems *it has created,* it must first be asked the right questions to isolate the various characteristics of information overload and its causes. Computer scientists have surely already begun the quest.

Leaving them to quest, I must finish trying to relate this chapter with one more observation. It predates but does not exclude the computer.

My reference is to missteps in higher education and particularly to one fundamental error that, in my judgment, has been repeated over and over for nearly a century.

There are data out there that show a correlation between level of education achieved and financial success attained. A book of statistics could be written on the fact that the correlation is there but that it does not prove a cause-and-effect relationship.

What is annoying and disappointing to me is the fact that academic torchbearers have consistently broadcast the statistics as ineluctable proof of the superiority of a four-year college education.

Bad enough, but "adding insult to injury," as my mother used to say, is the subliminal bottom line, *college education = wealth*. Perhaps not quite that boldly but leading to the easily accepted conclusion that a college education usually (true enough) produces a better job; and, worst of all, that a better-paying job, *ergo*, is *the* reason for attending college, the only reason for some.

What an unfortunate conclusion. A college education should help the student learn to think constructively, systematically, and sequentially; to relate, interrelate, and correlate; to analyze, synthesize, and classify; in a word, to learn how to learn, becoming educable; and, in a democracy, to attain the critical and discerning capability to guide one's choices at the polls.

If it also leads to higher postgraduate earnings, that's simply a bonus, an extra. Confusing that ancillary bonus with the *real* benefits of a college education is a hugely misleading mistake.

Students whose reasons for matriculating are primarily financial would be better off, ordinarily, avoiding college and immediately seeking employment. They would save, thereby, four years of lost income and avoid additional years of paying off loans.

Colleges, on the other hand, should shy away from singing this seductive song in anticipation of approaching days when costs of four-year college attendance may outweigh a student's financial benefits. This distinct possibility brings some urgency in view of the fact that each day more prospective students are choosing alternatives to a traditional college, online or otherwise.

Now, leaving the turmoil of headlong growth and spiraling costs, we must also part with the computer. Let it live out there, beckoning both the financially strapped institutions and the beleaguered students they seek. One may ask, will "the deity" eventually confer financial absolution upon both camps?

The answer should not be difficult: the computer's work is all but finished; the computer is just beginning. ◆

Chapter 23

FAREWELL, NEW ENGLAND. HAIL, CALIFORNIA.

◆ ═══════════════════════════════════════

Career ends. Reading, writing, travel, golf, tennis, music,
memories sustain.

*A*bout the time computers came to Eastern's offices, Andrée and I set sights westward. My very good friend and presidential colleague F. Don James had announced his intention of retiring, stating as he approached his 60th birthday that it was the proper time for him to leave Central Connecticut State University.

He didn't fool me. I knew that the dominant reason for his decision was that he had had enough of being told what to do by the messing minions of an overcentralized bureaucracy. I knew his views on the erosion of presidential authority and understood his vexation with a system where the board's central office *called* the shots but left *responsibility* with the presidents.

The critical factor for both of us was that a bad situation got worse when Jim Frost retired. He was the one who built the system and did so with great skill and manipulative acumen. His successor, the amiable Dallas K. Beal,

Talking with President Jimmy Carter at
Central Connecticut State University, in 1982.

inherited Frost's system but not his touch nor understanding of the subtleties of Connecticut politics.

Beal worked conscientiously with the board of trustees and with the presidents. But, perhaps because he was new, the members of his staff played an expanded role. Some of them seemed intrusive and a little officious, a situation under which Don James bridled, often voicing resentment, as did several of his vice presidents and deans.

Mainly for these reasons, Dr. James retired in September, 1987. I followed suit in April, 1988, for similar reasons and one significant local concern. Eastern was founded in 1889 and, therefore, its centennial would occur in 1988. Tradition and protocol, I felt, would be better served by having the new president inaugurate the university's second century. Tired too, I might have been daunted by thoughts of all the pomp and hoopla of a centennial celebration.

After retirement from Eastern, and as an adjunct professor of music at the University of Connecticut in 1989 and 1990, I'm playing the vibes with Dan Patrylak (trumpet) from UConn and Ed Drew (bass) and Fred Mirliani (tenor sax) of Eastern.

In concert on April 23, 1990, at UConn's Von der Mehden Hall, with Tom Pavone (guitar), Bruce Bellingham (bass), Dan Patrylak (trumpet) (hidden by me, on vibes), and Dave Wakeley (drums).

Andrée never once urged me to retire. Nor, however, did she object when I raised the subject. That was not her way. Alert to everything, she seldom initiated, especially in matters that related exclusively to Eastern or its faculty and administrators. Retirement? "It's *your* decision," she thought, but knew she didn't have to say. Likewise, it should be noted that in all she accomplished at ECSU, she invariably avoided taking the first step.

The Day for Women was probably the idea of Professor Anne Marie Orza. But Andrée and Carol Williams joined her in making it a success. The arboretum and campus beautification were definitely Andrée's idea, but it was Professor Kathy Nolan who followed through and was instrumental in bringing R. Buckminster Fuller on campus.

Kathy Nolan also invented (and named) the Green Leaf Review concert series to help finance campus beautification. It was she who persuaded me to bring "on-site" the Grooves of Academe to amuse the students and amaze the faculty. But Kathy's big student/faculty surprise was one that Andrée alone could pull off: the dance performance where she dared, inspired, and taught a gaggle of reticent faculty women to cast off their theatrical inhibitions, and some of their clothes, in a jolly, spectacular, relatively authentic, and very continental rendition of the cancan. Students stood and whistled, stomped, and hollered. Faculty sat and applauded, some vigorously, others somewhat restrained. Andrée was pleased with the student response and with the fact that some faculty members showed up.

Andrée topped all these activities with a formidable social agenda involving faculty and staff, local citizenry, and the University of Connecticut community. She was also elected president of the Willimantic/Storrs chapter of the American Association of University Women.

I have left out much of Andrée's many contributions so as to limit repetitions. Therefore, I see no reason to rehash here my career at Eastern. But one item keeps popping up, namely, the fact that so many of my decisions provoked widespread and vehement negative reactions. Accordingly, as a summation, I'll select three actions that brought me carloads of recrimination, vituperations, and threats.

First of these was the unprecedented lease/purchase of a dormitory complex, including the infamous eight-story apartment unit (the High Rise), all financed and constructed by the independent builder Gene de Matteo and all approved by our board of trustees, the local fire chief, and CHE. Recrimination, denunciations, obscenities, and every kind of "no, no" soon followed. Officers of the Department of Public Works were after our hides, immediately threatening injunctions, lawsuits, and outright intimations of having the partially constructed buildings torn down. In practically every state office, I was a bum. I was scarcely vindicated even after the job was done and hundreds of students accommodated.

Second, on the recommendation of the dean of Student Affairs, boxes of background information, and my own personal interview, I hired a convicted murderer, Warren Kimbro. Talk about unmentionables hitting the proverbial fan. I got it from Connecticut and about 49 other states. I was crazy, stupid, dishonest, and incompetent, and should be dismissed. By the time the abuse died down, Mr. Kimbro had performed beautifully as assistant to the dean, beloved by the students and highly respected by his faculty colleagues. I had, but did not need, vindication. Warren's four years of exemplary service were enough.

The third example resulted in the one most significant single advance in the fortunes of Eastern during my presidency, the closing of the Campus Laboratory School. It resulted in the longest and most sustained outcry against me and my ancestors that I had encountered, until 1975. Including a prolonged lawsuit and several private confrontations, the unending episode also extended the range of my vocabulary considerably. But despite the uproar, this action conferred far-reaching economic benefits and significantly helped to break the logjam on desperately needed faculty appointments.

Also, with Dr. Smith's encouragement, we established the Eastern Connecticut State College Foundation, unprecedented in the system and the long-term basis for the powerhouses developed by my successors David Carter and Elsa Nuñes. Eastern's foundation became, as well, the model for the other three colleges' foundations, created shortly after ours.

Despite a few relatively hassle-free transactions, the other presidents and I thought our relations with the central staff had become intolerable. Contact with the board only through Frost and Beal was humiliating and, worse, counterproductive. I knew that it was time for new blood in Hartford as well as in Willimantic.

My departure would soon be followed by turnover in the central office, bringing gradual amelioration of working conditions among the state universities, the board of trustees, and its staff. It is important to note, however, that while interrelationships had been strained at times, they did not interfere with development of the state university system.

In fact, the pace of progress never slackened during my last year at

Eastern. Beginning with the commencement address of Governor William O'Neill in June, 1987, we took a succession of steps that materially advanced the institution's prestige and effectiveness.

For example, we were able to appoint the first full-time director of Alumni Affairs, a move that greatly improved alumni relations and enhanced foundation effectiveness in support of alumni activities.

An "old" mainframe computer was replaced, small computers were secured for department heads and other administrative staff, and a word-processing center was set up for clerical personnel.

The new telecommunication system was installed and integrated.

Funds were secured for additional staff in advising, contract admissions, affirmative action, financial aid, and the

Andrée with William O'Neill, governor of Connecticut, at commencement exercises in the late spring of 1987.

data center. More than $400,000 was obtained for, and spent on, various improvements of the physical plant.

A major accomplishment of the year was the securing, at long last, of legislative approval in two areas. The General Assembly awarded funds to build the North Campus Classroom Building (renamed the Charles R. Webb Classroom Building in October, 1999), a large, highly computerized edifice providing classrooms and faculty offices. Funds were also made available to transform the old Noble School into a dormitory, a move that came to the rescue of a growing institution trying to house ever-increasing enrollments.

Oh. And I almost forgot. My year had almost ended. It was March, 1988. The students, faculty, and staff threw an elaborate party for Andrée and me at the Norwich Sheraton Hotel.

It was beautifully done, festive, colorful, well decorated, and highly entertaining, thanks to my good friend Dr. Edward Drew and the marvelous

Drew/Corcoran Orchestra. (They even brought a vibraphone and invited me to sit in on vibes several times during the evening.) There were speeches, of course, most of them good. Mine must have been the worst ever delivered. But people forgave me since it was short. And the presents! I won't elaborate. There were too many.

There were two, however, that stood out: one, a marvelous Xerox Memorywriter that probably was the idea of the late Angela Collison, my ever-thoughtful secretary for many years, who knew how much I enjoyed using a similar machine in our office. The other—pure and delightful—was sheer overload, a trip to Paris. Such a wonderfully loving tribute to Andrée.

Well, we took that trip, and we enjoyed it twice, both for the perfect gift itself and for the kindness and generosity of the gift-givers. We took other trips, notably travels south to meet spring, to Civil War country to wonder sadly. To Manchester, Connecticut, for a year's stay in a comfortable and relaxing apartment, and to Vermont and New Hampshire to slip, slide, and hope to glide on the slopes of the Green Mountains.

During our stay in Manchester, we had numerous opportunities to recall that the best gifts came from those who gave, both materially and of themselves. Mireille and Philip Clapp, professors, respectively, at the universities of Massachusetts and Connecticut, provided a timely example of this truism. Thus began the following episode at our apartment in Manchester:

Promptly at 7 pm, the doorbell rang. There, as expected, stood our host and hostess, properly adorned: she, a lady's maid, he a chauffeur. Mireille curtsied, and Phil announced tersely, "Your car is ready," as they solemnly escorted us to their stately Bentley sedan, Phil's pride and joy, bought in London years before.

Stopped at a traffic light in Hartford, on our way to the restaurant, the chauffeur graciously offered champagne to Andrée and me. Before we could answer, the maid turned and poured two glasses from a mysteriously hidden container, setting them on a retractable leather table in front of the backseat.

As we drank and appreciatively enjoyed the weird frolic, occupants of a car in the next lane were finding the adjoining commotion hilarious. Noting their laughter, Phil waved and rolled down his window. When the other window also lowered, he affected the British tone of a then-current TV commercial and asked,

"I say, by any chance do you people happen to have a bottle of Gray Poupon mustard handy?"

That broke up everyone. Fortunately, the light changed, else we might not have had enough champagne aboard to sustain the street party our canny chauffeur nearly provoked.

After selling our home in Storrs, we were off to California. There, we could contemplate retirement, enjoy the celebrated cuisine of the wine country and also its wine, on occasion.

But there, also, we'd soon become involved in such a whirlwind of social and civic activities that I often wondered petulantly, *this* is retirement?, lamenting, after poet François Villon (1431–65), "But where are the secretaries of yesteryear?"

Having sampled Berkeley and San Diego and finding them changed and crowded, we settled in Santa Rosa, where our good friends from San Diego days, Barbara and Ambrose Nichols, lived. Amby was the first president of Sonoma State University, in Cotati, about 10 miles south of Santa Rosa.

Another strong attraction was an extended family of cousins, nieces, and nephews scattered throughout Sonoma and Napa counties, all of them the progeny or grand-progeny of my brother, Gene, and his first and second wives, Aileen and Mary.

After a few more years in New York, Richard was able to transfer his burgeoning art career to the West Coast, coming out to join his cousins and his mother and father, nicely completing the circle.

The Sonoma County seat, Santa Rosa is a marvelous combination of new and old, sophisticated urban and charming rural, fragrant with scents of wine and roses. While slightly disturbed by automobile vapors and the rasp of motorcycles, the city of Luther Burbank still bestows the more earthly smells of horses, wild animals, and agriculture upon its grateful denizens.

I can still "hear" the powerful voice of John Yarian, formerly of the Episcopal Ministry of San Francisco and lately our next-door neighbor. Father Yarian enjoyed sitting on his front porch and cheerfully greeting passersby in stentorian tones, "Another miserable day in Paradise!"

Despite living in *Paradise*—or living next door to a neighbor who did—we traveled a lot, mostly in the United States. But when we were in France, driving through Languedoc, Provence, and Burgundy, looking out at those viticulturally vibrant acres and sniffing their familiar fragrance, Andrée exclaimed one day, with a half-smile, "We're home!"

I could only agree, and laugh appreciatively at her double entendre. Poignant, a happy moment; but with undertones. Here she was, reflecting ironically on being five thousand miles away from her Sonoma County

At the Chancellor's Office of the California State University System, in 1968.

home while wistfully aware that she was decades removed from her ancestral home, at the very moment of driving through it.

Whether in Paris or San Francisco or Yosemite or New York City, and no matter how much we enjoyed places like those four marvels, we were always happy to get back, anxious to be home in Yarian's Paradise. We had 14 years in Paradise, journeying to San Francisco often, Southern California occasionally, friends and family always.

PICTURE 266

*With our very good friends Jim and Jean Porter Thompson
in Yosemite, quite near their summer home, about 1998.
Photo by Muriel Porter Weaver*

Andrée became a member of the Santa Rosa Symphony League. She discovered her sorority, Pi Beta Phi, had a strong chapter in Santa Rosa. She transferred her membership in the Alliance Française from Connecticut to California. The social exchange was intense at times, especially considering there was always something going on at my brother's place in the quaint, historic town of Sonoma.

Although our travels were mostly to see new places or to rediscover old ones, they sometimes became convenient escapes. We had always enjoyed just being together, indulging frequently in a night on the town, which we defined as wine and dinner in a good restaurant, of which there are many in "wine country" and hundreds in San Francisco and surrounding communities.

One of Andrée's greatest delights was lunching with her brother, Charles H. Bonno—now always Jack Bonno—in San Francisco or Los Gatos, where he and his wife, Susan, live. Andrée frequently traveled the short distance by bus. I saw her off in the morning at the Santa Rosa bus depot. Jack picked her up at the bus station in San Francisco.

They'd go to some quiet place—working in San Francisco, Jack knew them all—and have themselves a great time talking French, drinking French wine, and observing the flow of nearby walkers in this most cosmopolitan of American cities. I'd pick her up late in the day, just in time for dinner somewhere in or near Santa Rosa.

My schedule was similar. Lots of new friends, some old. My new friends came mostly from music and golf. Music, first, was from playing at "tea dances" on Wednesday afternoons at Oakmont, a nearby retirement community. After several years, I fell in with a group—Traditional Ragtime And Dixieland Jazz Appreciation & Strutters Society (TRAD JASS) of Santa Rosa—meeting the first Sunday of every month.

Between these two groups and the musicians met therein, I found myself playing in trios and quartets for a number of popular and jazz music affairs, mostly dances. Golf and tennis combined with the music to swallow up much of my leisure. Fortunately, they left time for travel and wining and dining with Andrée.

Wining and dining took many forms, "out" and "in," with friends, relatives, out-of-town visitors, and so on. Jack and Andrée's San Francisco outings were often expanded. Richard and his wife, Georgia, frequently joined us on trips to Los Gatos, taking long walks with Jack and Susan and having lunches at gourmet spots, including the famous Saratoga Inn nearby where, incidentally, Andrée had fond memories of visiting as a child.

Then, the *tour de force*: Andrée decided the six of us should dine at the world-famous French Laundry. After scores of telephone attempts, she finally got through to the busy restaurant in Yountville, just over the Napa

County line, on January 19, 2005. She secured a reservation, *mon dieu*, for Saturday, March 19, 2005, at 8:00 pm, a mildly rainy night as it turned out.

The French Laundry was equal to the long wait for reservations and more than equal to its renown and cuisine. We all met there a little before eight and, shortly thereafter, were cordially and elegantly escorted to our table where six waiters waited.

The multi-coursed dinner, exquisite presentation, and elegant service were all beyond description. We thoroughly enjoyed the atmosphere and every delightful gustatory surprise. Incidentally, no one complained about the wine, a superb Burgundy. Two bottles at $120 per bottle and well worth the price as was everything else about the evening. We were home by 12:30 am, contentedly satiated; no one, apparently, noticed the rain.

We'd all had a great time. A great *family* time: we knew *that,* and we knew the French Laundry was the highlight of our many happy seasons together. What we did not know is that it was our last time as a group dining out together.

That night still lives in the memories of Andrée's survivors, while her spiritual presence continues to embrace Jack, Richard, and me. Reuniting with her, we three get together on a regular basis and have done so for more than a decade, drawing spiritual sustenance from her and brotherly support from each other.

Andrée and I with son, Richard, summer of 2000, in our garden on Alice Street, 100 yards from the Flamingo Hotel, Santa Rosa, California.

Andrée and I spent our first two years in Santa Rosa at a small condominium behind the Flamingo Hotel, next to the intersection of Farmers Lane and Fourth Street (Highway 12). Needing more space in 1992, we moved eastward to a townhouse in a gated community called Wild Oak.

My (young) cousin Gregory, Charles (Jack) Bonno, Andrée, and Susan at the Wild Oak Saddle Club, in the nineties.

Our new home was located near a polo area, later named Henry Trione Field. Its practice field bordered our backyard. There are beautiful views here, both short range and of the surrounding mountain ranges.

One day two neighbors, Stan Diamond and Phil Lurie, walked by our house. They were carrying tennis rackets, so I asked them where they played. "At the Wild Oak Saddle Club," Stan replied, inviting me to go there with him later to see the courts and to join him for a beer at the clubhouse, where he happened to be a member. I went and, of course, soon joined. Andrée and I would have many wonderful times there with its splendid facilities, festive parties, and many new and interesting friends.

But there was a strange part of the Saddle Club encounter.

As Stan and I walked toward the premises that day, I experienced a sense of *déjà vu*. Not *just* a sense. It was, quite literally, *déjà vu*. I had already

At the Place Vendôme, actually the Saddle Club, in the nineties. Richard Leger, Andrée, C.R., Sandy Temple-Raston, John Temple-Raston, Dianne Leger, Hal Marquis, and Nancy Marquis, at one of Andrée's creations.

seen it. Like Carole Lee's father rehearing Lionel Hampton, I had, in fact, "already been there."

Friendly people delighted in telling new members that the clubhouse had once belonged to the famous and fabulously wealthy shipping magnate Joe Coney. Interested, I nodded, thinking to myself, "I knew Joe Coney."

They proudly showed me that fireplace in the living room where Joe's friend, Alfred Hitchcock, had filmed wild feathered creatures swarming for his horror movie *The Birds.*

I listened "attentively" but was thinking of an ancient time when I sat before that very fireplace with Joe Coney's daughter, Pat, and her two brothers.

"Been there!"

Decades before, in my undergraduate days, when there was no polo field, no Star of the Valley Catholic Church, no Oakmont, just the Coney ranch house, a winery or two, and fields and pastures, Pat had brought me there. It was, I must not fail to add, *before* I met Andrée.

After Andrée and I moved to Wild Oak, I began playing tennis at the Saddle Club with multiple partners, including Stan Diamond, who became a close friend and a patient tennis teacher. Golf was different. That was where he fiercely delighted in extracting multiple quarters from my pockets in order to garner the rights to buy multiple beers at the conclusion of hostilities.

Andrée planned a number of club parties and, as a member of the social committee, introduced several examples of French cuisine to an always-appreciative membership. One of their favorite party settings was a reproduction of a Parisian bistro.

These were happy times, joyously busy days and nights.

Some sadness, too, my brother, Gene, having fallen ill with a variety of maladies, including amyotrophic lateral sclerosis, also known as Lou Gehrig's disease. The sadness was mitigated somewhat by the fact that Gene had let us know long before the event that the ALS was terminal.

He remained alert, busy, and creative to the end. I drove him to oncologists in Petaluma and, at a later stage, to the University of California hospital in San Francisco. Positive throughout, he maintained a clinical interest in the procedures, insisting on my presence at all medical interviews. We sorrowed in his death, at age 79, and gloried in the spectacular accomplishments that fanned the fires of his life.

Andrée and I had somehow managed, amid all the busy local activities, some travel, Andrée to France and both of us to Sacramento, Yosemite, San Diego, Arizona, Connecticut, and elsewhere; but the pace had slowed, quite naturally. There would be one last trip.

With a giant redwood, south of Benbow in the spring of 2005.

Marcelle Bonno was a very good photographer. Fortunately, she had taken photos at Benbow where the family had vacationed when Andrée was a child. Several times I had promised Andrée a return visit. Finally, the promise was fulfilled in late March, 2005.

We had a fun-filled drive north in our new Toyota Scion tC sport coupe on Monday, the 28th, lunching at Garberville and arriving at the Benbow Inn about an hour after noon. A beautiful room, with its own private patio, was awaiting us.

With hardly any time to enjoy the patio—it was raining—we scurried down to the main room, a gigantic hall quaintly decorated with native Indian artifacts and huge paintings where, promptly at four o'clock, scones of every variety and shape were served with tea steaming forth from hefty metal urns.

Too many scones, we delayed dinner as long as possible. Appetites returning after a damp but exhilarating walk through the wooded grounds in a misty downpour, we dined sumptuously and elegantly at the Benbow dining room.

Next morning, we revisited the scene of our gastronomic crime, breakfasting voraciously but a trace more circumspectly than at the preceding evening's feast. It was March 29, 2005, our 61st wedding anniversary. Energetic, and in high spirits, we both enjoyed good health. Neither of us imagined that this would be our last trip.

We checked out at noon. On a leisurely trip home, we stopped at Leggett Forest, driving through the grand redwood there and taking pictures of the site, particularly one great shot of Andrée standing within the cavernous base of that tree, one arm extended against its trunk as if to support the ancient giant hugging her. We were back in Santa Rosa in time for dinner at Monte's Bistro and, of course, champagne: *de rigueur* for the occasion.

It was a great little journey. We treasured the trip and for days afterward enjoyed reflecting on it and the anniversary it recalled. It had had its magic and its wistfulness. For Andrée it brought to life those photographs of early childhood showing her joyously frolicking in a beautiful place with her youthful mother and father.

Her thoughts must also have been tempered by fleeting twinges of remorse over the inevitable passage of time and parents. Quite naturally delighted at the time, I remain pleased and comforted to this day with memories of the trip and the fact that we managed to take it when we did. ◆

Chapter 24

THE SUN GOES DOWN IN THE WEST

◆ ══════════════════════

The days and months following the Benbow Lodge caper were neither sad nor wistful for Andrée. They were serene, spirited, and energetic in a life that admitted no discomfort, contemplated no obstructions, and brooked no thought of closure.

She enjoyed social and educational activities with friends and neighbors; courses at Sonoma State University with Nancy Marquis; movies with Nancy, with Beverly Jones, and with Sandy Temple-Raston; dining out (and "in") with Sandy and John Temple-Raston, Karen and Rheu Schwartz, Claire and Jack Killeen, Dianne and Dick Leger, Norma and Corrick Brown, and Gay and Lefty Stem, to name a few.

And there were friends in the Alliance Française, the Symphony League, and Pi Beta Phi. Additionally, she derived great pleasure from the fact that Richard and her daughter-in-law, Georgia, lived nearby in their new house, where we were frequent visitors.

Social engagements such as these were upstaged by two favorite enterprises, Andrée's garden—*mon petit jardin*—and our house. The latter soon became *the* project in the form of an upstairs bathroom and shower, the walls, ceiling, and floors of which had absorbed major damage courtesy of a thunderstorm.

Having two complete bathrooms on the lower level, we had endured the mess for months. The time to end the procrastination had come. Recalling the words of the late Stan Diamond, "Do it. Do it right. Do it right now," we decided on a complete renovation: new floor, repaired and repainted walls and ceiling, new bath and shower, new toilet, sink, cabinet, and mirror. We also raised the newly tiled cabinet surface 2½ inches to make it more comfortably accessible.

It became an exciting, creative, and enjoyable enterprise, demanding and all-encompassing but rewarding as well. Starting in April, we seemed to be in every industrial showroom and paint shop in Sonoma, Marin, and Napa counties; tiles here, floors there, shower and bath fixtures everywhere.

We were both at those shops most days, Andrée every day. Then the contractors came. And the plumbers. And the plasterers, electricians, tile men, painters, and detailers.

When Richard came over to help us choose among several floor tile samples, I knew we were about done. There'd be a few more weeks of tinkering; but by mid-June it was essentially finished, an architectural gem and an artful tribute to Andrée's perseverance and artistic vision.

She lived long enough to see it and to approve. She died before being able to make full use of it, sad to say. But there was no sorrow in the project. She enjoyed it, enjoyed every tiring minute and weary moment of it, every exhilarating day.

My records of those weeks, racing from retail pillar to wholesale post show us going out to dinner almost every evening. Andrée was enjoying herself. She also needed those gustatory outings as restoratives after the ceaseless explorations and negotiations of her days on the road. I may have needed them too.

Inspired by the progress on the bathroom renovation, and well before its completion, Andrée started—and finished—another task before tackling the temporarily neglected garden.

We had an upstairs living room and bedroom on either side of the bathroom so recently redone. Architecturally pleasing and nicely furnished, they needed a few touches to keep up with the spruced-up intruder in their midst. By deft rearranging and a few bright pillows, the never-slowin' arranger transformed the area.

Richard, a longtime fan of his maternal grandfather's favorite aperitif, got into the *spirit* of the moment. Finding an old but slick copy of a *Dubonnet* advertisement, he framed it:

    "DUBO DUBON DUBONNET"
    VIN TONIQUE AU QUINQUINA

We applauded the bright cryptic with its jolly little cartoon character traipsing through the expanding frames, placed it on the wall, and toasted its cheerful message . . . with Dubonnet, of course.

From that time on, as we toasted Gaby at every opportunity. Andrée's off-hand creation, with an assist from her son and the implied blessing of her father, would always be referred to as THE DUBONNET ROOM.

Well toasted, we were ready to return to *mon petit jardin*. Between June 29 and July 26, Kathleen, our gardener, came to our small garden five times. On each of these days, we had temperatures in the 80s or higher.

Despite the heat, Andrée was out there working along with Kathleen. All told, there were eight days in the 90s during this time, including the solid week from July 7 through July 17, the 16th (high 80s) being the only day below 90 degrees. Almost without exception, the incidence of her asthma attacks increased in hot weather. She had had asthma sporadically since childhood and usually knew how to handle it.

But with the continual heat in the summer of 2005, she'd been in and out of the office of Dr. Joe Miranda, who had her on and off prednisone as the asthma came and went. On Thursday, July 21st, we caught a day in the mid-seventies. Feeling better, she walked with me to the bank (round trip a little over a mile).

A week went by, up and down with the weather, and much time working in the garden. On Thursday, the 28th, the weather was down but, as it turned out, so was she. Unusually tired, she made an appointment for the next afternoon.

Alarmed at her condition on Friday, Dr. Miranda x-rayed her chest and sent her to the hospital for more tests and drainage from the right lung of a liter of fluid. She drove home alone.

She felt a little better on Saturday and Sunday but still very tired. So, on Monday, August 1st, I drove her to see Dr. Miranda again.

Still perplexed, he x-rayed her a second time and scheduled a bronchoscopy for Thursday at 7:30 am.

We arrived at 6:30 am for "prepping." At 8:00 am, Dr. Miranda postponed the procedure until the following morning because of Andrée's irregular pulse. She was admitted to the hospital after two more x-rays, an MRI, CT scan, electrocardiogram, blood tests, and drainage of another liter of fluid from her right lung.

More tests, and on Saturday, August 6th, the 83rd anniversary of Andrée's birthday, I picked her up at the hospital, and we headed for home together with a portable oxygen dispenser and prescriptions for five drugs.

By Tuesday, Andrée's back was hurting terribly, and she was tired but feeling a little better. We learned in the morning that the x-rays showed less fluid but that the fluid contained malignant cells. In the afternoon, we met with the oncologist, Helen Collins, MD, who confirmed the diagnosis and recommended chemotherapy.

Chemo began Monday, August 15th. The intervening week went well enough, filled with medical appointments, phone calls, and visits with family and friends. On Sunday afternoon, Jack drove up from Los Gatos. We all sat in the Dubonnet Room, talking earnestly, drinking Dubonnet, munching on Cheez-Its, and conjecturing on what "tomorrow" would bring. The next day, Jack telephoned to ask how the chemo inaugural had gone. "Not bad, easier than I expected," Andrée told him, explaining in some detail what happened, how she reacted, and the treatment she received (good, friendly, and helpful).

Actually, she had been in the chair seven hours. But it was a big easy chair, reasonably comfortable. We arrived at 10:30 am, the scheduled time. By 11:30 she was hooked up, medicine flowing, patient reading a magazine. I was in and out several times for errands and lunch, returning for her at 5:30.

The next few days went fairly well, some ups and downs, a little nausea off and on; a lot on the 18th. Phone calls came in steadily. Sandy Temple-Raston and others brought food. Saturday, the 20th, started out well enough. Georgia came over to help her change sheets and mats. By early evening, Andrée was tired.

Early to bed.

At about 3:30 the next morning, she awakened and tried to get out of bed. Together, we managed to get her up and to the bathroom. Back to bed was another matter. We finally gave up. Fashioning a bed on the floor, I called 911.

Two ambulances and several paramedics arrived by 4:30 am, taking her to the emergency room where she stayed until 2:15 pm.

She had a high pulse and an irregular heartbeat. Attendants took more than a liter of blood from her right lung, administered two x-rays and other tests, and admitted her once again to Memorial Hospital. I called Richard and went over to explain what had happened. Returning to the hospital that night, we found her much better and in high spirits.

Relieved and reassured, we returned to our respective homes, blissfully unaware that she would stay in the hospital for the rest of her days. The tantalizing part of those days was that so many of them seemed to promise the exact opposite outcome.

We teetered and we tottered for 36 more days as bad news trumped good about as often as Andrée seemed to be holding all the cards. The first hours back in the hospital were typical: sleepless nights and nausea all the time, gradual improvement, helpful therapists, and major confusion.

On August 25th, she was moved to the isolation ward because of a low level of white blood cells (presumably from the effect of chemotherapy on the immune system). Chemo was discontinued a few days later, and Andrée was removed from the isolation ward as her blood count improved.

By this time, her physical therapist, Stacy, had her walking several times a day. On September 3rd, she was moved across the street to the North Coast Rehabilitation Center. Official therapy started on the 4th. Day after day she walked with a therapist or alone in a walker.

There were a few setbacks, but apparently, Andrée was steadily improving, even thriving as she had many visitors, flowers, and plants. Karen and Rheu Schwartz sent her a nice bouquet of flowers, Penny and Terry Peterson gave her an orchid plant. Dick and Dianne Leger sent her a dozen yellow roses. Claire Killeen, Sandy Temple-Raston, and others sent me food. Sandy also invited me to lunch. The Legers invited me to dinner, as did Norma and Corrick Brown, and Grace and Frank Barner.

The above-mentioned were repeat visitors, along with family and others, too many to list, except for Marilyn Diamond who, with her late husband, Stan, had shared great times with us in Palm Springs; and Beverly Jones, who visited Andrée on almost a daily basis, often with her husband, Carl Flegal, one of my golf pals.

With all that collective support, Andrée's spirits were perking up. I was allowed to walk through exercises with her and to push her around in a wheelchair. She particularly enjoyed this tour when it was cool enough to ride outside.

She was doing so well that we were informed, rather abruptly, on September 9th, that rehab time was up. Dismissal would come on or before the 14th. Andrée wasn't ready. Dr. Miranda said, "You're not going anywhere," making it clear that major changes in therapy had to have the attending physician's approval.

An annoying confrontation with the resident dragon lady, it had its reassuring side: From then on, Andrée would be inquiring about home care and live-in help while I was visiting therapy outlets and prosthetic-device shops.

Meanwhile, we resumed our wheelchair rides and exercises.

Her impending dismissal, now planned for later, and under more convenient conditions, became a frequent but guarded part of our conversations. Several days went by, most of them good, with many visitors and phone calls, several from Connecticut. Back on therapy, Andrée was doing well, having learned how to get around by herself on the wheelchair.

On the 21st of September, I arrived early, prepared for a walk and a chance to see her demonstrate her solo skills on the wheelchair. She greeted me cheerfully while starting to get out of bed. Even with the nurse's help, once out of bed she had difficulty standing. Trouble with breathing followed.

Transported to the emergency room by ambulance, she was readmitted to the hospital that night. Next morning, she was strangely better. Dr. Miranda explained that a blood clot got into her "good lung." Coumadin and other drugs dissolved or dispersed the clot, allowing her to breathe more easily.

Dr. Miranda returned at about 6:00 pm and told us that the big problem was that there were just too many things going on at once. Andrée reminded us that the pain in her back was her worst complaint, whereupon Dr. Miranda prescribed morphine. When it took effect, she was much relieved, entertaining us all with her wit and vivacity: gratifying, but alarming, especially since she ate and drank little because of difficulty swallowing.

Jack and Susan drove up the next day. Andrée was groggy from the morphine and sleepy, hospital noise having kept her awake during the night. We saw little of her until late in the day. Then, relatively pain free and having had some sleep, she brightened as we came into the room, entertaining us charmingly but with an effort.

Next night, Saturday, September 24th, Drs. Collins and Miranda called a family conference. It was a sad and jolly time. Andrée was in top form, quick in repartee, alert to all questions "before the house" and responsive to the implications of the medical discussion.

She was holding court again, with her favorite courtiers. Soon, however, the discussion drifted into essentials, particularly the alternative treatments available. Andrée sharpened the interchange of ideas with four words, *sleep and back pain*. Worn out by too many sleepless nights from the clatter and clutter of a busy hospital, she said, "When sleep finally comes, back pain awakens me." Incontrovertible and critical, this observation crystallized the moment.

Responding to their marching orders, the physicians suggested a transfer to *palliative care* to address the noise problem. Pain, Dr. Collins pointed out, could be moderated by "self-administration" of morphine, a mechanical device whereby the patient can control pain with the push of a button.

Andrée agreed. We all did, certainly, to the palliative care, although there were concerns about morphine self-administration.

She was moved the very next morning to a pleasant, sunny room back at the rehabilitation center, with kindly and courteous nurses who would unobtrusively come and go during the day.

It was Sunday. Therefore, Jack and Susan were able to stay on, so Andrée had a quiet, peaceful day with her family. No more holding court, however. She was heavily sedated. I doubt that she had to push the morphine button—not even once—since she had been given a heavy dose before leaving the hospital room.

She never once complained of pain during the day, while she very gradually drifted off.

As she slept peacefully, Jack and Susan tiptoed out late in the afternoon.

Richard and I spent the night with her. Andrée died at six o'clock in the morning, September 26, 2005. ◆

EPILOGUE

My world seemed also to have ended that day. I could not fathom the enormity of this series of tragic events. In disbelief, I subconsciously sought the impossible, trying to rewrite the script.

Slowly becoming aware of this delusion, I resolved to rid myself of such aberrations. But awareness had not come quickly, and resolution was nowhere near. I needed help to clear my mind and find direction anew. Needed it badly.

Oddly, help was at hand or, more precisely, had been at hand for many years. Remote and unexpected, it would gradually change my life in several ways not apparent at the time. Elements of the process first appeared way back in 1988.

———— ♦ ————

Several months after retiring, I received a letter from Dorothy Payne, head of the music department at the University of Connecticut. She invited me to teach a class the following semester: Music 191, *The History of Jazz,* the current purveyor of the course having announced his plans to retire.

Surprised, flattered, and hesitant, I demurred for a while, enjoying the casual life at our Buckland Hills apartment in Manchester and intent on charting future directions without external distractions. But a return to teaching had its appeal, as did the pedagogical possibilities of such an assignment. So I eventually accepted the offer.

An upper-division course, it attracted advanced, capable students who were serious as well as interested in the subject. For me, it was a revelation. Here was a chance to use original documents—the historian's bread and butter—as the primary mode of instruction and, at the same time, to experience the pleasure of beholding a classroom of bright students enjoying the process.

Enjoying? How so? Because the Smithsonian Institution had just published a second edition of its *Collection of Classic Jazz* (Washington, DC: 1987), which I adopted as the class textbook. A book combined with tapes, it is systematically arranged in six cassettes illustrative of the history of jazz, augmented by explanatory statements side by side with each recording.

Students did their "homework" by listening to tapes and reading accompanying explanations. Discussions customarily moved along nicely. Generally well prepared, the students often responded with so much animation that getting through an assignment within the allotted fifty minutes could be difficult. The system worked well because the tapes were of the highest technical and musical quality. A minor drawback was the fact that the music was all recorded. "Canned," as they say. But the students didn't care.

Nor did they mind when a "fix" was found: live jazz. Friends in UCONN's music department, Dan Patrylak, Bruce Bellingham, and others, joined me, Ed Drew, "Doc" Merliani (from Eastern), and local guitar star Tom Pavone in an end-of-semester concert at Von der Mehden Hall, on campus.

A small success before a large audience, the performance was well-received by a mixture of students, faculty, and passers-by, including a sizable contingent of music majors and, presumably, those enrolled (about 20) in my Music 191 class. Everyone had a good time, musicians most of all. Faculty on hand must have recognized that the event was a significant example of innovative pedagogy integrating classroom instruction with onstage performance by musicians from two separate institutions. The concert probably assured my being reappointed for another semester. The ensuing "term-ender" concert, April 23, 1990, proved a bit grander than its predecessor. It was well planned, very well attended, and provoked the following letter:

August 8, 1990

Dear C. R.:

In cleaning off my desk, I happened across a copy of the inimitable Music 191 "Jazz Today" extravaganza, which left its mark in history on April 23 of this year. It reminded me that I am long overdue in expressing my appreciation to you . . . for your truly exceptional efforts. Praises for you and your course resounded through the corridors of our . . . building (and, I am sure, throughout the campus). I am also quietly hoping that I will be able to thank you in advance for agreeing to help us out once again in the Spring of 1991. . . . . If you can . . . assist us again . . . we would be delighted.

Once again, thanks so much for all you have already contributed to our program!

Sincerely,
Dorothy Payne, Head
Department of Music

A nice vote of confidence, but I declined the offer of a third year since, by 1991, Andrée and I were ready to depart for California. More than a boost, however, the teaching episode reaffirmed old friendships with musicians throughout the area, a reaffirmation solidified almost a decade later when in the fall of 1999, Andrée and I returned to celebrate the naming of Charles R. Webb Hall at Eastern Connecticut State University. During that ceremony, on October 15, 1999, from the speakers' platform I spotted musicians from off campus and as far away as Rhode Island. I puzzled over their presence, having failed to notice the small type in the program: "The Grooves of Academe will perform after the ceremony." And so we did. Two enormous tents—refreshments in one, the other clandestinely garnished with piano and my old set of Musser Vibes—enticed guests to gather, gab, and partake. I enjoyed coaxing sounds again from my ancient axe. But the musical high for me was at the piano, in trio between my good friends of yore Bruce Bellingham (velvet bass) and Dan Patrylak (brilliant horn): my high, because I thought we jelled harmonically and rhythmically.

Back again in California, I carried that piano "high" when rejoining my West Coast musical friends. In addition to playing in a weekly "tea dance," I had played for several years with a Santa Rosa organization called T.R.A.D. J.A.S.S. (Traditional Ragtime And Dixieland Jazz Appreciation & Strutters Society), which meets the first Sunday of every month, bringing in well-known bands to perform. During intermissions, featured bands surrender the stage to aspiring local instrumentalists. For years, on piano, I had joined this musical trade-off and had gradually gotten my "chops" back in the process.

Thus at the building-naming ceremony in 1999, I was ready to participate confidently on piano. More than that, in the years both before and after the naming event, T.R.A.D. J.A.S.S. got me involved in all sorts of gigs, trios, quartets, and traditional septets. Also, during these years, a group of T.R.A.D. J.A.S.S. musicians formed a "house band." I was invited to join, on piano. Our total purpose was to raise money for scholarships to help high school students attend summer workshops at the jazz society in Sacramento. An immediate success, the seven-piece band played so many engagements, we were constantly on call, year after year.

———— ◆ ————

Andrée's death had left me scarcely able to function. I was shocked, of course, and inconsolable; normal enough, but beyond that I felt numb and disoriented, like I had lost my way. Finding it again seemed unlikely.

The music, however, had not stopped. Nor had those scholarships. Nor the engagements. Nor the phone calls. Week after week they kept recurring until at last, instead of my usual "no, thank you," I heard myself murmur, "Yes. I'll be there." Performing regularly with fellow musicians requires time and provides distractions. While playing did nothing to ease the pain or assuage my sorrow, it did offer routine and social alternatives. Gradually, it forced me to deal realistically with my demons.

Disbelief and denial divert the grasp of grief. That may be a reason why we "cannot believe" someone is dead. It's a momentary gift, however. It diminishes in time. It atrophies with every unconscious resort to its soothing call. Music helped me awaken from its insidious grip: not music alone so much as all that went with it, the social side, the routine, the schedules, the tempos.

As time passed and the musical routine intensified, I steadily performed with the band, ate alone, slept alone, and gradually became a creature of routine or at least, of musical routine. Musical schedules and procedures impose order. Existing within that orderly framework, subject to its all-pervasiveness, I knew my daily life had changed. Music had taken over, rescuing me from a melancholy existence. I had become, primarily, a musical performer in a band that thrilled old people living in eleemosynary institutions, so we could raise funds for student scholarships.

It had become clear that mine was *now* the life, primarily, of a musician. I would perform as long as possible; even—possible or not—write a little; and henceforth strive to view life as a whole, not solely its parts.

Thus scored, here follows my chart for today and tomorrow:

> Acceptance, tolerance, serenity, service, and continued pursuit of that education ever sought and ever nearing attainment.

CPSIA information can be obtained
at www.ICGtesting.com
Printed in the USA
LVOW12*1236130418

573290LV00001B/1/P